Simon Mabon is Lecturer in International Relations in the Department of Politics, Philosophy and Religion at Lancaster University and a research associate with the Foreign Policy Centre. He holds a PhD in International Relations from the University of Leeds.

SAUDI ARABIA AND IRAN

POWER AND RIVALRY IN THE MIDDLE EAST

SIMON MABON

I.B. TAURIS
LONDON · NEW YORK

New paperback edition published in 2016 by
I.B.Tauris & Co Ltd
London • New York
www.ibtauris.com

First published in hardback in 2013 by I.B.Tauris & Co Ltd

ISBN: 978 1 78453 466 0
eISBN: 978 0 85772 907 1

A full CIP record for this book is available from the British Library
A full CIP record is available from the Library of Congress

Library of Congress Catalog Card Number: available

Typeset by Newgen Publishers, Chennai
Printed and bound by CPI Group (UK) Ltd, Croydon, CR0 4YY

Dedicated to my parents, George and Sally, without whom this project would not have been possible. I am forever in your debt. Thank you both.

CONTENTS

PREFACE TO THE PAPERBACK EDITION

If one stands in the southern part of the souk in Manama and looks up, the eye is drawn towards the towers of the Financial Harbour, which dominate the northern skyline of Bahrain's capital city. Underneath it, in the heart of the souk, political graffiti is sprayed across the walls, written in both Arabic and English, designed to get messages to the broadest possible audience. On a balmy May evening, while taking in the somewhat incongruent setting, I was forced to duck into a doorway to avoid an onrushing throng of riot police, seemingly comprised entirely of men from the Asian subcontinent. The hiring of Sunni Muslims from South Asia was a strategy employed by the Al Khalifa, the Royal Family of Bahrain, in an effort to respond to the violent clashes that were taking place along increasingly constructed sectarian lines across the country. Ultimately, this framing of protests along sectarian lines would help ensure the survival of the Al Khalifa regime.

Yet the manipulation of sectarian identities for political ends is not limited to Bahrain. Indeed, this has become a common tactic in the post Arab Uprisings Middle East, in an effort to both ensure the survival of a particular regime but also to locate political unrest within a broader geopolitical competition that was shaping the nature of Middle Eastern politics. In the aftermath of the Arab Uprisings, the rivalry between Saudi Arabia and Iran became increasingly influential in shaping the political dynamics of the region. While states began to fragment and regime-society relations were disintegrating and descending into violence, Riyadh and Tehran sought to use these opportunities to their own ends.

While the US-led invasion of Iraq created space for Saudi Arabia and Iran to engage in proxy competition in Iraq it was the fragmentation of states after the Arab Uprisings that provided new opportunities to increase their influence across the region. Revolutions and counter-revolutions occurred, in Egypt, Syria and Yemen, while protestors took to the streets and felt the force of regimes intent on ensuring their survival.

In the two years since the first edition of this book, the fragmentation of states and ensuing violence as actors fought for influence has dramatically increased. In Syria and Bahrain, where Riyadh and Tehran had already begun to engage in a degree of proxy competition, the Arab Uprisings provided scope for increased involvement in the domestic affairs of these states.

Yet it is not just direct intervention within neighbouring states that shapes the nature of the rivalry. Rather, it is the perception of intervention that is integral in understanding the responses of Saudi and Iranian leadership. While it is increasingly difficult to fully gauge perceptions, or indeed, the veracity of such perceptions, the behaviour of an actor is based upon its interpretation of a situation and, following this, as the quote from Epictetus that opens chapter 1 suggests, do what you have to do to achieve what you would be.

To this end then, history plays an important role in understanding the construction of perceptions. For Iran, a legacy of conquest and external interference such as the 1921 and 1953 *coups d'etat* within its territorial borders has furthered the belief that external actors are manipulating events across the state. For Saudi Arabia, the narrative of Karbala, in which Hossein was killed leaving a legacy of guilt and martyrdom that remains at the heart of Shi'a thought, coupled with the failed *coup d'etat* in Bahrain in 1981 carried out by Shi'a Bahrainis with support from the IRGC and the *Hajj* deaths in 1987, where 400 Iranian pilgrims were killed after violence broke out, have created the perception that Iran is behind any unrest across the region. While very little evidence is in the public domain to support this belief, anecdotally, this perception of Iran as a Machiavellian 'puppet master' exists in the minds of many across the Middle East and in the West.

In addition to the escalation of proxy conflicts across the region, two other issues have become increasingly prominent since the publication of the first edition. The first is the nuclear question and, although negotiations between Iran and the P5+1 reached an agreement, responses to this deal – across the region and in the US – have been mixed. Israel and Saudi Arabia have raucously condemned any such deal and many believe that Saudi Arabia will now attempt to create a programme of its own, or, to buy a bomb from Pakistan. Avoiding the nightmare scenario of nuclear proliferation across the Middle East in the months (and years) ahead will involve traversing precarious terrain.

The second issue, of course, the emergence of the Islamic State of Iraq and al-Sham, commonly known as ISIS in the summer of 2014. The group gained prominence after the declaration of a caliphate under Abu Bakr al-Baghdadi, who anointed himself as Caliph Ibrahim, and through gaining control of large swathes of territory in Syria and Iraq. ISIS is vociferously anti-Shi'a and has fought against the rule of Bashar al-Assad and Iraqi Prime Ministers Nouri al-Maliki and Haider al-Abadi. If the rivalry was just driven by sectarian tensions then the emergence of ISIS would seemingly provide an additional opportunity to weaken Iranian influence in Iraq. However, Riyadh's strong response to the group, which has included building a 600-mile long fence along its northern border,[1] suggests that it too is concerned by ISIS survival in the face of sustained military campaigns against it. Ultimately then, this suggests that there are many other factors at play than just sectarian divisions.

Given this, it is also important to remember the role that internal dynamics play in shaping the external rivalry. Saudi Arabia faces an increasingly marginalised Shi'a population in its Eastern Province, while Iran faces challenges on the periphery of the state, which, when combined with the perception of the other's influence in these areas, remain of concern. Furthermore, in the past two years, both states have undergone political transition. On 15 June 2013, Hassan Rouhani was elected as Mahmoud Ahmadinejad's successor as the President of Iran. Eighteen months later, on 23 January 2015, King Abdullah of Saudi Arabia died and was succeeded by his 79-year-old half-brother, Salman, setting in motion political transformation of key positions within the Al Saud. While many across the region – and in the US – hoped that Rouhani's election would facilitate a return to an Iranian foreign policy that was more in the mould of Mohammad Khatami than Mahmoud Ahmadinejad, this has perhaps not entirely been due to the power of other factions within Iran, such as the Iranian Revolutionary Guards Corps.

At the end of this book, I set up five areas that needed to be addressed in order to facilitate rapprochement between Riyadh and Tehran. Of the five, perhaps only one has come close to resolution, although this may bring with it the nightmare scenario of nuclear proliferation across the Middle East. Following this, the role of the US in the region remains of concern, with Riyadh apprehensive about the apparent thawing of relations between Washington and Tehran. Given this, Washington faces a difficult balancing act of ensuring success in the nuclear deal with Iran while maintaining positive relations with Saudi Arabia. The resolution of domestic problems within both states is necessary in order to ensure the long-term stability of each state, but also to close down the perception of external interference. Coupled with this, of course, are notions of tolerance for other doctrinal belief systems, which are increasingly important in light of a growth in sectarian divisions across the region. Lastly addressed was the notion of both actors behaving with restraint in light of a fragmenting region; however, given the importance of perception in shaping an actor's behaviour, restraint may not be enough. Indeed, the need for trust building in order to demonstrate restraint appears imperative. Ultimately, both actors face serious challenges in the coming two years. How they choose to respond to them will shape the region in the coming decades.

ACKNOWLEDGEMENTS

When starting out on a project such as this, one is unaware of the depth of support and friendship required to see it through to the end. I am grateful to have received a great deal of both, from many people, and am delighted to have the opportunity to thank them here.

First and foremost, my heartfelt thanks go to my PhD supervisors, Professor Clive Jones and Dr Hugh Dyer, who offered a huge amount of support and guidance at every stage. The process was more enjoyable for your insight and I could not have wished for better supervisors.

Secondly, I wish to thank my examiners, Dr Graeme Davies and Dr Asaf Siniver, for an incredibly thorough vivá voce and their insightful comments. You have both helped make this a stronger work.

Thirdly, I wish to thank my friends and colleagues who offered encouragement, guidance, distraction and amusement throughout the project. In particular, I would like to thank Alan Craig, and Gordon Clubb; your friendship has been hugely valued. I would also like to thank Stefanie Bray for her friendship and support, for taking the time to read through the book and for her insightful comments.

MAPS

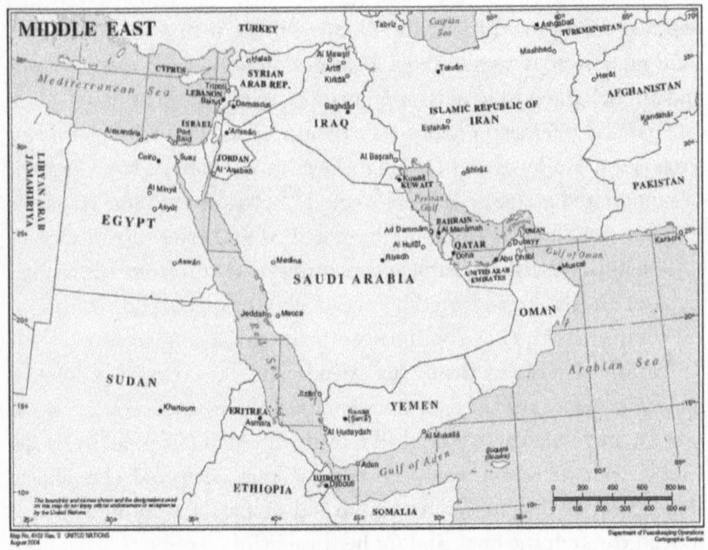

The Midde East
Taken from: http://www.un.org/Depts/Cartographic/map/profile/mideastr.pdf

Iran
Taken from: http://www.un.org/Depts/Cartographic/map/profile/iran.pdf

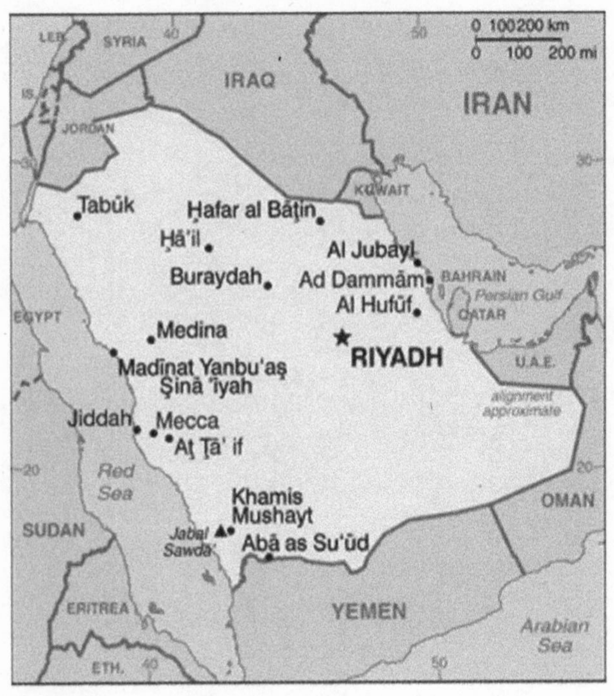

Saudi Arabia
Taken from: https://www.cia.gov/library/publications/the-world-factbook/geos/sa.html

INTRODUCTION

On 11 October 2011, Eric Holder, the US Attorney General, accused Iran of attempting to assassinate the Saudi Arabian ambassador to the United States. In a somewhat brazen attempt, the scheme involved an Iranian-American used-car salesman with alleged family ties to senior military personnel in Iran, hiring assassins from a Mexican drug cartel at a cost of $1.5 million. The assassins ultimately proved to be agents of the US Drug Enforcement Agency, who were able to foil the plot. Holder alleged that the assassination attempt was "directed and approved by elements of the Iranian government and, specifically, senior members of the Quds Force",[1] the wing of the elite Iranian Republican Guard Corps tasked with action abroad. This event was yet another incident in an increasingly complicated rivalry between Saudi Arabia and Iran.

Four years earlier, the President of Iran, Mahmoud Ahmadinejad, landed in Riyadh to attend the third Organization of the Petroleum Exporting Countries (OPEC) summit. The same year, Ahmadinejad also received an invitation to attend the Gulf Co-operation Council (GCC) meeting in Doha, the first time an Iranian president had received such an invitation. These meetings reflected a thawing in hostilities that had occurred in the preceeding years. During the GCC meeting, Ahmadinejad made reference to Iranian desires for regional security, free from external actors. Upon leaving, Ahmadinejad stated that it "seems that a new chapter of cooperation has been opened in the Persian Gulf".[2] Ahmadinejad was two years into his first term in office, having succeeded the more reform-minded Mohammad Khatami in 2005. Across the region, states hoped that the new president of Iran would build upon the work of Khatami, leading to an increase in positive relations across the Gulf. Unfortunately, this proved not to be the case.

Ahmadinejad's rise to power from Mayor of Tehran heralded a change in Iran's position within the region, becoming more assertive in foreign policy calculations. Ahmadinejad combined the Shi'i identity of the revolution with a strong sense of Persian nationalism, and under his leadership, Iran assumed a more prominent role within the regional security environment. This assertive foreign policy coupled an alleged nuclear weapons programme with the provision of support for groups such as Hizballah in Lebanon, the Assad regime in Syria, and Shi'i groups in Iraq, Bahrain and Saudi Arabia. In the process of supporting these groups and regimes, Iran alienated members of the GCC, other Middle Eastern states and the international community.

In the same year that Ahmadinejad was elected, Abdullah bin Abdul Aziz Al Saud ascended to the throne in Saudi Arabia. Abdullah, the tenth son of Saudi Arabia's founder, Ibn Saud, became the kingdom's sixth king at the age of 81. Under Abdullah, Saudi Arabia sought to maintain the status quo of a regional power, subsuming much of the power from Iraq post 2003. Saudi Arabia's leaders, the Al Saud family, have long derived much of their legitimacy from Islam, initially through the alliance with the fundamentalist Wahhabi movement, but also through custodianship of the two holy places of Islam, Mecca and Medina. Given the importance of Islam for the Al Saud, the revolution of 1979 in Iran and the establishment of an Islamic Republic would dramatically alter the dynamics of the Persian Gulf, resulting in competition for Islamic supieriority.

Thus, with both states aspiring to leadership over the Islamic world, coupled with perceived Iranian expansionist aspirations, the emergence of competition between the two states on ideological and geopolical grounds appeared a logical outcome. The ideological schism between the two states has manifested itself in the provision of support for groups across the region, wherein Saudi Arabia and Iran have found themselves providing support for opposing sides in conflicts, as seen in

Iraq, Bahrain and Syria. However, relations between Saudi Arabia and Iran have not always been hostile.

Prior to 1979, the rivalry between Saudi Arabia and Iran was predominantly characterised by concerns regarding the regional order, wherein both Al Saud and Pahlavi dynasties aspired to control of the Gulf region. Ideological competition within the rivalry stemmed from pre-existing Arab–Persian tensions and a degree of sectarian antagonism rather than fundamental doctrinal religious differences. The relationship was, however, characterised by suspicion between the royal families of the Al Saud and the Pahlavis.[3] This suspicion stemmed predominantly from competition over regional dominance and prior to 1958, was in part due to the involvement of the Hashemites in Baghdad, whose presence complicated relations within the regional order.[4]

Post World War Two, Iran was seen as a close ally of the United States. Writing in 1979, Fred Halliday noted:

> [T]he USA has guaranteed the Iranian regime since 1945 and has, since the late 1960s, been willing to back Iran in its drive for regional dominance by providing most of the diplomatic and military support that Iran has requested. Without US support Iranian foreign policy would not be conceivable in its present form: indeed, it would be impossible.[5]

Halliday suggested that despite a vast wealth, Saudi Arabia was unable to compete for regional power, given the size of Iran's population and military potential.[6] Despite the emergence of ARAMCO (the Arabian American Oil Company) in the early 1930s, strong ties between Riyadh and Washington were not fostered until after World War Two, by which point the United States had both realised the strategic importance of oil and feared the spread of Communism throughout the region.[7] This resulted in the emergence of military ties between Saudi Arabia and the United States,[8] providing Washington with increased influence within the region and Saudi Arabia with the military support to counter the threat posed by Nasser's Egypt.[9] Given ties to both Riyadh and Tehran, combined with space stemming from the British withdrawal from the Gulf,[10] the United States attempted to foster a "twin pillar" alliance between Saudi Arabia and Iran, although this never achieved formal status.[11]

In the aftermath of the British withdrawal from the Gulf in the 1970s, Iran was presented with an opportunity to assert its dominance over the region, immediately reviving the "historical Persian claim to sovereignty over Bahrain".[12] However, Saudi Arabia was opposed to this idea; indeed, the case of Bahrain is one of the instances where Saudi Arabia and Iran were in disagreement prior to 1979. The issue was resolved, with Iran saving face, by the Shah suggesting that the Bahrainis should be able to determine their own fate, opening the door for a UN mission to discover that the people of Bahrain desired independence.[13]

Despite the areas of competition and friction, including competition within OPEC over oil prices, as Halliday notes, "the Iranians and Saudis, though suspicious of each other had learned to live together".[14] Furthermore, the role of the United States demonstrated the reliance of both Saudi Arabia and Iran on external forces to guarantee their security.[15] The events of 1979 in Iran, however, dramatically changed the nature of both the rivalry and regional security.

The rivalry between Saudi Arabia and Iran can be characterised by two areas of competition, namely ideological and geopolitical. The first area of competition is driven by competing identities, in particular, ethno-national and religious identities. Historically, relations between Arab and Persian have been strained, as a consequence of the legacy of both Arab and Persian influence across the region. Religious competition occurs as a consequence of the dominance of Wahhabism[16] within Saudi Arabia, which is often categorised as part of the Sunni sect of Islam and Iran's adherence to the Shi'i sect of Islam. The two major facets of Islam are ideologically opposed to each other, with some holding Sunni and Shi'i doctrines to be incompatible, given Islamic history. The Iranian revolution of 1979 proved cataclysmic for regional security and was followed by a torrent of rhetoric articulating Iran's desired position within the Islamic world. Saudi Arabia was especially vulnerable to this rhetoric, given the importance of Islam within the Kingdom and the Al Saud's desire to control the Islamic world.

Particularly damning was Tehran's postulation that the Al Saud was not a legitimate Islamic dynasty and thus could not be accepted as the guardian of the two holy places of Islam.

The notion of being the guardian of Mecca and Medina is an integral aspect of the Al Saud's legitimacy, both internally and across the Islamic world. As such, the emergence of Iran as a major power within the Islamic world adhering to a diametrically opposed interpretation of Islam offered a further source of entanglement in relations between the two. Furthermore, the Iranian leadership used a large amount of rhetoric against the Al Saud, which had a two-fold effect upon internal stability within Saudi Arabia: firstly, in delegitimising the Al Saud, and secondly, unsettling the Shi'i population within the Kingdom.

Within the second area of competition, Riyadh and Tehran both lay claim to influence over the Persian Gulf region and the wider Middle East. These claims are especially pertinent, given the decline of Iraq as a regional power post 2003. This geopolitical competition is illustrated by a dispute over the name of the body of water separating Saudi Arabia and Iran, denoted the Persian Gulf and Arabian Gulf by Tehran and Riyadh, respectively.[17] Moreover, Tehran perceives that it is uniquely qualified to occupy a position of influence over the region through its belief that Iran is a natural state, derived from the notion that many states throughout the Middle East were created at the whim of colonial powers. The belief that Iran is a natural state is a consequence of Persian history stretching back to approximately 700 BC, and the emergence of organic borders.[18] Additionally, within the geopolitical sphere is an economic rivalry, stemming from Saudi Arabia and Iran's roles as the dominant suppliers of both oil and natural gas, both within the Middle East and the world. This competition has manifested itself within OPEC and has proved to have wide ramifications.

Current Debates

Much has been written on Saudi Arabia and Iran, with debates ranging from foreign policy making to the nature of civil society. While the array of literature is vast, the literature examining the security aspect of the relationship between the two countries is limited[19] and also employs a narrow conception of security. This book seeks to broaden this conception of security, in particular of the security dilemma. Furthermore, while there exists a deep pool of literature on both Saudi Arabia and Iran that discusses the impact of identity upon each state, the authors do not place the conclusions in the wider context of the relationship between the two countries.

This book considers the rivalry between Saudi Arabia and Iran from an alternate perspective. Much has been written examining the nature of hard power competition across the Middle East, however this work stresses the importance of soft power. In addition, it challenges the notion that states within the Middle East are coherent, unitary actors, suggesting instead that in order to fully understand the behaviour of a state, one must consider the importance of internal dynamics. The internal challenges that a state faces, if severe enough, can result in an internal security dilemma, the resolution of which has the capacity to complicate the external security environment.

The population of Saudi Arabia is around 28 million people (including approximately 5 million expatriate workers). The vast majority of Saudis are Sunni Arabs, although there are a number of Shi'i Muslims, located mainly within the Eastern Province of the country. The main cause of identity incongruence within Saudi Arabia occurs between the state and the Shi'i Muslims within the Eastern Province, although there are also strong tribal tensions. The state of Saudi Arabia was created in 1932 by Ibn Saud, who unified a collection of tribes through a combination of force and ideology, antagonizing numerous tribes who believe their claims of legitimacy of rule over the Arabian Peninsula to be greater than the Al Saud's.

Within the Iranian population of approximately 70 million, Persians account for only half the population. In addition to Persians, there are numerous different ethnic groups, spanning Azerbaijanis, Kurds, Arabs, Turkmen, Baluchis and Lors. This has led John Bradley to refer to Iran as a "multinational empire dominated by Persians".[20] The various groups transcend purely ethnic characteristics and include religious groups. Although the vast majority of Iranians subscribe to the Shi'i strand of Islam, there also exist small numbers of Sunni Muslims, Christians and Jews.

In order to fully understand the nuances of the rivalry, and indeed of Middle Eastern security, one needs to have an awareness of the impact of internal dynamics upon external relations between states. To this end, the book is split into seven chapters. The first chapter offers a critical analysis of literature within International Relations and an approach to explore the nature of the rivalry. The second chapter provides a contextual and historical background to the relationship between Saudi Arabia and Iran in the post-1979 period, detailing the major events in the relationship and discussing the pressures emanating from both the domestic and international system that shaped the relationship. It does so by separating the rivalry into two spheres: ideological and geopolitical. Chapter three analyses the nature of state formation and the role of narratives in the state-building process, while offering a location of the state in the regional security environment.

Chapters four and five examine the nature of identity incongruence and internal security dilemmas within each state. In doing so, the argument considers identities located within both Saudi Arabia and Iran, with particular focus upon ethnic, tribal and religious identities. Chapters four and five seek to achieve two goals: firstly, presenting those identities existing within Saudi Arabia and Iran; secondly, considering how these identities have impacted upon regime stability. The fourth chapter examines the role of religion within each state, discussing the main religious identities. Chapter five examines the plethora of ethnic and tribal identities, within Iran focussing upon ethnic identities and within Saudi Arabia focussing upon tribal identities. This chapter also considers the impact of irredentism within the region, with an examination of issues stemming from the process of state formation.

Chapter six examines the resolution of internal security dilemmas, with a focus upon the use of narratives. It also explores the manipulation of internal security dilemmas across the region and the implications for regional security. The seventh chapter considers how internal security dilemmas within Saudi Arabia and Iran have led to an external security dilemma driven by soft power. It considers how this external soft power security dilemma guides both the nature of the rivalry and of Middle Eastern security.

1

THE MIDDLE EAST IN INTERNATIONAL RELATIONS

"First say to yourself what you would be; and then do what you have to do."

Epictetus

The field of International Relations (IR) is concerned with explaining the interaction of actors, operating at state, sub-state and trans-state levels. As the late Fred Halliday notes, "the task of social science, IR included is [. . .] namely to *explain*, in as persuasive a manner as possible, what has occurred and to identify what constitute significant contemporary trends" within the discipline.[1] The heterogeneous theories of IR suggest that the behaviour of a state is determined by various factors ranging from security concerns to state institutions, from identity to the construction of the international system.

This book examines the impact of identity incongruence upon regional security across the Middle East, with a particular focus upon the rivalry between Saudi Arabia and Iran after the Iranian revolution of 1979. The phrase *identity incongruence* stems from the work of Raymond Hinnebusch, who articulates incongruence between identity and territory;[2] however, this book expands upon the idea of identity incongruence to include tensions between states and national identities, sub-and trans-state identities, and to consider the ensuing problems of legitimacy. The notion of identity incongruence is often overlooked when considering the Middle East; it is not possible to fully understand the nuances of Middle Eastern politics without understanding the true essence of identity groups and, thus, identity incongruence. Indeed, there are very few states within the Middle East that do not possess a degree of identity incongruence, which challenges the notion of a coherent nation-state that underpins several approaches to IR. When the level of identity incongruence challenges the sovereignty of a state, either territorially or ideologically, and necessitates a response from the ruling elite, then identity incongruence results in an internal security dilemma. The nature of this response, in turn, can impact upon the regional security environment, given both a shared normative environment and the incongruence of identity and territory. Thus, understanding identity incongruence can explain the impact that internal dynamics have upon external relations, namely in the form of an internal-external security dilemma.

Given the pervasive nature of conflict and the prominent role played by identity within the Middle East, the book focuses upon security, building upon three of the five security issues articulated by Barry Buzan,[3] notably military, political, and societal, leaving examination of economic and environmental security issues to other scholars. These three understandings of security are the focus of the work, due to the prominent role played by identity within each conception of security, and it is through analysing the impact of identity incongruence that the work explains the nature of the rivalry. In undertaking this task, the book draws predominantly upon the modified Realism of Hinnebusch and the Constructivism of Michael Barnett,[4] seeking to offer a new framework for analysing Middle Eastern IR and broadening understandings of security.

Within each state are a plethora of identities, several of which are conflicting in nature; indeed, national identities are often challenged by different ethnic, tribal or religious identities. Given the existence of myriad identities within the region, it is irrefutable that these identities will impact both upon internal stability and relations and competition between states. Nevertheless, analysis of the influence of these identities has been hitherto scant, particularly with regard to the impact that identity has upon the relationship between Saudi Arabia and Iran. Despite the importance of identities across the region, literature examining Middle Eastern security has predominantly been focussed upon hard power calculations.

In contrast, this book concentrates upon how competing identities within Saudi Arabia and Iran have impacted upon relations between the two states, specifically how the state's response to internal challenges, stemming from identity incongruence, has complicated the rivalry. It suggests that the state's response to identity incongruence has ramifications for regional security, in an internal-external security dilemma, where the external security dilemma occurs in the guise of a soft power security dilemma. The move from the internal to the external is referred to as "the Incongruence Dilemma".[5]

The Middle East in International Relations Theory

Much has been written on IR theory, with recent work seeking to resolve ontological and epistemological disputes both within and across theories. However, very few scholars have applied IR theory to the Middle East. Those scholars who have undertaken such a task include luminaries such as Anoushiravan Ehteshami, Raymond Hinnebusch and Fred Halliday.[6] Many of the applications of IR theory to the Middle East apply Realist approaches to the region, yet adopting a singular position belies the complexity of the region and fails to appreciate the importance of identity.

The existing literature examining the IR of Middle Eastern states attempts to bridge the gap between the theoretical world of IR and the empirical world of regional studies in order to provide a comprehensive analytical framework for examining the IR of the Middle East. While recent work in IR has employed Sociological or Constructivist approaches, it is beneficial to begin analysis with one of the more celebrated yet contested theories of IR.

The Realist Tradition

The main starting point for most IR scholars is Realism, which, although as a theory contains numerous different interpretations, is predominantly concerned with power.

Numerous authors have contributed to the theory of Classical Realism, notably Edward Hallett Carr[7] and Hans Morgenthau.[8] For the Classical Realist, the main unit of analysis is the state,[9] which is taken to be a rational actor and the main driving factor within IR is the state's pursuit of interests, defined as power. Understanding interest as power provides continuity for analysing different actors,[10] and circumvents problems of defining national interest.

Carr's 1939 work, *The Twenty Years' Crisis*, offers a damning critique of liberal utopianism, which had prevailed post World War One. Carr suggests that one should be more concerned with how the world is, than how it ought to be.[11] At the heart of Carr's work is a concern with the notion of scarcity, the ensuing conflict between the haves and have-nots and a desire to maintain the status-quo of the haves.

Morgenthau's *Politics Among Nations: The Struggle for Power and Peace* extrapolates on Carr's ideas, offering a theoretical development of Classical Realism. Morgenthau articulates how different accounts of world politics demonstrate a dispute between two schools who:

> differ fundamentally in their conceptions of the nature of man, society, and politics. One believes that a rational and moral political order, derived from universally valid abstract principles, can be achieved here and now. It assumes the essential goodness and infinite malleability of human nature [...] It trusts in education, reform, and the sporadic use of force to remedy these defects. The other school believes that the world, imperfect as it is from the rational point of view, is the result of forces inherent in human nature.[12]

For Morgenthau, "politics, like society in general, is governed by objective laws that have their roots in human nature".[13] Indeed, for Morgenthau, this Realist tradition can be traced back through history, notably in the work of Sun Tzu, Thucydides, Machiavelli and Hobbes.

While Morgenthau's work is compelling, there are several criticisms that must be noted. Firstly, Morgenthau holds the state as a unitary actor, ignoring internal dynamics and ideology. Secondly, Marxists contend that Realism is concerned with a reproduction of capitalist relations of production and that the theory lacks engagement with the impact of economic factors upon foreign policy. Lastly, post-modernists reject claims of objectivity. This book builds upon the first criticism, of the state as a unitary actor, seeking to unpack this notion and give credence to the competing identity groups existing within the state. The argument also addresses aspects of the post-modernist criticism, accepting that while there are objective and verifiable facts, often narratives and events within the Middle East are contestable.

Kenneth Waltz's 1979 work, *A Theory of International Politics*,[14] introduces Neo-Realism, also known as Structural Realism, as a theory that examines the relationship between the states and the international system. In contrast to Classical Realism, Neo-Realism focusses upon the nature of the international system, rather than the nature of states. The international system Waltz describes is a trans-historic, anarchic system within which states are free from the threat of coercion from a higher rule. Accordingly, the international system is governed by security concerns, defined by the distribution of power within. States are again held to be unitary actors who behave in a rational way, seeking to maximise their own security; the international system is one of self-help, wherein states are required to guarantee their own security.

Waltz argues that security is preserved through a balance of power, which holds that states counter threats facing them, with the aim of introducing parity into a relationship. A further way states can improve their security is through bandwagoning, particularly relevant to weaker states, who struggle to counter threats through a balance of power. Thus, weaker states can bandwagon with the stronger states or coalitions who can guarantee their security; consequently, alliances are born.[15]

While Neo-Realism revitalised the Realist tradition, it does incite several serious criticisms,[16] in particular stemming from its state-centric approach. Waltz rejects the idea of reducing examination of the international system to anything beyond the state level, arguing that by doing so one encourages a proliferation of variables. Yet, in undertaking analysis based on a state-centric position, Waltz's theory ignores much of the context needed to truly understand the IR of the Middle East.[17]

Furthermore, the Neo-Realist rejects the impact of trans-state ideologies, which seems counter-intuitive, as Pan-Arabism pervaded Middle Eastern states throughout the 1960s. Pan-Arabism greatly influenced the behaviour of Arab states, which can be seen with regard to the 1967 War with Israel. However, a counter argument to this suggests that Arab leaders, motivated by self-interest and a desire to maintain internal and external legitimacy, led to what Michael Barnett refers to as the symbolic dance to war.[18] Indeed Barnett suggests that the 1967 War was a result of symbolic competition rather than of Pan-Arabism.[19]

Additionally, given the security-dominated paradigm of Neo-Realism, alliance building should have pervaded the region, yet no Middle Eastern state has formally allied itself with Israel, arguably the dominant military power in the region. This appears to suggest that adopting a theory grounded purely in power politics is counter-intuitive, further, that ideological imperatives must, to a certain degree, govern a state's behaviour. However, it is possible that alliance formation across the region may occur through the medium of covert diplomacy. This suggestion has been supported by the release of WikiLeaks cables that allege Israel is engaging in dialogue with the United Arab Emirates, despite not possessing official diplomatic ties.[20] Further, Waltz's assertion that the international system is *ahistoric* poses problems. The Neo-Realist holds that the international system has remained constant since the time of Thucydides,[21] an assertion that seems questionable, given the evolution of the state, of economics and of military affairs.

A more contemporary aspect of the Realist tradition is an attempt to fuse the Classical and Neo-Realist positions in what has been termed "Neo-Classical Realism" by Gideon Rose.[22] Neo-Classical Realism seeks to fuse both internal and external dynamics, with Rose suggesting that:

> [T]he scope and ambition of a country's foreign policy is driven first and foremost by its place in the international system and specifically by its relative material power capabilities [. . .] the impact of such power capabilities on foreign policy is indirect and complex, because systemic pressures must be translated through intervening variables at the unit level.[23]

While Neo-Classical Realism appears to combine the best aspects of both Classical and Neo-Realism, it fails to adequately address the focus upon material understandings of power and of ideologies.

Constructivism

One response to the ontological and epistemological claims made by the various Realist positions is Constructivism. Constructivism is especially relevant to understanding Middle Eastern IR, given the emphasis placed upon non-material factors, such as identity and ideology. While Constructivists agree that inherent to the approach is a focus upon the construction of International Relations, within Constructivist thought are several strands, they differ over the extent to which there is an empirically verifiable reality.[24] Constructivists differ from Realists (be they Classical or Neo) by rejecting objective facts, suggesting instead that facts are dependent upon socially established conventions. These conventions can be characterised by the credence given to normative and social factors, moving away from a purely material analysis. As Nicholas Onuf argues, facts are "not reflective of an objective, material reality but an inter subjective, or social, reality".[25] As such, the structures within which actors operate are defined by social norms and ideas.

Given the prominence of the state within the Middle East, one of the most captivating Constructivist theories for examining Middle Eastern IR comes from Alexander Wendt. In Wendt's seminal work "*Anarchy is what states make of it*",[26] the argument is predominantly concerned with the nature of identity and the ensuing impact on relations between states. Wendt argues that the identity of a state is created through the process of interaction with other actors, rather than existing inherently, and argues that international structure does not exist except for the process of states interacting. As a consequence, international politics is created rather than given.[27]

Wendt offers a state centric view of IR,[28] suggesting that the behaviour of states is influenced by inter-subjective relationships. Wendt's Constructivist holds that people act on the basis of meanings that objects and other actors have for them, and that meanings are not ontologically inherent, but develop through the process of interaction. While Wednt's international system is one of anarchy, because states' identities are created, not innate, anarchy is what states make of it. Consequently, identities are developed and maintained in interaction; these interactions determine the nature of anarchy and the ensuing security environment.[29]

Despite the initial appeal of his work, one must question certain aspects of Wendt's theory. Maja Zehfuss is critical of the exclusion of domestic politics from Wendt's theory, while also attacking the notion of collective identity and drawing attention to the "malleable, contingent and elusive"[30] nature of Wendt's identity. A further criticism draws upon the issue of identifiable identities, for according to Wendt's framework, it must be the case that a state must be identifiable with a particular identity. This causes problems for insecure identities, and shifting identities. When considering the level of identity incongruence within and across Middle Eastern states, this appears problematic.

This is illustrated by the case of Saudi Arabia, which maintains a strong Islamic identity through the alliance between the Al Saud family and Wahhabism, yet through an alliance with the United States the ruling elite has arguably caused a dichotomy between those who support the Al Saud dynasty and the followers of Wahhabism.[31] Moreover, there are those within Saudi Arabia who reject the legitimacy of the Al Saud, thus rejecting the Al Saud's position as tantamount to a national identity. Indeed, the Middle East is a breeding ground of identities hostile to those deemed national identities.[32] Accordingly, there are some who may reject Wendt's state-centric approach on the grounds of choosing the *wrong* identity. Indeed, a prime example of this is Syria, whose ruling family, the al-Assad, belong to the Alawite Shi'i minority, while the majority of the Syrian population is Sunni.

Further, one must also consider the arbitrary imposition of state boundaries across the region, wherein there are many instances of the evisceration of collective identities, be they tribal, ethnic or religious. Moreover, this challenge to collective identities is best seen in cases of irredentism[33] and secessionism. Thus, the idea of all states within the Middle East being "nation-states" is inaccurate. Consequently, it must be questioned to what degree is a collective identity possible, both theoretically and empirically. Thus, it is necessary to explore the internal dynamics of states to ensure a full awareness of malleable, contingent and elusive identities.

Historical Sociology

A further approach is offered by Fred Halliday, who suggests that IR should be examined through the lens of Historical Sociology, which contains two distinct stages: a historicisation of the state and a location of that history within an international context. Halliday details the theory of Historical Sociology in *For an International Sociology*,[34] in which he suggests that Historical Sociology should play both an analytic role and an emancipatory role, which attempts to "denaturalise the inevitable". Within Historical Sociology, Halliday gives credence to the role of agency and the relationship with structure. Stressing the importance of agency is especially important for Halliday, given that IR has traditionally denied the question of agency.

Halliday applies his theory to the Middle East in a work entitled *The Middle East in International Relations*,[35] which attempts to bridge the gap between the theoretical and empirical. In this work, Halliday gives prominence to the state, while examining the core components of the political and social orders, with particular focus upon the formation and maintenance of institutions. Additionally, given the existence of regional norms and the trend for shared political systems, Halliday argues there is a "low salience of sovereignty",[36] which results in constant interference.

While Halliday's framework of analysis is both fascinating and insightful, particularly through application of an interpretation of the structure-agency debate to the region, there are several issues to address. Halliday attempts to open the proverbial "black box of the state", in essence attempting to explain why the norms, nuances, institutions and identities located within constitute a state and determine foreign policy. The work necessitates complete knowledge of society and historical context, and while the results may be of some merit, there is also the capacity for inaccuracy. Given that at no time is there access to unabridged information, the potential for missing elements is great and the conceivable consequences for the theory may be severe. Moreover, the relationship between institutions and identity is not always clear, with institutions not always reflecting the identities of a particular state.

Alternative Approaches

There are numerous alternate ways of explaining the behaviour of states in the Middle East, in particular through using Structuralist theories. One of the more compelling of which is World-Systems Analysis, which, as proposed by Immanuel Wallerstein, is a "knowledge movement" that takes world system to be the main unit of analysis, rather than the nation state.[37] World-Systems Analysis suggests that within the international division of labour, different regimes of labour control between multiple states determines the strength and geopolitical location of a state within the world economy. As such, there are three classes of states: core, semi-periphery, and periphery. However, this approach moves the focus of analysis from the state, which in the Middle East is problematic.

An additional approach that can be used to explain the behaviour of states that possess internal problems is Diversionary Theory,[38] sagaciously discussed in the context of the Iranian case by Graeme Davies.[39] Given the high levels of unemployment and economic problems within Iran, Davies suggests that in accordance with Diversionary Theory, the "Iranian foreign-policy elite therefore has two incentives to engage in aggressive acts with another state (1) divert attention from problem's at home and revive a 'rally-round the flag' effect and (2) demonstrate a competence in foreign affairs".[40] Given the internal challenges facing states across the Middle East, it seems that Diversionary Theory possesses a strong explanatory power. However, while Diversionary Theory possesses the capacity to explain behaviour, it fails to adequately address the internal conflict that the diversionary tactics seek to circumvent. Although diversionary tactics have most certainly been used as part of a strategy to tackle these problems, the severity of internal challenges across many states in the Middle East requires direct action. Indeed, with the case of Iran, there are strong challenges to the territorial and ideological sovereignty of the state, which necessitate a direct response from the ruling elite. While diversionary tactics have undoubtably been used in an attempt to circumvent economic problems, these tactics cannot adequately explain the foreign policies of Saudi Arabia and Iran, given the levels of identity incongruence within each state.

Theoretical Underpinnings to the Incongruence Dilemma

Thus far, the chapter has considered celebrated singular theoretical approaches, yet the application of a singular theory to examine the IR of the Middle East appears problematic. In an attempt to circumvent these problems, this chapter offers a pluralist approach, entitled the "Incongruence Dilemma". The Incongruence Dilemma builds upon a Classical Realist position, while adding a Constructivist dimension that stresses the importance of identity. It suggests that, in order to fully understand the IR of the Middle East, one must examine internal identity groups and the behaviour of the state towards those groups. This book focusses on the importance of identity and how this drives the behaviour of states across the region. The work is set over three stages, with particular consideration of both the interaction of identity groups, which may contain incongruence, and of state-society relations. Before expanding on the Incongruence Dilemma, it is essential to examine the work of several authors who wrote directly on the Middle East.

Hinnebusch's Realism

Raymond Hinnebusch, in a work entitled *The Foreign Policies of Middle Eastern States*,[41] co-edited with Anoushiravan Ehteshami, articulates an analytical framework based on a position of modified Realism, taking the state to be the main actor in the international system, intent on maximizing both autonomy and security across domestic, regional-systemic and global levels. A move away from the Realist position sees Hinnebusch hold that the Middle Eastern regional system is still in the process of consolidation and so has less effect on the behavior of states within the system than other, consolidated regional systems. The argument occurs across five stages: core-periphery relations, identity and sovereignty, state formation, foreign policy making, and the regional state system. [42]

Hinnebusch begins his analysis by portraying the Middle East as a penetrated system, subject to high levels of interference yet resistant to subordination, drawing upon Structuralist theory, in particular, Johan Galtung's *Structural Theory of Imperialism*.[43] The second stage of Hinnebusch's framework considers the relationship between identity and sovereignty, rejecting the Realist assumption of a secure, defined national identity. Hinnebusch argues that with arbitrary boundaries emerging from the artificial imposition of states in the Middle East, loyalty to the state is tempered by loyalty to sub-state and trans-state identities. Indeed the "resultant embedding of the state system in a matrix of fluid multiple identities"[44] causes problems for Realist assumptions of national interest. The discussion of the relationship between identity and sovereignty occurs on two levels: firstly, an examination of irredentism, a dissatisfaction with the incongruity of imposed borders and communities. Irredentism can lead to the emergence of strong trans-state movements and in an effort to provide support for an ethnic community, can incite states to interfere in another state's domestic affairs. Secondly, the nature of trans-state identities in the Middle East results in the emergence of a duality between *raison de la nation* and *raison d'état.* The examples of Pan-Arabism and Pan-Islamism are used to emphasise this point, showing that collective ideals contained within the pan "isms" can supersede state identity.

The third stage of the framework examines state formation, refuting that states always contain internal cohesion. Hinnebusch suggests that if strong institutions are developed through the process of state formation, then the will of the leader can be constrained; however, if such institutions have not developed to a satisfactory level, the leader has the potential to rule with very little accountability. In the fourth stage of the framework, Hinnebusch turns to an examination of the making of foreign policy, notably, "omni-balancing": a need to defend the regime from external threats while maintaining internal legitimacy. States face pressures from both sub-and trans-state ideologies, and from external actors. As such, the location of the threat dictates the nature of the response.

The final stage of Hinnebusch's framework contains analysis of the regional states' system, in particular the relationship between states when conflict occurs, and the consequence of the interaction between a state's domestic needs and systemic pressures for foreign policy. Hinnebusch discusses how the efforts of states to maintain internal stability and fend off pressures from sub- and trans-state ideologies have increased tensions within the region. As states consolidated, they "enhanced the potential threat each posed to the other".[45] Given the increased level of distrust, Hinnebusch suggests that Middle Eastern security is dependent upon a balance of power, stressing that Realist solutions are of particular relevance to the Middle East.

While Hinnebusch's framework, especially concerning the impact of identity upon IR, is compelling, there are several issues that need to be raised. While giving credence to internal identity groups, this framework does not examine the interaction of these internal identity groups, but rather focusses upon the challenge posed to the territorial integrity of the state. This misses the challenge posed by identity incongruence to the ideological sovereignty of the state, pertinent to the cases of both Saudi Arabia and Iran.

Barnett's Constructivism

Supplementing Hinnebusch's theory is a compelling development of Constructivist theory provided by Michael Barnett. *Dialogues in Arab Politics*[46] draws heavily on Constructivism but supplements the position with sociological arguments. Barnett rejects the assumption that Realism is the most appropriate prism through which to view Middle Eastern IR, suggesting that arms races are not the dominant guiding factor within the Middle Eastern security dilemma, thus rejecting that security concerns govern action. Rather, Barnett suggests that the self-image of leaders determines action, holding that the ruling elites of Middle Eastern states are more concerned with perception, particularly the perception of impropriety and, thus, hold symbolic politics over military politics.

Barnett's argument is concerned with norms and how these norms regulate relations and express identity, with the notion of a "dialogue" born when "an event triggers an intensified discussion among the members of the group about the norms that are to guide their relations".[47] These dialogues are governed by two ways through which Arab leaders attempt to engender support: firstly, by attempting to frame events in a particular way, and secondly, by using symbolism to convey their message. Barnett portrays Arab leaders as motivated by self-interest and self-image, as "actors [who] stand distant from their social roles and can manipulate them for ulterior purpose".[48]

The framework presented by Barnett covers three stages: an examination of normative structure, an examination of the technologies of power, and an analysis of how actors draw upon structural properties as they make and unmake relations. The first stage of Barnett's framework considers the nature of the international system and the relationship between the material and the normative. Barnett rejects the position of several IR theorists who attempt to reduce IR to the material, arguing that combining the social element to the material is imperative. The argument continues with an examination of how the international environment is a source of identity and interests, providing conditions for the possibility of action. Here, Barnett is rejecting the *asocial* concept of actors offered by many microeconomic approaches, but is not advocating a view of actors as both completely socialized and domesticated. For Barnett, actors are not solely the bearers of social roles and enactors of social norms, they also have the capacity to interpret them.[49] Within this stage, Barnett draws upon the work of Erving Goffman,[50] arguing that actors interpret structure and norms for both "audience" and the "self".[51]

The second stage shows Arab leaders' attempts "to define the social situation, determine the norms of Arabism, and control the actions of their rivals through strategic framing and symbolic exchanges".[52] The stage rests upon the premise that the more entrenched the actor is within the normative environment, the more dependant the actor is for social approval and, conversely, the more susceptible the actor is to "normative suasion and symbolic sanctions".[53] The logic behind this argument is thus: Barnett argues that events do not have objective meaning, so leaders attempt to give events political meaning through locating the event within an overarching narrative, which provides a link between an interpretation of the past and an image of the future.[54] Barnett posits the idea of a "symbolic security dilemma"; however, rather than the notion of a threat provoking an escalation, the idea of a spiraling flux of symbolic moves motivates ruling elites to act, as demonstrated by the build up to the 1967 War. This flux of symbolic moves can be seen within the Islamic world, notably over claims to Islamic leadership. This notion of a flux of symbolic moves plays an important role within the Incongruence Dilemma.

The third stage of the framework examines how normative structures are "produced through social and strategic interaction"[55] and how changes in normative structure can result in changes in identity. Indeed, "crises and dialogues in this regard can be a place of 'punctuated equilibrium', a point of passage from one identity to another".[56] Barnett suggests that the structure of Arab politics ultimately led to its demise. Arabism was a tool that propagated stability and legitimacy, however its transnational nature proved threatening to the sovereignty of states. As such, ruling elites sought to portray themselves as the bastions of Arabism, often attempting to employ its norms, coupled with the events of the day, in a way that would preserve the interests of the regime. Moreover, this portrayal was often combined with the framing of other Arab states as seditious to the collective cause. Drawing from this, it is easy to see how the fractious nature of Arabism resulted in a fragmentation of norms and consequently changes in identity.

Ontological Compatibility

As previously noted, the Incongruence Dilemma builds upon work within both Realist and Constructivist areas. While there appear to be several problems existing at an ontological level when combining Realism and Constructivism, this book builds upon an existing trend within IR,[57] holding that it is possible to circumvent these problems. While the Constructivist starting point was a response to Realism, this was to Waltz's Neo-Realism, leaving scope to bring Classical Realism and Constructivism closer together, especially given the credence placed upon morality by Classical Realists. Moreover, power, albeit in different guises, underpins both Classical Realism and Constructivism. As J. Samuel Barkin states, even Wendt "notes that to the extent Realism is about power, he too is a Realist".[58] This suggests that there is common ground between Realism and Constructivism, and that while traditionally Realist understandings of power have been focussed upon the material, this is not explicit. However, a point of difference emerges when considering the ontological claims made by both positions. The Realist accepts the existence of objective facts, whereas the Constructivist rejects this, holding that the facts about the international system reflect an inter subjective reality.

When resolving this ontological compatibility, one must differentiate between strands of Constructivist thought, achieved through considering whether there is an "empirically identifiable reality to be identified and studied".[59] Those who argue that there is such a reality are referred to as Neo-Classical Constructivists, contrasted with Post-modern Constructivists. It is predominantly the Neo-Classical position that permits ontological compatibility.

Barkin suggests that there are typically three areas of Classical Realist thinking that demonstrate an incompatibility between Realists and Constructivists: firstly, a focus upon material capabilities; secondly, viewing human nature as materialistic; thirdly, the charge that Classical Realism is "positivist" or "empiricist". In responding to these charges, first one must allow for complex understandings of power, giving scope to both material and non-material factors. Indeed, by using more malleable interpretations of power, one is able to permit analysis of the role of morality and ideas within power structures. Thus, using a Realist-Constructivist position, one is able to examine the relationship between normative structures, political morality and the use of power. Secondly, the Classical Realist position does not require human nature to be infinitely malleable. Rather, for the emergence of insecurity and fear that are inherent within Realist schools of thought, all that is needed is for some individuals to be aggressive or driven by self interest. In responding to the third challenge, it is worth quoting Barkin in full:

> [T]he acceptance of the importance of ideas, and the insistence that historical context matters found in the works of Morgenthau

> fit quite well into a statement of constructivist epistemology, whther Neo-Classical or postmodern. And the ontology of classical realism, accepting a reality separate from subjective opinion but not, as a result, denying the role of unobservables such as morality, is hardly the sort of brute materialism that constructivist critics sometimes associate with realism. [60]

As such, it appears possible to fuse the Classical Realist and Neo-Classical Constructivist positions, which allows for greater analysis of the role of non-material factors in power structures.

Security Dilemmas and the Incongruence Dilemma

Much of the analysis of Middle Eastern IR and, indeed, of the rivalry between Saudi Arabia and Iran has been written from a Realist perspective, be that Classical or Neo-Realist; both offer appealing theories, given that the Middle East is a region governed by security concerns and is possibly best described as an anarchic region. However, these positions are open to several serious criticisms, one of the main critiques being concerned with the lack of credence given to the impact of identities and ideologies. Given the plethora of identities and ideologies existing within the region, this appears to be a serious problem. A potential way around this is to employ a Constructivist framework that acknowledges the importance of these identities; however, again, there are problems with this position. Thus, it appears that the application of a single theory to the Middle East region has serious pitfalls.

While there appears an incompatibility between Hinnebusch and Barnett, through their subscription to modified positions of Realism and Constructivism, respectively, the two positions are closer than initially considered. Indeed, both Hinnebusch and Barnett stress the importance of identity within the discipline of IR and both are concerned with the accumulation of power, albeit through different methods.[61] Furthermore, if one adapts the Realist and Constructivist positions, assumes that the state is not a unitary actor and gives credence to the role played by identity groups within the state, then it appears possible to synthesise the Realist and Constructivist approaches.

Given this ability to draw Realist and Constructivist positions together, there remain important criticisms of the theories posited by Hinnebusch and Barnett that must be addressed by any proposed framework: any approach must accept the prominence of the state within Middle Eastern IR while also appreciating the importance of identity. By building upon and adding to the theories of Hinnebusch and Barnett, it is possible to avoid the problems of subscribing to a Constructivist school of thought while utilising facets of Realism. Moreover, the use of power, albeit in different guises, illustrates how the Constructivist and Realist can potentially be brought closer together, also facilitating appreciation of the importance of identity within IR. As such, building upon the theories of Classical Realism and Constructivism, this book applies a three-stage conceptual framework to explain the rivalry between Saudi Arabia and Iran, referred to as the Incongruence Dilemma.

At the heart of the Incongruence Dilemma is a modified form of the security dilemma.[62] Standard understandings of the security dilemma hold that two or more states, concerned with potential threats posed by other states, act to increase their own security. Given the lack of omniscience, other states perceive these moves as acts of aggression and move to increase their own security. As a consequence, despite neither state necessarily desiring an escalation in tensions, the potential for conflict has been exacerbated. Thus, the security dilemma is perceived as a feature of anarchy, defined by Ken Booth and Nicholas Wheeler as "the existential condition of uncertainty in human affairs".[63]

Booth and Wheeler outline how the security dilemma emerges from a two-level strategic predicament, through a dilemma of interpretation and a dilemma of response. The dilemma of interpretation is born from the uncertainty of attempting to understand the "motives, intentions and capabilities"[64] of another's military policies and posturing, while the dilemma of response concerns the nature of the reaction. If the dilemma of response increases hostility, then the two states are embroiled in a security dilemma.

While general understandings of the security dilemma employ a hard conception of power, there are, however, additional aspects to the security dilemma. One of these can be understood in terms of soft power. The work of Joseph Nye, notably *Bound to Lead*[65] and *Soft Power*,[66] differentiates between two different types of power, hard and soft. Hard power is taken to be the ability to get others to change their position through military and economic might, in the guise of inducements or threats. In contrast, soft power "rests on the ability to shape the preferences of others",[67] through the power of attraction: "in behavioral terms soft power is attractive power".[68] Accordingly, these different conceptions of power can be applied to the security dilemma, with the Incongruence Dilemma focusing upon soft power, namely attractive power and legitimising power.

While the security dilemma is generally applied to relations between states, it can also be applied internally, where identity groups challenge the territorial integrity and/or ideological sovereignty of the regime. Indeed, as Barry Posen correctly notes, security dilemmas affect relations between identity groups as well as between states.[69] Internal security dilemmas differ from their external counterparts, as they are not necessarily concerned with military policies and posturing, but, rather, exist when the ruling elite feels threatened by the existence of an identity group that challenges the territorial integrity or ideological sovereignty of the state. Given that there is a degree of uncertainty as to the motives intentions and capabilities of the group, then there is a dilemma of interpretation.

The state is then faced with a dilemma of response: leave the identity group alone, at which point the identity group may seek to secede, prompting other groups to embark along a similar path; or to address the threat posed by the group, through referring to nationalist or religious narratives, restricting political space, the use of force, or other means. Either option reduces the security of a particular group, be that a particular identity group or the ruling elite. As such, the two dilemmas remain, yet instead of the uncertainty of attempting to understand the rationale behind military policies and posturing, the uncertainty emerges from concerns about the ambition of the identity group. If the dilemma of response increases hostility, then the ruling elite is embroiled in an internal security dilemma, with an identity group existing within the state.

Efforts to resolve internal security dilemmas often result in ruling elites employing rhetoric and referring to narratives in order to demonstrate legitimacy. This use of rhetoric to resolve internal security dilemmas can lead to external security dilemmas, given the entrenchment of actors within a particular normative environment. The premise of a relationship between internal and external security dilemmas is supported by the empirical work of Clive Jones, who, in an article entitled 'Saudi Arabia after the Gulf War: the internal-external security dilemma',[70] suggests that Saudi Arabia is subject to an internal-external security dilemma. Jones posits an internal-external security dilemma where the drive to secure external security has significant implications for the internal security of the Kingdom.

However, this internal-external security dilemma can be inverted to suggest that internal security threats can have consequences for external security. This builds upon the notion of identity incongruence and the response of the state when the sovereignty of the state is challenged, either ideologically or territorially. This position is supported by Hinnebusch, who discusses how the efforts of states to maintain internal stability and fend off pressures from sub- and trans-state ideologies have increased tensions within the region, suggesting that as states consolidated they "enhanced the potential threat each posed to the other".[71] Indeed, given the importance of Islam for both Saudi Arabia and Iran, any reference to Islam and leadership within the Islamic world from either state necessitates a response from the other. The importance of Islam is coupled with legitimacy sourced from the "Arab Street", explored in greater detail within chapter two.

Thus, as a consequence of an internal security dilemma (and shared normative environments), states can become embroiled in an external security dilemma, driven by soft power concerns. The responses to the threats posed by identity incongruence often invoke rhetoric that place a state in direct competition with neighbouring states. A prime example of this can be seen in the use of religious rhetoric by both Riyadh and Tehran, both of whom seek to reduce internal security dilemmas. Indeed, given the prominent position of Islam within both Saudi Arabia and Iran, religion is often used as a legitimising tool for ruling elites to circumvent domestic challenges. As such, Islamic rhetoric is often employed to demonstrate the legitimacy of the regime and to reduce the threat posed by an identity group or groups. The importance of Islamic rhetoric and claims of legitimate rule over the *umma*, necessitates ruling elites of neighbouring states to also employ such rhetoric, thus beginning a process of strategic framing and symbolic exchanges that constitute a soft power security dilemma.

The use of soft power seeks to increase legitimacy for two reasons: firstly to reduce the threat posed by internal security dilemmas, and secondly to mould self-image in ways beneficial to improving external perception. This increases a state's standing within the region, which, in turn, impacts upon domestic stability and legitimacy. External perception is often aimed at populations of other states, rather than leaders of said states. Given the entrenchment of actors within similar normative environments, notably across the Islamic world, the use of soft power provokes responses from the rulers of the second states, concerned at diminished legitimacy within their own states, thus creating a soft power security dilemma.

The Incongruence Dilemma is thus built upon two security dilemmas, namley an internal security dilemma and an external security dilemma. Initially, there is an internal security dilemma, between identity groups and the state, which builds upon the dilemmas of interpretation and response, as previously articulated. In the internal security dilemma, building upon the dilemma of interpretation, the state faces a dilemma of response as to whether to accept the political manouverings of a group, which would reduce the security of the state, or to respond to the moves of the group, which would reduce the security of the group. Given the shared normative environment and the overlapping of identities across the region, these responses trigger the external security dilemma, where a seond state, uncertain as to the behaviour of the first, makes moves to secure its own identity. Further, given the shared normative environment and the importance of identity within the region, this can lead to a spiralling flux of identity moves, which increases the insecurity of each state.[72] In explaining the move from the internal security dilemma to the external, the Incongruence Dilemma employs a three-stage framework.

Stage One

The first stage of the framework is predominantly concerned with structure, notably the impact of structure in offering conditions for the possibility of agency to act. It is important to note that here structure predominantly refers to the constraints placed upon identity groups operating within a state, rather than Waltz's understanding of structure, the international system.[73] The argument contains an examination of state formation and the political environment before expanding on the structure of both domestic and regional systems. This permits an accurate location of a state within a regional and international system. In addition, the argument considers the role played by external actors.

State Formation and Political Strucutre

This first stage begins with examination of the process of state formation. As Halliday suggests, the conflict between Arabs and Persians, (and Gulf States) "is a product not so much of imperialist interference or of millennial and atavistic historical antagonisms, but of the two interrelated modern processes of state formation and the rise of nationalism".[74] While considering state formation, it is important to consider political structure, given its impact upon the capacity for action. This political structure reflects and shapes the norms and identities of a particular regime, which can be used in an attempt to resolve security dilemmas. In addition to discussing the nature of state formation, one must discuss the role played by ideology, in the form of both religion and nationalism. Indeed, both religion and nationalism, operating at either a state or trans-state level, have a strong normative capability.

As such, examination of state formation facilitates an awareness of norms that pervade society; these norms are often found within history, constituted by both religion and nationalism. Indeed, the process of state formation and the necessity of deriving legitimacy for new regimes often results in leaders referring to myths and tales that evoke nationalist sentiment. Yet, given the nature of the Middle East state system, these myths and tales often have a trans-state character. This reference to myths and tales is often supported by reference to Islamic values. As such, religious and nationalist norms play an important role within processes of state formation and can demonstrate how normative power has a symbolic trans-state capability within the region.

Regional Security

The regional security environment serves both as a source of norms and as a source of conflict for Middle Eastern states. The nature of state formation in the region, combined with the importance of trans-state identities and ideologies, means that states have the capacity to be involved in the action of others. Building on this, it does not always follow that states have the capability to withstand normative pressures. Indeed, irredentist movements and trans-state identities have the capacity to separate the nation from the state, eroding territorial integrity and potentially fostering interstate conflict and border disputes. Furthermore, the notion of interference can be demonstrated by the pervasion of Pan-Arab and Pan-Islamist ideologies across the region. The challenge posed by identity groups is especially relevant if one considers that several states within the Middle East can be considered state-nations rather than nation-states.[75] The term "nation-states" reflects the existence of predetermined national identities, which were then manifested in the process of state formation, while "state-nation" reflects how the state is building the nation, wherein "authority and sovereignty have run ahead of self-conscious national identity and cultural integration".[76] The idea of a state-nation can be seen when considering Iraq, Syria and Lebanon.

The US and Regional Security

The argument then turns to a consideration of the impact of the United States upon each state. The role of the United States is especially important, given that with the end of the Cold War the United States remains the dominant power within the international system and has a legacy of action within the Middle East. In addition, relations with Middle Eastern states are complicated by US–Israeli relations and by US foreign policy throughout the region. Moreover, the role of the United States within regional security calculations is seen in diametrically opposed views by Saudi Arabia and Iran.

In addition to the role played by the United States within the region, the importance of natural resources cannot be understated. As such, it is necessary to consider the impact of these resources, also questioning the role played by international organisations such as OPEC.

Stage Two

The second stage of this framework is concerned with the role of agency, notably those identity groups who comprise identity incongruence and, thus, the internal security dilemma. The second stage of this analytical framework is concerned with an examination of the nature of the internal security dilemma and the threat posed to each state.

The mosaic of identities across the Gulf region presents a unique challenge to ruling elites, providing tests of both an internal and external nature. Primarily, ruling elites are concerned with retaining domestic stability; as such, managing identity groups, particularly those with irredentist or trans-state agendas, is imperative. The management of these identity groups, who comprise an internal security dilemma, has the capacity to impact upon relations with neighbouring states directly or indirectly through the use of rhetoric, in the form of an external security dilemma. As such, identity groupings play a key role in determining domestic and foreign policy, and legitimising rule.

Thus, the argument necessitates an analysis of the identity groups who constitute identity incongruence, who engage in social interaction[77] and who comprise an internal security dilemma. Underpinning all of the aforementioned areas is the notion of legitimacy, targeted at identity groups at an internal and external level. The argument will be utilising a Realist[78] approach to identity, defining identities as "socially significant and context-specific ideological constructs that nevertheless refer in non-arbitrary (if partial) ways to verifiable aspects of the social world".[79]

The Relationship between Identity and Sovereignty

Before considering the nature of agency, it is essential to consider the relationship between identity and sovereignty. Hinnebusch argues that with arbitrary boundaries emerging from the artificial imposition of states in the Middle East, loyalty to the state is tempered by loyalty to sub-state and *trans-state* identities. Indeed the "resultant embedding of the state system in a matrix of fluid multiple identities"[80] causes problems for Realist assumptions of national interest and unitary state identities. Irredentism can lead to the emergence of strong trans-state movements and, in an effort to provide support for an ethnic community or to divert attention from their own domestic challenges, can incite states to interfere in another state's domestic affairs. The nature of trans-state identities in the Middle East can thus lead to the emergence of a duality between *raison de la nation* and *raison d'état*, which further complicates the Middle East security environment.

However, in addition to this territorial understanding of sovereignty, it is possible to understand sovereignty in ideological terms. As such, one must also consider the impact of identity incongruence upon the ideological sovereignty of a regime. Ideological sovereignty is understood as maintaining an ideological dominance over a particular territory, which is used to maintain the legitimacy of the regime. Thus, when identity groups challenge the ideological sovereignty of the ruling elite, this also poses a threat to the stability of the state. The existence of challenges to the ideological and territorial integrity of the regime demonstrates the potency of identity incongruence and the emergence of an internal security dilemma.

Political Space, Interaction and Violence

One of the most important aspects of a discussion of the impact of identity incongruence upon stability and legitimacy concerns the notion of political space. Indeed, in order for there to be identity incongruence, there must be a degree of space for identity groups to operate within. It is this space that is referred to throughout as political space. The notion of *space* is taken to be a form of negative freedom, that is, a freedom from state interference in the political, religious and/or cultural lives of individuals.[81]

The notion of political space is discussed by Mohhamed M. Hafez in *Why Muslims Rebel*, albeit in the guise of political system accessibility, with specific focus upon social movements. The argument within this book holds that this need not be exclusive to social movements, but rather can hold for all forms of identity groups. Hafez builds upon the 1986 work of Herbert Kitschelt, defining the political system as "the set of formal institutions of the state- parliaments, government ministries, policy-implementing agencies-and informal channels, procedures, and 'policy styles' by which the state elite governs".[82] Hafez also speaks of accessibility: "A political system is accessible to a movement when the state grants it the possibility to influence policymaking through governmental institutions; it is closed when the movement is prohibited from influencing public policy through institutional channels".[83] As Hafez correctly articulates, it is possible that certain movements may perceive the system to be open, whereas others may perceive it to be closed. While there must be a degree of space in order for identity incongruence to exist, this space is often limited, with identity groups often challenging the boundaries of the space.

It is generally held that if an organisation, group, or coterie, has the necessary political, cultural and religious space in which to operate, then this group will behave in accordance with the norms and laws of a state. While groups may disagree over ideologies, religious beliefs and agendas, be they of a political or social nature, their interaction will generally occur in a legitimate manner. As such, within most liberal democracies, stability is maintained through the provision of space within which groups can operate and oppositional grievances can be legitimately channelled. This is what is also understood as civil society, which, as Augustus Richard Norton articulates, is a "mélange of associations, clubs, guilds, syndicates, federations, unions, parties and groups [which] come together to provide a buffer between state and citizen".[84] Norton suggests that civil society has the capacity to imply a "shared sense of identity, by means of, at least, tacit agreement over the rough boundaries of the political unit",[85] which demonstrates the importance of civil society for both identity formation at a state level and for tolerance within a state, given this shared sense of identity. Moreover, feeding into the argument that civil society aids the fostering of shared identities, Norton articulates how "the individual in civil society is granted rights by the state, but, in return, acquires duties to the state".[86] One such duty is to accept the existence of views that are in opposition to those held by the individual.

When disagreements occur within societies that possess political space, or civil society, disputes are predominantly aired tolerantly within legal frameworks; consequently, the interaction of these groups maintains a degree of legitimacy. However, when such space is restricted, or no such space ever existed and legitimate channels within which grievances can be heard are lacking, one must question what the next move of an organisation can be. Indeed, this is similar to Mohammed M. Hafez's argument contained within chapter two of *Why Muslims Rebel*, in which Hafez speaks of how "the absence of institutional channels for conflict mediation and political contestation encourages rebellion by delegitimizing the ruling regime and disempowering moderate voices within the movement".[87]

Given the lack of space to air grievances through legitimate channels, and the inability to act within the political structure of the state, opposition groups are left with three options. Firstly, to accept their position, ignore their grievances and continue with day-to-day life. Secondly, assuming they have the capacity to do so, to leave the state. Thirdly, to engage in illegitimate interaction,[88] be that in the form of civil disobedience, or in the form of violent opposition.

The Internal Security Dilemma

As a consequence of a perceived lack of political space, identity groups may challenege the legitimacy and stability of the state, potentially resulting in an internal security dilemma. Several authors have considered the emergence of internal security dilemmas, with Barry Posen suggesting they occur in an emerging anarchy,[89] while Brian Job suggests they occur in weak states.[90] The argument holds that when the level of identity incongruence challenges the sovereignty (either territorial or ideological) of the regime, then a state becomes embroiled in an internal security dilemma. As previously discussed, this internal security dilemma transcends purely armed groups and considers those groups with strong identities that challenge the regime. While internal security dilemmas can initially be considered as societal security dilemmas,[91] concerned with the erosion of a state identity, there are additional understandings of this dilemma, notably those challenges posed to territorial and ideological sovereignty.

The two stages of the security dilemma also apply to internal security dilemmas. If the state feels threatened by the presence of strong identity groups operating internally and *interprets* the intent of a group in a malignant way, it *responds* by moving to reduce this threat. This demonstrates how a security dilemma can manifest itself internally. Of course, it is possible for a state to become embroiled in several different security dilemmas at the same time, of different natures, with different groups. In order to gain awareness of internal security dilemmas, one must consider the interaction of those groups operating within the state and the response of the state to each group.

Types of Interaction

Legitimate interaction is taken to be interaction in accordance with the laws and norms of the state, while illegitimate interaction is interaction that transcends laws and norms. Adding to understandings of interaction, one must question between which groups the interaction occurs. Again, there are several answers to this question: initially, interaction exists between identity groups within a state, yet in addition to this, interaction occurs between a particular identity group and the state. A further level of interaction occurs between the state and a target identity group within the state, while supplementary levels of interaction can occur between a state and an identity group or groups located within a different state; between two states; between a state and an international organisation; between a state and non-governmental organisation. Indeed, there are numerous levels of interaction. This Incongruence Dilemma initially considers two kinds of interaction, although in achieving this, an additional layer of interaction occurs.[92] The interactions initially considered are between the state and an identity group or groups. In considering the interaction between the state and a single identity group, it is possible that this in turn will impact upon an identity group (or groups) in a neighbouring state, given the existence of irredentist characteristics or shared ethno/religious ties.

Stage Three

The third stage of the Incongruence Dilemma explains how internal security dilemmas manifest themselves at the external level, thus impacting upon regional security. It achieves this through building upon the analysis of internal security dilemmas contained within the second stage of the framework, offering an analysis of the state's response to both individual groups and identity incongruence as a whole. The response to an internal security dilemma results in the manifestation of an external security dilemma, driven by soft power. The third stage also considers how internal security dilemmas can be manipulated by external actors seeking to undermine legitimacy and stability and questions the implications for regional security.

Resolving the Internal Security Dilemma

The second stage of the framework outlined the identity groups comprising internal security dilemmas. Building upon this, the third stage considers the response of the state to these internal security dilemmas. Given the trans-state nature of numerous identity groups across the Middle East, coupled with identity groups possessing irredentist agendas and shared normative environments, it is undeniable that these internal security dilemmas manifest themselves at the external level. The response of the state is two-fold: firstly, responding to identity groups that threaten the territorial integrity of the state; and, secondly, responding to identity groups that threaten the ideological sovereignty of the regime. Assuming that a state chooses to respond to the dilemma of interpetation, rather than accepting and addressing an identity group's concerns, there are two responses typically used by states. These responses thus lead to the manifestation of internal security dilemmas at an external level.

A first potential response to both of these problems is to employ nationalist and/or Islamic rhetoric to foster increased cohesion under a unifying banner. Within this strategy, states may also seek to create an external other. This response makes reference to shared identities, norms – notably national identities and religious rhetoric – and collective grievances. Indeed, the increased entrenchment of actors within shared normative environments provides tools to resolve internal disputes; however, existing within this environment leaves states open to "normative suasion and symbolic sanctions".[93] The use of strategic framing and symbolic exchange are used to mould self-image for perception, for both internal and external identity groups, yet this external perception may be aimed at the populations of neighbouring states, seeking to propagate the stability and legitimacy of the regime. However, this move may provoke a response in kind, resulting in a security dilemma, albeit stemming from soft as opposed to hard power, as demonstrated by the symbolic moves within Pan-Arabism and Pan-Islamism.

A second response to identity challenges is through de-politicisation, which occurs in several guises. Francesco Cavatorta[94] discusses a growing trend towards the de-politicisation of citizens across political systems and the convergence of governance. Cavatorta focuses on the idea of de-politicisaion, defined thus:

> The inability to have meaningful access and the sentiment that liberal reforms do not truly equate with genuine change de-politicise the citizenry, which ultimately switches off from political engagement and either refrains from participating or finds alternative ways of engaging that may be overtly less political.[95]

Cavatorta suggests that this helps rulers of liberalised autocracies retain power through the destruction of political society. However, the idea of de-politicisation can be developed beyond Cavatorta's understanding. Indeed, de-politicisation programmes can be undertaken by states who feel threatened by certain identities, groups or organisations.

This type of de-politicisation may result in different responses from opposition groups, less apathetic, more vociferous, and potentially more violent. Regimes may seek to de-politicise groups in several ways: firstly, through encouraging political apathy; secondly, through limiting political space; thirdly, through banning an organisation; fourthly, through exporting an organisation, thus removing a potential threat; and lastly, by expelling an organisation. Different strategies are undertaken when considering the nature of the threat posed by the group. Given the trans-state nature of many identities across the region, this may lead to an increase in tensions between neighbouring states over the treatment of an identity group.

Through examining the composition of the state, as outlined in the first stage of the framework, one has a solid understanding of the nature of the political system. Yet groups also can operate outside of the political system. While these groups may not necessarily have the space or capacity to act within the current political system, it is prudent to recognise that space often exists outside of the system. Indeed, these groups may search for other means to assert political views, perhaps through engaging in illegitimate interaction, which often exacerbates the internal security dilemma.

A Soft Power Security Dilemma

When resolving internal security dilemmas, states typically refer to nationalist and/or Islamic rhetoric, which leads to a security dilemma at the external level, between states. This is a consequence of the importance of identity as a legitimising tool within each state and across both the Gulf and Middle East, which necessitates other states responding to identity moves. This can be seen when considering claims to Islamic leadership, whereby both Saudi Arabia and Iran, fearing the ambitions of the other for dominance within the Islamic world, move to increase their own standing. This, in turn, has the capacity to lead to a series of symbolic exchanges that may increase security concerns, both for regimes and regional security. As such, it is possible to see how one can move from soft power concerns, stemming from identity incongruence, to hard power concerns, which manifest themselves as tensions within the regional security environment.

This soft power security dilemma is predominantly seen within the religious sphere, although it can also be seen when looking at the "Arab

Street" and Iran's attempts to increase its power across the region. In an effort to counter Iranian gains across the Middle East, Saudi Arabia has also employed soft power tactics. As such, despite the lack of a conventional, hard power security dilemma increasing tensions within the rivalry, this book holds that ideological competition feeds into a soft power security dilemma, which increases tensions between Saudi Arabia and Iran. This increase in tensions has manifested itself in several proxy conflicts, particularly in Lebanon, Iraq, Bahrain and Syria.

Interaction and Legitimacy

Although the state remains a key player within IR, it is remiss to consider it as a coherent, solitary actor, given the numerous identity groups operating within each state, often in conflict with each other. The nature of interaction, between identity groups and between state and society, determines the degree of legitimacy bestowed upon the state, which in turn impacts upon the stability of the regime. Given the provision of space and capacity for identity groups to act in accordance with the law, it is foreseeable that a state may be perceived as legitimate, both from internal and external audiences. However, if a state impinges on this space, or restricts the capacity for a group to act, these claims to legitimacy may be reduced. Indeed, the nature of the response to these identity groups also impacts upon a state's claims to legitimacy.[96]

The differing nature of identity groups results in different spheres of impact. Indeed, a group rejecting the legitimacy of a ruling elite, assuming the space and capacity to act, could impact upon domestic policy, while a group with an irredentist agenda could impact upon both domestic and foreign policy spheres.[97]

Manipulating Internal Security Dilemmas

The final area to consider within the third stage of the framework is to what extent internal security dilemmas are manipulated by other actors, seeking to destabilise a regime/state. As such, one must consider to what extent external actors provide support, be it ideological, financial or logistical to actors operating within internal security dilemmas. Given the trans-state nature of identities and ideologies across the region, many states share affinity with groups in neighbouring states, on the basis of shared ethnic or religious ties. In offering support for a particular group, the external state may be hoping to further destabilise a regional rival or enemy, providing opportunity to increase its own standing within the region. The manipulation of internal security dilemmas is not limited to the internal security dilemmas within Saudi Arabia and Iran. Indeed, actors can seek to manipulate internal security dilemmas in other regional states in an effort to either increase their own standing within the region, or destabalise another. However, the consequences of seeking to manipulate internal security dilemmas may have severe repercussions for regional security.

2

ARABIAN GULF VS PERSIAN GULF

Since the Iranian Revolution of 1979, the relationship between Saudi Arabia and Iran has been characterised as belligerent, with Riyadh and Tehran suspicious of the other's actions and intentions, within the Persian Gulf and across the wider Middle East. Many authors have posited arguments as to the roots of the rivalry, with some suggesting that the antagonistic nature of the relationship is a consequence of historical events, be they conflict between Arab and Persian, or between Sunni and Shi'a.

Anoushiravan Ehteshami rejects the idea that tensions between the two countries emanate from theological and ideological differences between Sunni and Shi'a, or from historical disputes between Ottoman/ Arab and Persian.[1] Rather, Ehteshami suggests that tensions between the two countries are of a contemporary nature, derived from the Iranian Revolution. However, Halliday, in *Nation and Religion in the Middle East*,[2] rejects the claim that tensions between Saudi Arabia and Iran, and indeed tensions between all Gulf States, are a product of atavistic belligerence, or of imperialist interference, instead arguing that these tensions are a consequence of the state-building process and of the rise of nationalism.[3]

In contrast, Shabram Chubin and Charles Tripp suggest that structural factors, such as geopolitical differences, notably demographic and geographic disparitiesm and national, cultural, ethnic and sectarian problems limit the possibility of security cooperation.[4]

Given these areas of competition, it is possible to define two spheres in which Saudi Arabia and Iran compete, namely ideological and geopolitical. Indeed, these two spheres of competition have played a central role in defining the rivalry post 1979 and although they can be viewed as separate entities, feed into each other.

Prior to 1979 while Saudi Arabia and Iran were engaged in competition within the geopolitical sphere, the revolution of 1979 and the emergence of the Islamic Republic of Iran "considerably worsened Iran-Saudi relations, not least by expanding their rivalry to Islamic leadership".[5] The emergence of the Islamic Republic increased the level of competition occurring within the ideological sphere, while also affecting the nature of geopolitical competition. Geopolitical competition has further been complicated by a dramatic shift in Tehran's relationship with Washington, which was damaged initially by the removal of the Shah, who upon leaving Iran sought medical attention in the United States and then by the hostage crisis at the US embassy in Tehran in November 1979.[6] The United States hostage crisis had domestic ramifications within the US, culminating in President Jimmy Carter failing in his bid for re-election. Further, an interesting point to note is that there are some who suggest that current Iranian President Mahmoud Ahmadinejad was one of a number of students responsible for taking 52 American students hostage.[7]

Ideological Competition

Arab–Persian tensions, sectarian tensions and the impact of the 1979 Iranian Revolution all play a role in the ideological part of the Iranian-Saudi relationship. As such, the discussion of ideology will firstly consider Arab–Persian tensions; secondly, a discussion of sectarian differences; thirdly, an examination of the impact of the revolution of 1979 and its consequences; and lastly, a discussion of the impact of both the revolution and attempts to export revolutionary goals upon legitimacy and stability, with particular focus upon the *Hajj* deaths of 1987.

Arab–Persian Tensions

Arab–Persian tensions have historical roots, stemming from a history of military activity and conquest across the region, by both Arab and

Persian armies. Indeed, this history of conflict, which can be traced back to before the time of Muhammad, has helped shape attitudes towards each other for centuries. In around 559 BC, Cyrus became king of Anshan upon the death of his father. Cyrus has played an important role within Iranian history, as discussed in greater detail within chapter three; however, he also played an important role in shaping Arab–Persian relations, through creating a vast empire that Michael Axworthy suggests was "perhaps the greatest empire the world had seen up to that time",[8] spanning from the eastern coast of Greece, on the Aegean Sea, to the banks of the Indus.

In contrast, Arab military successes came some 1100 years later. Arab armies, buoyed after the defeat of a Byzantine army near Gaza in 634, moved east, defeating Persians in Mesopotamia in 637.[9] Arab generals persuaded the *caliph* (ruler) to continue with their campaign and, as a consequence, Arab armies captured and controlled most of Persia by 654.[10] The most important aspect of the Arab conquest was the coming of Islam to Persia. Although the Arabs did not generally engage in a programme of mass murder or forced conversion, the existence of *jizya* (taxes for non-Muslims) led to many Persians converting to Islam.[11] Whilst this is in no way a comprehensive history of Arab–Persian tensions, this historical grounding underpins much of the suspicion directed towards the other.

Sectarian Differences

Adding to this history of mutual suspicion are sectarian differences between Saudi Arabia and Iran, which occur as a result of adherence to two ideologically opposed Islamic sects. Whilst being careful to avoid essentiallising the two states, the regime in Saudi Arabia subscribes to Wahhabism, which many hold falls within Sunni Islam although sits outside of the four *madhahib* of orthodox Sunni thought, whereas Iran subscribes to Shi'i Islam. The dispute between Sunni (and Wahhabi) and Shi'a is rooted in debates regarding the nature of succession, notably questioning who was to lead the *umma* in the years after the Prophet. Post 1979, religion occupied a salient position within both Saudi Arabia and Iran, whereas prior to the revolution, religion had not figured heavily within Iran. After 1979, both states gained legitimacy through religious posturing, often at the expense of the other, reflecting a zero-sum game in operation. In understanding the nature of sectarian differences, one must firstly locate Sunni and Shi'i schools of thought within a broader understanding of Islam.

A Brief History of Islam

There are myriad texts on the history of Islam;[12] as a result, discussion of the formative stages of the world's second largest religion will be kept brief. There are approximately 1.3 billion Muslims in the world,[13] 60 per cent of whom are located in Asia, with 20 per cent in the Middle East.[14] Muslims are typically split into two sects, Shi'a and Sunni, with a large majority of Muslims adhering to Sunni doctrine.[15] Shi'i Muslims are primarily located within the Middle East, particularly within Lebanon, Iraq, Bahrain and Iran, while Sunni Muslims have a worldwide presence.

The Role of Muhammad

The Islamic message was brought to the people of Arabia by the Prophet Muhammad, who was born in Mecca around 570 AD. Brought up by his uncle after the death of both his parents, Muhammad received his call to prophecy from God around the age of 40.[16] It is said that the Prophet's revelation came in a dream, or vision;[17] however, in order to safeguard "the 'objectivity' of the Revelation",[18] some believed that an external figure should be referred to. As such, within *ahadith*[19] (singular *hadith*) there exist portrayals of "the Prophet talking to the Angel in public".[20]

Muhammad's role as Prophet began in Mecca, where he encountered opposition but gained enough support and politico-religious influence to receive an invitation from the Medinese to move to their city as the political and religious leader. The emigration to Medina, known to Muslims as the *hijra*, proved to be a pivotal moment within the formative years of Islam, reflected in the present day by the anniversary of the *hijra*, marking the start of the Islamic calendar.

Muhammad's time in Medina was spent striving for two main ideals: monotheism, and justice of an economic and social nature. Yet underpinning Muhammad's work in Medina was a desire "to win Mecca itself for the cause of Islam and from Mecca to work outwards".[21] Moreover, this desire can be conflated with the moves to create "conditions for a universal brotherhood on the basis of faith".[22] After the death of the Prophet, there followed a period in which several *caliphs* ruled the Islamic *caliphate* (political community). It is the dispute over succession after the Prophet's death that is at the heart of the dispute between Sunni and Shi'i Muslims.

The Sunni-Shi'i Split

During the rule of the fourth *caliph*, a schism emerged, dividing Muslims into those who adhere to Sunni doctrine and those who adhere to Shi'i doctrine. Shia'at Ali (The Party of Ali), henceforth referred to as Shi'ism, began as a political movement but morphed into a religious organisation. The schism stems from the issue of succession: who was to lead the *umma* following the Prophet's death? Shi'i Muslims hold that Ali, the cousin and son-in-law of the Prophet, was the true successor to Mohammad and declared him the first *Imam*; however, Ali ruled over the fourth *caliphate* of Islam, dating 656 to 661. Prior to Ali's time as the *Imam*, the Islamic *caliphate* had accumulated enormous power, having conquered vast territories. Given this, inordinate power was bestowed upon certain Arab families, including those who had opposed the prophet in Mecca, forcing him to flee. In contrast to those who had accumulated such power, Ali "held himself aloof, maintaining a pious life of austerity and prayer. He became a natural focus for dissent, and in turn was resented by those around the *caliph*: bringing forth the austerity/piety conflict within Islam itself for the first time".[23] This conflict would have severe repercussions for Islam, resulting in the murder of Ali, and the emergence of the Yazid court.

Ali had six children, one of whom, Hosein, was to become central to Shi'i thought. Hosein derived legitimacy both directly from blood links to the Prophet and indirectly from the impropriety of the Yazid court.

Hosein was the third *Imam* of Shi'ism and rebelled against the Yazid rule, in an attempt to purify Islam. Hosein plays an integral role within Shi'i thought, as reflected in the festival central to Shi'i beliefs, Ashura, which commemorates the death of Hosein at Karbala. In rebellion against the Yazid rule, Hosein's forces were killed, leaving Hosein, holding the lifeless body of his infant son, to be killed last. Many hold that Hosein sought martyrdom at Karbala, believing that he could "only bring about the renewal [of original Islamic values] he desired by sacrificing himself".[24] Further, the failure of "Kufa supporters to help Hosein added a strong sense of guilt to the Shi'a memory of Karbala".[25] Hence, ideas of guilt and martyrdom are inherent within modern Shi'i thought.

Within Shi'i thought are three different strands: Twelver; Ismaili; and Zaidiyyas. The three strands of Shi'i thought differ predominantly with regard to belief about legitimate succession. After the death of the 11th *Imam* with no apparent heir, Shi'ism was split into various factions who coalesced around the premise that the 11th *Imam* did have an heir who was hidden away to avoid persecution. At the correct time, "a time of chaos and crisis, this twelfth Emam [sic], the hidden Emam, would reappear to re-establish the righteous rule of God on earth".[26]

In contrast to Shi'ism, there are four *madhahib* (singular *madhab*) existing within orthodox Sunni Islam. The four *madhahib* are Hanafi, Shafi'i, Maliki and Hanbali.[27] While there are differences between the four orthodox *madhahib*, these differences are negligible, stemming from different interpretations of the Qur'an and *ahadith*. In addition to the four *madhahib*, there are several schools of Islamic thought deemed illegitimate by scholars belonging to the *madhahib*. One such school of thought is Wahhabism, which will be considered in greater detail in chapter four.

Doctrinal Differences

In addition to the political aspect of the Sunni-Shi'i split, there are several doctrinal differences between the two strands. Indeed, Shi'i Muslims have a preference for particular *ahadith* and Sunna literature, namely stemming from those credited to the Prophet's family and close associates, whereas

Sunni Muslims consider all *ahadith* and Sunna from the Prophet's companions to be equally valid. While all Muslims are required to pray five times each day, Shi'i practice permits some prayers to be grouped into three daily prayer times. It is possible to distinguish Sunnis and Shi'a at prayer by the use of a small clay tablet from a holy place, generally Karbala, which Shi'i Muslims place their forehead on while praying.

The Wahhabist movement was born in the Najd region, from the ideological beliefs of Muhammad ibn Abd al-Wahhab.[28] While some refer to Wahhabism as a conservative or extreme form of Sunni Islam, it is important to note that few Sunni scholars accept that Wahhabism is part of Sunni doctrine; rather, these few suggest it should be considered Sunni as it is not Shi'a. Wahhabism is based upon the belief that "there is no god but God",[29] stemming from a rejection of intercession: none can intercede with God on behalf of a believer. The Shi'i practice of venerating shrines of the Prophet's family, *Imams* and other key individuals within Islam is thus viewed as heresy by Wahhabis; thus, Wahhabis do not accept Shi'i Muslims as true believers. This belief led to the destruction of numerous shrines and the prohibiting of the act of prayer at the Prophet's tomb.[30] Given the weaving of Wahhabi beliefs within the fabric of the Saudi state, these beliefs have complicated relations between the Al Saud and the Shi'i population of the Kingdom's Eastern Province, but moreover, with Iran.

Islamic Teachings

Within Islam, there are several key values held by all Muslims, regardless of ideological or doctrinal persuasion. The Qur'an is the main source of Islamic beliefs and is especially concerned with the issue of *tawhid* (monotheism). Islamic values are reflected in the Five Pillars of Islam, which although are subtly different depending on doctrinal interpretation, encompass similar beliefs.[31]

Shari'a Law

The Shari'a Law, henceforth referred to as the Shari'a, is a consensus of Islamic law, based upon the relationship between Qur'an, Sunna, *ijma*, and *qiyas*. The Shari'a differs from other legal frameworks, given that it offers guidance on all facets of life, as opposed to purely offering religious guidance. In understanding the Shari'a, it is imperative to first comprehend the four aspects that comprise the Shari'a.

The Qur'an is the primary Islamic text, comprising of 114 *suras* (chapters), and is "the most consummate and final revelation of God to man".[32] While the Qur'an is all encompassing on ethical and religious matters, legal matters are barely touched upon. Indeed, of "some 6000 Qur'anic verses, only 200 have a legal aspect, that is, approximately one thirtieth of the Qur'an".[33]

The Sunna, literally translated as the "trodden path",[34] is taken to mean the way of the Prophet, although Fazlur Rahman suggests there are three possible understandings of the term. The "Sunna of the Prophet, the living tradition of the earliest generation, and the deduction from these – [which] created a wealth of material, especially through individual interpretations of the law and the dogma".[35] In understanding the Sunna, Muslims examine *ahadith*, literally translated as a story, or narrative. Indeed, a *hadith* "is a narrative, usually very short, purporting to give information about what the Prophet said, did, or approved or disapproved or, of similar information about his Companions".[36] As Rahman articulates, *ahadith* is a "religious methodology in the absence of the living guidance of the prophet and of the earliest generation of his Companions".[37] In an attempt to prevent the conflation of the "Word of the Prophet" with the "Word of God", the Prophet forbade his followers from transcribing his words, thus leaving *ahadith* open to interpretation.

The third area comprising the Shari'a is *ijma*, taken to be a consensus of the Islamic community. *Ijma* proves to be somewhat ambiguous through the notion of a consensus of community, with no clear definition of what the community currently entails. While in the early stages of Islam the community was much smaller, located within a singular geographical area, the community in the present day spans the entire world, leading to problems of interpretation.

The fourth aspect of the Shari'a is *qiyas*, which are used when neither Qur'an nor *ahadith* make reference to a certain issue. In this event, the *faqih* (Islamic Jurist) can extrapolate on texts within the Qur'an, drawing analogies to facilitate guidance on a certain issue.

It is the relationship between Qur'an, Sunna, *ijma* and *qiyas* that comprises the Shari'a. Given that both *ijma* and *qiyas* possess a subjective element, it is thus possible for there to be a plethora of interpretations and, thus, understandings of the Shari'a.

Ideological Interpretations

As previously outlined, within Islamic jurisprudence there is one text that offers explicit guidance on ethical and moral issues, while there are several other aspects that are open to interpretation. The science surrounding *ahadith* is vast, yet to a certain degree is able to test the veracity of *ahadith*. With regard to *ijma* and *qiyas*, there is no test for Islamic values. Given this, it is possible for numerous interpretations of Islam to exist, differing across several levels: the individual, the community, the state, and the doctrinal.

The interpretation of Islamic credence is referred to as *ijtihad*, especially useful when no guidance is offered in either Qur'an or Sunna.[38] Thus, the process of *ijtihad* permits Islamic guidance within contemporary spheres. There are some who reject the process of *ijtihad,* instead taking a fundamentalist stance with regard to the Qur'an and Sunna.

Revolution

The Iranian revolution proved to have repercussions reaching far wider than the borders of Iran; the revolution would have a detrimental effect upon regional and international stability, manifesting itself in both geopolitical and ideological spheres of competition. The ensuing emergence of an Islamic state with an explicit proselytizing agenda "disrupted the regional order and also ended the slowly emerging alliances of moderate forces in the Middle East".[39] The aftermath of revolution saw Iran pursue an aggressive foreign policy that claimed to export the ideological beliefs of Ayatollah Ruhollah Khomeini. This foreign policy would leave "a trail of devastation in regional relations, littered with spontaneous utterances and unfettered intervention in neighbouring states".[40]

Khomeini's religious views were enshrined and protected within the concept of *velayat-e faqih*,[41] a system of government that gave credence to the values of Shi'i thought and derived rules directly from the *Sharia*. Given this belief, Khomeini argued that in the absence of the 12th, or Hidden *Imam*, only jurisprudents, or those with the correct religious training, were able to interpret the *Sharia* and thus rule.[42]

The ideological nature of Khomeini's *velayat-e faqih* was to prove antagonistic within both the Middle East region and the international system. Furthermore, Khomeini's vision ran against years of Shi'i political thought, which had previously attempted to avoid the involvement of clerics within the political sphere. This can notably be seen by the absence of clerics in the events of 1953,[43] which were predominantly driven by nationalist concerns. Khomeini's unwillingness to become involved in the events of 1953 is alleged to have stemmed from a reluctance to offend the then-leading Ayatollah, Mohamad Hossein Borujerdi. After the death of Borujerdi, Khomeini became more vocal, eventually leading to his expulsion from the state.[44]

Indeed, the revolutionary goals encapsulated within *velayat-e faqih* set Iran on a path of hostility with former allies and neighbours. Khomeini's Islamic vision was anti-monarchical and anti-Western, and would provide to support for Shi'i groups across the region, including those with belligerent and militaristic aims. Within five years, Khomeini's discourse and emphasis had [...] "widened the gap between the predominantly Shi'i population of Iran and Sunni majorities elsewhere [...] and exacerbated sectarian feeling throughout the Muslim world".[45] As such, the revolution of 1979 brought Islamic competition to the rivalry, which was complicated by competition for Islamic supremacy and the provision of support for Shi'i groups across the region, further widening the gap between Sunni and Shi'i states across the region.

Exporting Ideology

Iranian foreign policy post 1979 sought to export the revolutionary goals of Ayatollah Khomeini, thus locating Tehran in ideological conflicts with Islamic regimes across the region. These conflicts transcended the ideological sphere, resulting in military action, demonstrated by the outbreak of the Iran–Iraq War in 1980. Despite the ideological conflict appearing to be rooted heavily within the sectarian, Chubin and Tripp suggest that sectarian rhetoric hides strong nationalist sentiment.[46] Saudi Arabia was a prominent target for Tehran, through being both a powerful Islamic state and a Gulf neighbour with whom relations were not always cordial. Saudi Arabia's position as the leading Islamic nation stemming the location of Mecca and Medina within its borders, and the legitimacy derived from the Al Saud's custodianship of the two holy places, would explain the burgeoning sectarian competition between the two states. This stems from the importance of Islam for both states, serving as a legitimising tool for regimes in both Riyadh and Tehran.

Organisation of Islamic Conference

Although referring to the Islamic world or *umma* appears to suggest a coherent entity, as previously discussed, this is not the case. Instead, within the Islamic world are several strands of theological debate, combined with geopolitical competition. Seeking to foster dialogue within the Islamic world is the Organisation of the Islamic Conference, based in Jeddah, Saudi Arabia, which is the second largest intergovernmental organisation in the world after the United Nations.[47] The organisation was created in 1969 and its inception was seen as an attempt to both safeguard Islamic interests across the world and to foster space for Pan-Islamic discourse. However, given the numerous different interpretations of Islam within the organisation, the efficiency of the OIC has been criticised. Additional criticisms suggest that state interests and rhetoric tend to be more prominent than Islamic issues or the engendering of Islamic unity.[48] Furthermore, as Peter Mandaville argues, the OIC is a "useful vantage point from which to observe the evolution of relations between the "core" and "periphery" of the Muslim world, and the competition for influence of various Muslim powers".[49]

The creation of the OIC was steeped in geopolitical competition, with Saudi Arabia seeking to counter the power of Egypt's Pan-Arabism in the 1960s by using Islam as a means to demonstrate their legitimacy.[50] This competition can also be seen in the present day, notably between Sunni and Shi'i states, led by Saudi Arabia and Iran, respectively. As Martin Kramer notes, "Iran conducted a vigorous campaign against Saudi Arabia's claim to organize the consensus of Islam. For a decade Iran virtually ignored the OIC, and convened frequent conferences of its own clients and supporters from abroad".[51] However, competition within the OIC is not restricted to competition between Saudi Arabia and Iran. Indeed, many states, seeking to demonstrate their own Islamic credentials, organised their own conferences, evidenced in 1990 with the outbreak of the Second Gulf War, and Iraq and Saudi Arabia both convening Islamic conferences in an attempt to demonstrate their Islamic legitimacy.[52]

Despite the tensions within the OIC, and Iranian criticisms of the organisation, Henner Furtig suggests that Iran is more interested in employing the OIC to its own ends on two issues. Firstly, on the back of the revolution of 1979, Iran sought to offer support for Islamic movements across the world, notably in India, Kashmir, Bosnia and Lebanon. Secondly, Iran attempted to limit Saudi Arabia's influence within the organisation.[53] In undertaking a leading role in offering support for Islamic movements across the world, Iran attempted to demonstrate legitimacy over the Islamic *umma*, while also reducing the legitimacy of Saudi Arabia, given the zero-sum nature of Islamic competition.

The *Hajj* Deaths

The fifth pillar of Islam requires all able-bodied Muslims to undertake the *Hajj*[54] (pilgrimage) to Mecca once in their lifetime, a process that occurs every year during the month of Dhu al-Hijjah. During the *Hajj* of 1987, 450 pilgrims were killed in clashes with Saudi Arabian security forces; 275 of the pilgrims who died were Iranians. Over 150,000 Iranian pilgrims undertook the pilgrimage to Mecca, although it is suggested that of this number, 25 per cent were Revolutionary Guards, 40 per cent suicide actors, 13 per cent members of the generation of the revolution and only 22 per cent were true pilgrims.[55] In response to the Iranian deaths, protesters in Tehran ransacked the Saudi embassy, resulting in the death of a Saudi diplomat.[56]

Riyadh and Tehran blamed the events upon each other, with rhetoric emanating from both capitals articulating the guilt of the other. The *Hajj* has an integral role to play for Saudi Arabia and Iran, with both states using the event to demonstrate legitimacy, political vitality and to "implicitly trumpet their regional primacy".[57] Moreover, although the *Hajj* is phrased in religious terms, the tensions surrounding the event and ensuing recriminations are political.[58]

In response to these deaths, Riyadh capped the number of licences given to Iranian pilgrims at 45,000 in an attempt to prevent such atrocities occurring on ensuing pilgrimages. Furthermore, the Saudi regime imposed a ban on political and religious demonstrations during the *Hajj*, which was duly ignored by Iranian pilgrims. This can also be seen as an attempt to prevent Iranian challenges to the legitimacy of the Al Saud. In light of this, Saudi Arabia broke ties with Iran, perhaps, as Chubin and Tripp suggest, in an attempt to provoke Iran to boycott the *Hajj*.[59] Whilst this was successful, the boycott would only last three years. Despite hoping that the lack of an Iranian presence on the *Hajj* would reduce tensions, the 1989 pilgrimage saw two explosions near the Grand Mosque in Mecca, which were later attributed to Kuwaiti Shi'a of Iranian origin.[60]

Legitimacy and Regional Security

Iranian rhetoric had a three-fold impact upon Saudi Arabia: firstly, offering ideological support for the Shi'i minority in Saudi Arabia; secondly, serving to increase instability within the Kingdom; and thirdly, seeking to undermine the legitimacy of the Al Saud. Iranian efforts to undermine the legitimacy of the Al Saud involved employing rhetoric rejecting the Al Saud's claim to be the legitimate protector of the holy places of Islam. This sought to demonstrate the Iranian regime's political vitality and position as the leader of the Islamic world. In response to the Iranian verbal attacks, the King Fahd changed the title of the monarch, in an attempt to re-establish Islamic legitimacy.[61] Prior to 1986, the Saudi monarch was referred to as "His Majesty"; however, this connotes impious parallels with God. King Fahd thus changed the title to the "Protector (also custodian or servant) of the Two Holy Places", reaffirming Saudi Arabia's importance within the Muslim world. It is worth noting that the rhetoric used by Iran against the Al Saud regime mirrors that of dissident Saudi nationals,[62] despite Saudi dissidents and Iran occupying polar positions within the Islamic world.

In addition to the attacks on the Al Saud, Iranian rhetoric was often directed at the Shi'i minorities of neighbouring countries, in an attempt to engender wider support for the revolution across the region. As such, those states with large Shi'i communities were concerned by the potential for sectarian uprisings.

Saudi Arabia has a large Shi'i population, located within the oil-rich Eastern Province. Responding to the concern of increasing Iranian influence within the Shi'i community, coupled with uprisings by its Shi'i population, the Saudi regime resorted to the use of force to suppress its Shi'i population. The late 1970s and 1980s saw a spate of riots and some of the worst repression of Shi'i Muslims in the Kingdom's history, highlighted by the use of 20,000 members of the National Guard to end the Ashura celebrations of 1979, which were the first public celebrations of the prestigious Shi'i festival since 1913.[63] The Shi'i riots across this period "were products of the success of the Iranian revolution whose leadership began to attack Saudi Arabia for corruption, alliance with the West, and above all questioned the Saudi leadership's claim to protect the two Muslim shrines in Mecca and Medina".[64]

The ruling elites of several states across the Middle East are concerned that Iran seeks to unite the Shi'i populations of the Middle East and North African (MENA) states in what has been termed the "Shi'i Crescent" by King Abdullah of Jordan. King Abdullah stated how "pro-Iran parties or politicians dominate the new Iraqi government, [and how] a new 'crescent' of dominant Shia movements or governments stretching from Iran into Iraq, Syria, and Lebanon could emerge".[65] Furthermore, rhetoric supporting Shi'i organisations also has the capacity to undermine internal legitimacy within the respective states. The suspicion surrounding Iranian actions was exacerbated through Tehran's suspected involvement in subversion in Bahrain and Kuwait, amidst accusations of providing support for groups such as the Islamic Front for the Liberation of Bahrain,[66] which provoked Prince Nayef, then Saudi interior minister, to refer to Iran as the "Gulf's terrorists".[67]

Geopolitics

When examining the rivalry between Saudi Arabia and Iran, one must first consider the geography of the Gulf region. As Henner Furtig articulates, the Gulf is a major lifeline for both states, given each economy's reliance upon oil. As such, secure transit routes through the Gulf and Strait of Hormuz are essential.[68] When considering the geopolitical nature of the Gulf regional system, it is possible to examine the environment in terms of regional security. The argument within this chapter shall utilise such an interpretation of geopolitics in order to facilitate greater understanding of the role played by identity incongruence.

Historically, the Gulf geopolitical environment has traditionally been dominated by Iran and Iraq. Post 1979, three serious conflicts occurred: the 1980 War between Iran and Iraq, and two conflicts between Iraq and the United States (leading coalition forces). Saudi Arabia's position during these conflicts helped shape the nature of the Gulf security environment, especially considering Riyadh's reliance upon external powers for security. The 2003 invasion of Iraq saw the removal of a strong, belligerent power from the region, an actor that had behaved antagonistically towards both Riyadh and Tehran in the years following 1979. In addition, the insurgency and power struggles within Iraq after the removal of Saddam Hussein fostered an opportunity for Saudi Arabia and Iran to engage in proxy competition.[69]

Prior to the events of 2003, several issues dominated the regional security environment, beginning with the Iran–Iraq War, the two conflicts with direct US involvement in the Gulf, Iran's nuclear aspirations, proxy conflicts, Iran's involvement in perceived Arab spheres of influence, and the debate between internal and external provisions of regional security. Post 2003, it is suggested that the "fundamental driver of the relationship is a struggle to shape the regional balance of power".[70]

Iran–Iraq War: The First Gulf War

Iran's war with Iraq during the 1980s had a profound effect upon regional security, resulting in both the development of the Gulf Cooperation Council (GCC), and the further involvement of the United States in the region. The war with Iraq began on 22 September 1980, with a cease-fire signed on 20 August 1988. The conflict was preceeded by increased suspicion of Iranian actions to undermine the Ba'athist regime in Baghdad, through attempting to assassinate key members of the regime, including Tariq Aziz, the Christian vice president.[71] Neither Iran nor Iraq appeared ready for conflict, with Iran in disarray after the revolution and key components of the Iraqi navy undergoing maintenance when war broke out.[72]

The conflict saw the use of chemical weapons, with the number of deaths and nature of warfare suggesting comparisons with World War One. Iran perceived the conflict to be an attempt to quash the revolution, a belief furthered by the support of Gulf States and the United States for Iraq. The war would result in a generation of Iranians losing their lives, with casualty estimates ranging to over 1 million, and many more left maimed or as refugees.[73] While neither side was fully prepared for the conflict, it was assumed by the Iranian leadership that the Shi'a of Iraq would rally around Iran, rather than side with the "Godless Ba'athists"; however, this did not occur. Tehran also feared that the Arabs of the Khuzestan province would side with Iraq, given shared ethnic ties. Again, this was a misreading of the situation.

In addition to impacting upon Middle Eastern stability, with Gulf States offering support to Iraq,[74] the war contained an international component. During the war, Iraq began to attack Iranian ships, seeking to provoke Iran into behaving irrationally and draw the international community into the conflict. In retaliation, Iran attacked the ships of Iraq's allies, Saudi Arabia and Kuwait.[75] This launched a new stage in the conflict, known as the "tanker war", which forced the United States' navy to participate in the conflict.[76] Further complicating matters was the Iran-Contra affair,[77] in which arms were transferred from the United States to Iran, to secure the release of US hostages in Lebanon. The proceeds from the sale of arms were then diverted to the Nicaraguan opposition, known as the Contras, at a time when US support for the Contras was prohibited. Domestically, the scandal rocked the Reagan administration, but also, internationally United States credibility was eroded, having broken its non-negotiation policy.

The war between Iran and Iraq had serious implications for the rivalry between Saudi Arabia and Iran. In the early stages of the conflict, it appeared as if Saddam Hussein's military goals had failed, demonstrated by the survival of the Iranian navy and air force.[78] This led to a fear within Saudi Arabia for its continued safety, particularly given ties to Iraq. As a consequence of this and a perceived inability of Baghdad to guarantee security, King Fahd negotiated the AWACS (Airborne Warning and Control System) agreement of 1980–1 with the United States.[79] This agreement proved significant, leading to an increased US presence within the region, and the shooting down of two Iranian military aircraft in 1984, along with a civilian plane in 1988.[80] Thus, in addition to concern regarding Riyadh's alliance with Washington, Tehran was suspicious of Saudi Arabian military spending, which outstripped that of both Iran and Iraq,[81] suggesting the existence of a conventional security dilemma.

The Second Gulf War

The Iraqi invasion of Kuwait on 2 August 1990 had a dramatic impact upon regional security, with repercussions felt 11 years later in New York. When 700 Iraqi tanks and 100,000 Iraqi soldiers crossed the border with Kuwait,[82] Saudi Arabia turned to its largest military arms dealer for protection: "Impressed by America's resolve to reverse Iraqi aggression, King Fahd unabashedly welcomed into the Kingdom a half million members of the American armed forces".[83]

The defeat of Iraq in 1991 dramatically changed the balance of power within the region, leading to an expansion of US power in the region, given that "Arab Gulf states were less reticent about enhancing their security ties with the US".[84] This burgeoning regional influence coincided with a diminishing of US forces within the Kingdom, to a figure around 20,000.[85] Yet, in an often-overlooked event, Saddam Hussein threatened Kuwait again in 1994, which would result in the dispatch of 36,000 US troops to the Gulf to participate in Operation Vigilant Warrior.[86] Tehran perceived this continued military presence as a frustration to "Iran's sense of importance as the largest regional state. For Iran, a strengthened US presence distorted the natural order of regional relationships".[87] Disputes over the nature of regional security remain central to understanding the rivalry between Saudi Arabia and Iran.

The Third Gulf War

Twelve years after the end of the Second Gulf War, US (and coalition) forces again were engaged in military action within Iraq. American foreign policy in the aftermath of 9/11 and as part of the Global War on Terror, sought to preserve US security based on the pillars of pre-emptive strikes and the spread of democracy. On 20 March 2003, a US-led coalition entered Iraq, with victory proclaimed by George W. Bush on board the USS Abraham Lincoln within a month. The presence of coalition forces within the region would again prove antagonistic to many, with Iran especially concerned about US intentions, given the rhetoric emanating from Washington positing Tehran as part of an "axis of evil" in early 2002.[88] This was despite increased coopeartion between the United States and Iran over the US-led intervention in Afghanistan in the previous few months.

The removal of Saddam Hussein and the Ba'athist regime from power in Baghdad resulted in a redistribution of power, both within Iraq and across the Gulf region. The removal of Iraq from Gulf security calculations presented Saudi Arabia and Iran with greater scope to increase their influence across the region, both in terms of hard and soft power; however, both Riyadh and Tehran are aware of the importance of events in Iraq and the consequences for the political and economic landscape across the Gulf.[89]

Regional Security: Internal v External?

The struggle to achieve regional dominance has been an area of competition for Saudi Arabia and Iran, with Riyadh and Tehran attempting to attain this through different means. For both states, existential security concerns are paramount; however, security is sought in diametrically opposed manners. Saudi Arabia perceives itself "to be surrounded by real or potential enemies, most of whom are bigger and more powerful",[90] and thus seeks external security guarantees. In contrast, Iran seeks to provide its own security. To this end, Saudi Arabia looks externally to balance asymmetrical threats within the region, whereas Iran "favours a 'Gulf-centred' view that excludes outsiders".[91]

This tension as to the nature of regional security is exacerbated by the role of the United States within the region. Indeed, the "actual power of the US in the Gulf is seen in diametrically opposite ways by Riyadh and Tehran – for Iran it constitutes a military threat; for Saudi Arabia it is the best guarantee of its military security".[92] Furthermore, as a consequence of both the Saudi alliance with the United States and Tehran's dispute with Washington, the Iranian leadership believed that negotiations with Riyadh would be a slippery slope to détente with the United States.[93]

Despite the prominent position of US forces in contemporary Saudi security calculations, Riyadh's relations with Washington were not always affable. Indeed, Riyadh and Washington have held differing positions on the role of US forces, as demonstrated by perceptions of the role of US forces in the Kingdom. For the United States its role in Saudi Arabia is as a protector, while many in Saudi Arabia were opposed to the form the US presence had taken.[94] Furthermore, the Kingdom's reliance upon the United States to preserve its security has antagonised facets of its population who are vehemently opposed to the West, in particular the United States. This has resulted in the United States maintaining an "over the hill" presence within Saudi Arabia, in an attempt to preserve the Kingdom's security while appeasing domestic dissent.

In contrast to Saudi Arabia's desire to balance threats in the Gulf with the help of external powers, Iran is opposed to the presence of external actors in the regional security environment. This stems, Ehteshami suggests, from Iran's history and geography, as "Iran sees itself as uniquely qualified to determine, at the very least, the destiny of the Gulf sub region".[95] The perception of such a role is due to the belief that Iran is a "natural state", with a history dating back many centuries, surrounded by "artificial states", those states created either by or with tacit support from the West in the twentieth century. Indeed, the idea that Iran is a "natural state" is important when considering Iran's perceived role within the Persian Gulf and Middle East region.

In addition, this notion must be combined with Iranian history and "Iran's historic impotence in the face of foreign influence {which} has left a deep and seemingly permanent scar on the Iranian psyche".[96] As such, the desire for autonomy is an important factor in determining foreign policy in Tehran. Thus, Iranian self-perception, combined with historical impotence has driven the perceived self-reliance for regional security.

Nuclear Fears

The desire to provide its own security and to counter military asymmetry throughout the region may be used as justification by Tehran for the commencement of a nuclear weapons programme. However, combined with fears about the ideological goals of the regime in Tehran,[97] Saudi Arabia, Sunni states, Arab states, Israel and the West all have strong concerns about Iranian nuclear aspirations. Despite Tehran being a signatory of the Non-Proliferation Treaty (NPT) of 1970,[98] the international community remains suspicious of Iran's intentions. This suspicion is especially directed at Iran's uranium enrichment programme,[99] wherein "Iran has installed 1,640 centrifuges and is injecting uranium gas into about 1,300 of them and running them simultaneously".[100] This provides a means for producing highly enriched uranium,[101] which is not deemed necessary for use in civilian reactors.[102] The origins of the Iranian nuclear programme are rooted in the reign of the Shah, who desired a nuclear Iran in possession of both civilian and military nuclear weapons programmes. The initial motivation for attaining nuclear weapons arguably stems from a desire for prestige, given the Shah's "grandiose program for rapid modernisation, economic development, and investment in Iran's military forces".[103] One should note that in the aftermath of the revolution, the development, stockpiling and use of nuclear weapons was prohibited by Ayatollah Khomeini, who issued a *fatwa* to this effect.[104]

Given Riyadh's perception that a nuclear Iran is an existential threat, there are concerns throughout the region that Saudi Arabia may, in turn, seek a nuclear deterrent.[105] Indeed, Dennis Ross, a senior US diplomat, stated that in a conversation with King Abdullah in April 2009, Abdullah threatened the following: "If they get nuclear weapons, we will get nuclear weapons".[106] Publicly, Saudi Arabia has distanced itself from talk of a US-led pre-emptive strike, which would prove damaging to the Al Saud's legitimacy, also engendering opposition support.[107] However, the release of diplomatic cables between Riyadh and Washington by the WikiLeaks organisation seemingly contradicts this position, with suggestions that King Abdullah called upon the United States to "cut off the head of the snake",[108] alluding to Iran.

Tehran has sought to carefully manage the perception of its nuclear programme for its Gulf neighbours.[109] This considered approach has seen Iranian sources portraying Saudi Arabian acceptance of the "peaceful" nature of Iran's nuclear programme, with Tabnak, an Iranian newspaper, suggesting that 73 per cent of Saudis "support" the Iranian nuclear programme, a figure higher than in any other Arab state.[110] However, the veracity of such claims remain in doubt and certainly do not include members of the Al Saud.

Whilst the argument is neither attempting to discover the veracity of claims that Iran is in the throes of developing a nuclear weapons programme,[111] nor to discuss ways to prevent such an achievement, it is necessary to consider the importance of perception. Although the existential consequences of an Iranian nuclear weapons programme appear potentially catastrophic for Middle Eastern security, the mere perception of a nuclear weapons programme can also play an important role in determining Iran's position within the region, and in engendering support.[112] Indeed, one can hold that in order to possess a nuclear deterrence, one does not need a nuclear weapon; rather, one needs the perception of possessing or even having the capacity of building a nuclear weapon. Achieving the status of a nuclear weapon state can solidify a position within the international system and can increase bargaining power during negotiations;[113] however, the drive to such a position risks severe ramifications, be they in the form of economic sanctions or military action. Given this, there is perhaps a more achievable target for Tehran to aspire to: the perception of possessing nuclear weapons, or possessing a break out capability. Indeed, once this perception is attained, provided that the regime survives sanctions or military action, the position of Iran within both the regional and international system is greatly increased. However, the notion of an "Islamic" bomb,[114] specifically a "Shi'i" bomb, has been of great concern for numerous states within the international system,[115] regardless of the success (or indeed aspirations) of Tehran's programme. Given this, much discussion has occurred as to how to behave towards a nuclear Iran.

The consequences of Iran achieving the perception of possessing nuclear weapons are twofold, and can be categorised as pro-Iranian and anti-Iranian. Those who reside within the pro-Iranian camp would fall under the protectorate of the Iranian nuclear umbrella, which would offer both a strong deterrent and degree of legitimacy, as befits a "member of the club". Indeed, in accordance with a basic tenet of Neo-Realism, state (and non-state) actors have the capacity to bandwagon with Iranian power. It is important to note that despite the anti-Israeli/US rhetoric employed by Ahmadinejad and the attempt to speak directly to the "Arab Street", it has been predominantly non-state Shi'i actors that have fallen in line with Iran,[116] notably in Lebanon and in Iraq. However, the degree of support for Iran within Iraq's population appears to be falling.[117] Despite this, several Sunni non-state organisations have also developed ties with Iran, notably Hamas, which may be a consequence of increasing soft power, in the guise of financial support and opposition to Israel, rather than through pure hard power.[118]

The second categorisation, as anti-Iranian, is comprised initially of the United States, Israel, and immediate allies. However, what is interesting to note is the burgeoning shift of Arab states towards the anti-Iranian category. Indeed, this has been demonstrated by the emergence of US diplomatic cables by WikiLeaks, which document the desire of certain Arab states (notably Saudi Arabia) to launch an attack on Iran.[119] When this is coupled with attitudes towards Hizballah in Lebanon, whom it is widely accepted that Iran is supporting, it is possible to see a shift in the balance of power across the Middle East.

Given this, it is possible to suggest that Iranian power exploits have facilitated a redistribution of the balance of power across the region, through both hard and soft understandings of power. Informal, transient alliances have been developed, which separate Iran from Sunni Islamic countries, who appear to be engaged in a form of bandwagoning with Israel and the United States, although this is covert. Conversely, there appears to be some semblance of bandwagoning occurring with Shi'i states and organisations fostering strong ties with Iran, on the back of both ideological support and the perception of a nuclear programme within Iran.

It is, however, interesting to consider the nature of alliance formation below the official state level. As previously noted, much Iranian rhetoric has been directed at the "Arab Street", which is predominantly concerned with the populations of neighbouring Arab countries. As such, one must consider to what extent alliances with the United States and Israel will impact upon legitimacy and stability within Arab states, for whom both the United States and Israel have been generational enemies. However, the process of alliance formation within the Middle East is often kept covert.

The "Arab Street"

Iranian foreign policy, as noted by Paul Aarts and Joris van Duijne, has been predominantly focussed upon the Palestinian cause, while also attempting to disrupt US hegemonic aspirations in the region. As Aarts and van Duijne articulate, there is "nothing particularly Shi'a about the two issues".[120] As a consequence, Iranian foreign policy has been undertaken within what are typically Arab spheres, particularly the Arab–Israeli issue and the Levant. This strategy is referred to as the "Arab Street",[121] in which Iran attempts to speak directly to the populations of Arab nations, "undermining the rulers' legitimacy by portraying them as sclerotic lackeys of Washington, and upstaging them on the Palestinian question through provocative rhetoric and support to such groups as Hamas and Hizballah".[122] This "Arab Street" foreign policy has been aggressively non-sectarian, and, rather, has been aimed at external targets. Yet, despite this, it the parallels with causes typically endorsed by Sunni Arab states are clear to see.[123]

Indeed, Aarts and van Duijne suggest that the symbolic importance of the Arab–Israeli issue and events in the Levant play an integral role within Saudi-Iranian competition for the support of the "Arab Street",[124] yet one can also add the events in Iraq to this calculation. To some within the Arab world, Tehran's aspirations over the "Arab Street" are antagonistic, leading to claims that Arab portfolios have been stolen and are now in Iranian hands. Yet, questions remain as to the motivation for such a foreign policy: a proof of influence or an attempt to end its isolation from the rest of the region?

A key aspect of the "Arab Street" is the Arab–Israeli issue. For many Middle Eastern states, including Saudi Arabia, the Arab–Israeli question has been utilised as a tool to engender domestic legitimacy and to undermine regional political rivals.[125] Saudi Arabia had been a prominent player in anti-Israeli sentiment across the region, having been a leading member of the coalition of Arab states opposed to Israel. This role, coupled with the demise of Nasser's Pan-Arab power and Riyadh's burgeoning economic power, had helped to establish the Kingdom as a dominant power within the region.[126]

Tehran appreciates the symbolic importance of the Arab–Israeli issue, with Ayatollah Khamenei referring to Palestine as a "limb of our body".[127] Tehran's rhetoric seeks to position Iran as a dominant actor within the issue, with its actions attempting to demonstrate the languid efforts of Saudi Arabia to resolve the issue. In addition to this rhetoric, financial support is given to the likes of Hamas and Palestinian Islamic Jihad, provoking Saudi diplomats to question why Iran is involved in an Arab issue.[128]

A secondary aspect of the "Arab Street" concerns action in the Levant. Iranian action within the Levant proved assertive, if not belligerent, prompting a more confrontational response from Saudi Arabia.[129] The actions of Hizballah in the summer of 2006, kidnapping two Israeli soldiers for prisoner exchanges and the ensuing conflict, proved to galvanize Arab opinion, undercutting Sunni Arab regimes, "who had long evinced opposition to Israel, but with little to show for it".[130] In accordance with the "Arab Street" policy, Iran's support for Hizballah would engender support across the region. In response to this, the Al Saud faced a dilemma: to do nothing and risk looking weak while

Iranian power grew, or to support Hizballah. In attempting to reclaim Arab portfolios, the ruling elite in Saudi Arabia discussed providing support for Hizballah; however, this idea of providing support evoked strong debate within the Kingdom, exposing the conflict between Arab leadership aspirations and the doctrinal aversion to Shi'ism of the Wahhabist, Salafi clerics.[131]

The 2006 War in Lebanon demonstrated the success of this Iranian strategy, with the exploits of Hizballah providing scope for Tehran to challenge the Al Saud's legitimacy on both regional and domestic stages.[132] Riyadh's criticism of Hizballah's actions was viewed by some as an acceptance of the US–Israeli strategy of eliminating threats within the region,[133] yet this would be contradicted by strong public opinion in support of Hizballah.[134]

It is important to note that some hold the 2006 War in Lebanon to be a success for Israel and the Israeli Defence Force (IDF), not Hizballah. Indeed, this can be seen predominantly in the military losses sustained by Hizballah and an apparent weakening of status.[135] Furthermore, the IDF's destruction of the Dahiya suburb of Beirut, a predominantly Shi'i suburb, facilitated the emergence of the "Dahiya Doctrine", wherein the IDF would use heavy force against civilian areas believed to be pro-Hizballah.[136] Indeed, as Israeli Northern Command chief Gadi Eisenkot stated, in a 2008 interview:

> What happened in the Dahiya quarter of Beirut in 2006 will happen in every village from which Israel is fired on [. . .] We will apply disproportionate force on it and cause great damage and destruction there. From our standpoint these are not civilian villages, they are military bases.[137]

This suggests that the Dahiya Doctrine could be applied writ large across the region.

Proxy Conflicts

In addition to competition on the Arabian Peninsula, Riyadh and Tehran engage in numerous proxy conflicts, notably in Palestine, the Levant, Iraq and Bahrain. The political structure and nature of Palestine, the Levant and Iraq invite external influence, permitting open competition between Saudi Arabia and Iran, while the events of the "Arab Spring" of 2011 fostered a form of proxy conflict in Bahrain and Syria. The behaviour of Saudi Arabia and Iran within these arenas has differed, with Iran providing financial support for non-state actors and Tehran's "assertiveness and patronage of non-state actors [...] largely unabated".[138] Furthermore, clerical ties between Iran and Lebanon, in particular within actors in southern Beirut, have long been utilised to support and spread Iran's ideological agenda.

Through efforts to counter Iranian support for non-state actors such as Hamas and Hizballah within Palestine and the Levant, Saudi Arabia has attempted to cultivate multilateral support from other Arab states, "each of whom regards Hamas as a threat to its own stability and Iran's rise as a danger to the region as a whole".[139] These burgeoning alliances also featured unofficial *rapprochement* with Israel, in an effort to counter Iran's alliance with Hizballah; however, Operation Cast Lead in December 2008 may have undermined any potential shifting of alliances.[140] In addition to Israel, Syria is the other variable within the region: despite its Sunni Arab majority, Syria has strong ties to Hizballah and remains a key ally of Iran.

The Levant

Lebanon has long been important for both Saudi Arabia and Iran, with the existence of clerical ties between Iran and Lebanon that predate the 1979 revolution. For Saudi Arabia, Lebanon has provided scope to counter regional dynamics, namely the threat of Nasser in the 1950s and 1960s.[141] The political arrangement of Lebanon leaves the state open to interference and, as a consequence of ties between Hizballah and Iran, Saudi Arabia has been concerned about increasing Iranian involvement. Given the ties between former Lebanese Prime Minister Rafik Hariri and Saudi Arabia,[142] the aftermath of Hariri's assignation and the Cedar Revolution of March 2005 appeared to foster outright competition between two factions within Lebanon: the March 8th Alliance, comprised of Iran, Hizballah, Syria and several

Lebanese actors; and the March 14th Alliance, the pro-Hariri coalition, supported by Saudi Arabia.[143] Yet, despite the emergence of these two factions, neither Iran nor Saudi Arabia necessarily favoured conflict between the two alliances. Furthermore, given that many in the international community believed that Syria was the main protagonist in the assassination of Hariri, Riyadh believed that Tehran was a more desirable negotiating partner than Damascus, in both ensuring stability in Lebanon and reducing Syrian influence. However, this period of détente was broken by the 2006 War between Hizballah and Israel, the aftermath of which saw Saudi Arabia attempting to counter Iranian gains achieved through the actions of Hizballah by the provision of $1.5 billion for postwar reconstruction. In contrast, Iran provided around $120 million.[144] Furthermore, Saudi Arabia has offered support for Salafi organisations within Lebanon, seeking to reduce the ideological power of Hizballah and also Iran.

A key aspect of Saudi Arabia's strategy within Lebanon is to attempt to isolate Syria from Iran, and in doing so, reduce Iranian influence in Lebanon, the Israel-Palestine sphere and close an Iranian door to the Arab world. Saudi Arabia has also sought to reduce Syrian power, thus also reducing Iranian influence. The crisis in Syria has provided Saudi Arabia with an opportunity to reduce both Syrian and Iranian power. While protests in Syria initially emanated from the "Arab Spring", which facilitated the expression of long-standing grievances against the regime, the crisis has strong sectarian overtones, with sectarian differences being used by regime and opposition groups alike.[145] The ruling elite of Syria subscribes to the Alawite form of Twelver Shi'ism, while opposition groups are predominantly Sunni Muslims.

Opposition movements, while not a coherent group, are comprised of armed groups, peaceful protest groups and army defectors. It is suggested that armed groups emerged to protect the peaceful protesters from security forces, who were using forceful counter-insurgency tactics.[146] Part of this strategy also included regime forces bombarding civilian populations across the state, particularly seen in Homs, which appears tantamount to collective punishment.[147]

The "Arab Spring" uprisings in Syria provided Saudi Arabia with scope to reduce the Assad regime's power, as Madawi Al-Rasheed notes, presenting Saudi Arabia with an opportunity to "win Syria back to the Arab fold".[148] To this end, Saudi Arabia, alongside Qatar, has allegedly offered support to opposition groups fighting the Assad regime.[149] Indeed, the Saudi foreign minister, Prince Saud al-Faisal, stated that "arming the opposition is a duty", although Saudi sources have denied that they have provided arms to opposition groups.[150]

In contrast to Saudi Arabia, Iran sees the security of the Assad regime as integral to its own standing within the Middle East, alongside continued support for Hizballah. As such, it has sought to support the regime through the provision of military and technical support. A senior figure in the Qods wing of the Iranian Revolutionary Guard Corps (IRGC)[151] is quoted as admitting that members of the IRGC are operating in Syria to support the Assad regime.

In an interview with the Isna news agency, that was later removed, Ismail Gha'ani, the deputy head of the Qods force, stated:

> If the Islamic republic was not present in Syria, the massacre of people would have happened on a much larger scale [. . .] Before our presence in Syria, too many people were killed by the opposition but with the physical and non-physical presence of the Islamic republic, big massacres in Syria were prevented.[152]

However, the exact extent of Saudi or Iranian involvement within Syria is difficult to ascertain.

Iraq

In addition to the Levant, the political situation in Iraq post 2003 witnessed much sectarian conflict between Sunni and Shi'i agents, with those of Sunni persuasion operating with the support of Saudi Arabia, and those of Shi'i persuasion operating with the support of Iran. The ethnic constitution of Iraq means that aspects of the population are open to interference from neighbouring states, particularly in light of the the US withdrawal. Indeed, a strong concern exists amongst policy makers and analysts that "tribes would turn to neighbouring states for help, thus becoming a vehicle for the conflict's further regionalisation.

Arab states, seeking to promote their influence, counter Iran's or pursue a sectarian Sunni agenda might pick up where the U.S. let off".[153]

It is believed by Riyadh that Iran possesses strong ties to members of Shi'i parties in Iraq, in part stemming from shared religious views, but also because many Iraqis from Shi'i communities were expelled to Iran during the 1970s and 1980s on the grounds of perceived Iranian loyalties.[154] Moreover, it should be noted that for the most part, "Iraq's Shiite actors engage only with external Shiite parties just as Iraq's Sunnis deal exclusively with Sunni states. By the same token, neighbouring states are inclined to deal with their co-religionists".[155] Saudi Arabia is also concerned about ties between the Shi'i community of Iraq and Iran and, while Riyadh accepts that the Iraqi government is predominantly Shi'a, Saudi Arabia desires a nationalistic government, free from Iranian influence.[156]

While Iranian influence within Iraq is undeniable, namely through the IRGC and the Qods force,[157] Saudi Arabian involvement is less easily discerned. Although there is a precedent for Saudi Arabian interference in the conflicts of neighbours,[158] the extent of Saudi involvement in Iraq is not as clear. Despite reports in 2006 claiming that if the United States was to withdraw from Iraq, the Saudis would intervene to protect the Sunni population from Shi'i militias,[159] it is difficult to ascertain the extent of this involvement. However, anecdotal evidence exists supporting the notion that Saudi Arabia has provided financial support to Sunni organisations across Iraq. Indeed, the Iraq Study Group Report detailed "current but private Saudi involvement in the funding of the Sunni insurgency in Iraq".[160] In addition to seeking to counter Iranian gains, it is pertinent to note that the Al Saud have faced increasing pressure from within Saudi Arabia to protect Sunnis within Iraq on the grounds of shared religious beliefs, tribal ties and ethnic bonds.

This suspicion of the other's action within Iraq is also prominent within Iran. Indeed, Tehran is concerned at Riyadh's increasing involvement within the state. Frederick Wehrey, Theodore W. Karasik, Alireza Nader, *et al.*, detail how various facets of Iranian media, possessing close ties to the regime, have stated concern at the level of Saudi involvement within Iraq.[161] Thus, it is clear that Iraq is important when understanding both ideological and geopolitical competition between Saudi Arabia and Iran.

Bahrain

The case of Bahrain offers rich scope for analysing the relationship between Riyadh and Tehran, on both ideological and geopolitical grounds.[162] Firstly, the Kingdom of Bahrain is perceived to be the epicentre of the Peninsula's "sectarian disenfranchisement",[163] thus providing scope for analysis of ideological competition. Indeed, Bahrain is rife with sectarian tensions, with some reports suggesting that as much as 75 per cent of the population are Shi'a.[164] This Shi'i population is perceived to have ties to Iran on the grounds of shared religious affiliation. The ruling tribe, the Al Khalifa, emanates from the Arabian Peninsula and, in contrast to the majority of the population, are Sunni. Secondly, Bahrain's geographic location provides opportunity to analyse geopolitical competition within the rivalry.

The Kingdom of Bahrain is an archipelago of 33 islands, the largest of which is Bahrain, located some 16 kilometres from Saudi Arabia. Bahrain is linked to Saudi Arabia by the King Fahd Causeway, which was opened in 1986. The population of Bahrain, according to the 2010 census, stands at 1,234,571, of which 568,399 are Bahraini nationals and the remainder non-nationals,[165] making Bahrain the smallest GCC state. The Al Khalifa came to power in the eighteenth century, arriving from Qatar and, with the help of tribal allies from the Arabian Peninsula, overthrew the Persian rulers.[166] In 1820, claims to Bahrain were uttered by the then-Persian rulers;[167] however, claims to ownership over Bahrain also possess a contemporary aspect, as demonstrated by Hussain Shariatmadari, the editor of the Iranian newspaper *Kayhan*, in an editorial suggesting that "Bahrain was an inseparable part of Iran".[168]

Saudi Arabia also possesses strong ties with Bahrain, stemming in part from the Al Khalifa's tribal roots in Saudi Arabia and also from economic ties, facilitated by the sale of oil.[169] However, there also exists a strong level of concern within Saudi Arabia at how the Al Khalifa has responded to the Shi'i question within Bahrain, namely that political accommodation may result in similar demands from the

Shi'a of Saudi Arabia, while also fostering increasing Iranian involvement within Bahrain. The importance of Bahrain for Saudi Arabia transcends solely providing support for the Al Khalifa[170] and reflects geopolitical concerns about increasing Iranian power within the Persian Gulf and across the wider Middle East. Indeed, the Al Saud are eager to prevent increasing Iranian involvement within Bahrain, given such close proximity to Saudi Arabia; thus, Riyadh perceives the stability of the Al Khalifa to be the best way to achieve this.[171]

While the Al Khalifa and Al Saud possess shared ethnic and religious ties, the Bahraini Arab Shi'i population possess close ties with the Shi'a of Saudi Arabia. Furthermore, it is believed by the Al Khalifa that, much like with the Shi'a of Saudi Arabia, the Shi'a of Bahrain possess a dual loyalty, to both Bahrain and Iran. Despite this suspicion, the actual level of ties between the Shi'a of Bahrain and Tehran is difficult to ascertain: "Despite the occasional discovery of domestic plots with confirmed or suspected links to Tehran, Arabic-speaking Saudi and Bahraini Shiites have generally expressed cautious, even wary, attitudes towards their Persian-speaking Iranian coreligionists across the Gulf".[172] This suspicion can be traced back to the legacy of ethnic conflict between Arabs and Persians.

Furthermore, much like Saudi Arabia's Shi'i population, the Shi'a in Bahrain are perceived by some as a potential Iranian fifth column. This perception stems from shared religious views and the legacy of a failed 1981 *coup d'état* by the Islamic Front for the Liberation of Bahrain (IFLB), which received support from Iran.[173] It is also alleged by the ruling elites in Bahrain that Iran was behind political unrest during the 1990s.

In the aftermath of the "Arab Spring" of 2011, Saudi Arabia and Iran became engaged in a proxy competition within Bahrain, offering support for the ruling elite and protesters respectively. The roots of the "Arab Spring" in Bahrain can be traced back to the ascension of Hamad Al Khalifa to Emir, then King, in 1999.[174] Upon his ascension, King Hamad offered a programme of reforms in an attempt to move Bahrain away from its authoritarian tradition,[175] although the lack of implementation of many of these reforms added to the growing unrest across Bahrain, culminating in the events of 2011.

While the majority of the protesters were Shi'a, this was not initially a sectarian protest; rather, the protests were driven by calls for political and democratic reform and the devolution of a degree of power from the palace to the elected parliament.[176] Protests were generally peaceful and avoided directly criticising King Hamad, although the response of the state's security forces was heavy handed, further incensing the protesters.[177] After a prolonged period of skirmishes with security forces and numerous deaths, the protesters occupied Pearl Square in Manama.

On 14 March, one month after the protests began, Bahrain invoked a GCC security clause that triggered the arrival of Saudi and GCC forces, under the guise of the Peninsula Shield Force. According to an International Crisis Group report, an estimated 1,000 Saudi Arabian troops crossed the King Fahd Causeway, along with police and troops from the UAE and Qatar.[178] Their presence was to ensure the survival of the Al Khalifa regime, which is viewed as a red line by Riyadh. Furthermore, the presence of Saudi troops was also an attempt to prevent the Shi'a of Bahrain from gaining more power, fearful of the domestic consequences of an increasingly powerful Shi'i population. While some believe that the Saudi presence within Bahrain is to counter the increasing Iranian influence towards the Shi'i majority,[179] others, such as Jean-François Seznec, suggest that the presence of Saudi troops was to protect elements within the Al Khalifa family from more liberal members,[180] who are more open to ideas of reform. The consequence of this would undeniably lead to increasing Shi'i empowerment within Bahrain.

While Saudi Arabia's presence within Bahrain was undeniable, Iranian involvement within the kingdom is less easily observed. Many Bahraini officials, along with members of the GCC, have accused Iran of interfering within Bahrain, although empirical evidence to support this is difficult to locate. While ascertaining the exact level of Iranian involvement within Bahrain is troublesome, the notion that Iran has supported, if not instigated these protests appears probable. Indeed the United States, amongst others, has acknowledged Iran's "propensity for mischief"[181] within Bahrain. It is, however, possible to understand the nature of Iranian involvement by looking at historical ties between

Iran and opposition groups within Bahrain, namely al-Jabha al-Islamiyya li Tahrir al-Bahrayn (the IFLB). The IFLB were accused by the Al Khalifa of attempting a *coup d'état* in 1981, along with allegations that the group received help from Tehran in order to undertake the *coup*. The Bahraini government suggested that the IFLB received support and training from the IRGC,[182] which echoes Tehran's behaviour across the region in the immediate aftermath of the revolution.[183]

Hasan Alhansan's study on the IFLB provides valuable insight into ties between the group and Iran, suggesting that there are five areas in which Iran has been linked with the IFLB, namely: ideology, leadership, offering media support, logistics, and military training.[184] Indeed, many of these ties are perceived to remain between Iran and Bahraini opposition groups.

Although there is ambiguity as to the extent of Iranian involvement in the protests across Bahrain, the veracity of ties between Bahraini Shi'i clerics and Tehran is undeniable. Sheikh Isa Ahmad Qassem, the spiritual leader of the main opposition party, Wafa, and the leader of Friday prayers at a mosque in the predominantly Shi'i populated Diraz City, "is a religious representative of Khamenei, collecting taxes for the Supreme Leader, propagating his religious authority, and encouraging people to follow him rather than other 'sources of emulation' ".[185] Qassem has been described by Khamenei as a "star in the sky" of Shi'ism. However, not all Bahraini clerics possess ties to Iran; indeed, some maintain close ties with clerics in Najaf in Iraq,[186] demonstrating the differences within Shi'ism. Yet, despite this, most Bahraini clerics were trained in Qom and, thus, speak Persian.

While there is no solid evidence as to Iran's role within the uprisings in Bahrain, there exists a strong belief that the Shi'a of Bahrain would be more receptive to Iran if the protesters gained power,[187] and, conversely, the influence of Saudi Arabia within Bahrain would diminish. This demonstrates the importance of securing the Al Khalifa and preventing reforms that would empower the Shi'a for the Al Saud.

As Gregory Gause notes, the sectarian aspect is becoming increasingly open within the rivalry, a process facilitated by the events in Bahrain.[188] However, in allowing the sectarian issue to become more prominent in strategic calculations, the Al Saud are risking inflaming internal tensions within its Eastern Province. Furthermore, while Sunnis dramatically outnumber their Shi'i counterparts across the region, the power of Shi'i groups is undeniably growing, leaving Saudi Arabia in an increasingly hostile neighbourhood, surrounded by powerful Shi'i states. However, in contrast to this position, Mehdi Khaliji suggests that "Tehran wants to avoid being seen as igniting sectarian conflict in the Arab world, whether in Bahrain or elsewhere",[189] as a consequence of the different demographics of Sunni and Shi'i populations, respectively.

Given the increase in Shi'i power across the region, perhaps this adds even more weight to the Al Saud's calculation that the security of the Al Khalifa regime is a red line. As such, given the perception of increased Iranian involvement within Bahrain and the ensuing empowerment of the Shi'a, and thus Iran, Saudi Arabia has been left with little choice but to become involved in securing the regime of the Al Khalifa. This suggests that, while the ideological aspect is important in understanding the rivalry, it cannot be separated from the geopolitical.

The existence of Saudi troops in Bahrain, regardless of the explanation for their presence, increased tensions between Riyadh and Tehran. Part of Khomeini's rhetoric, both pre and post revolution, focussed upon being "an enemy to the oppressor (*mustakbarin*) and a helper to the oppressed (*mustazefin*)".[190] This responsibility to protect the *mustazefin* is often stressed by Tehran when reaching out to Shi'a beyond Iran. As such, given that Saudi forces are present in Bahrain to protect the Sunni ruling elite from the Shi'i protesters, Iran perceives this in a negative way. In contrast, Saudi Arabia fears that Iranian actions across the region are an attempt to disrupt the status quo and part of an agenda to increase Iranian power in both ideological and geopolitical spheres. As such, the perception of interference from the other has increased tensions within the rivalry.

Economics

Within the geopolitical sphere, one must also consider the role played by economics in determining the nature of the geopolitical environment.

When examining economic competition, it is important to examine three areas: natural resources, the role of OPEC, and the provision of financial support to proselytizing agendas.

The economies of both Saudi Arabia and Iran are driven by the sale of natural resources, with oil a primary source of income. Both states are members of OPEC and are the two largest producers of oil since the early 1980s.[191] Indeed, Saudi Arabia's oil reserves alone account for one-third of the oil in OPEC.[192] Given this position of power within OPEC, it is unsurprising that Iran finds itself "unable to achieve its own economic and political goals [without Saudi cooperation], which are not necessarily compatible with those of Saudi Arabia".[193] As a consequence of the nature of domestic demands, the two states require different prices in order to fulfil financial requirements, with Iran requiring the price of oil per barrel to be much higher than Saudi Arabia.[194] In addition, Iranian production capacity is much smaller than that of Saudi Arabia and, as such, Tehran is far more willing to supply less oil than Saudi Arabia, at much higher prices.

One of the defining factors in determining the level of oil production is found in domestic usage. Iran has historically used a greater proportion of its oil production internally than does Saudi Arabia;[195] however, as a result of increasing population and economic growth, usage in Saudi Arabia is expected to increase by 10 per cent over the next decade.[196]

A further concern for Riyadh is the suggestion that crude oil reserves "may have been overstated by as much as 300bn barrels-nearly 40 per cent".[197] Aside from the obvious long-term implications for a Rentier state reliant upon the sale of goods for most of its income, short-term implications include not being able to pump more oil if increasing prices pose threats to demand. These claims emanate from Sada al-Husseini, a geologist and former head of exploration at Saudi Aramco, detailed in a series of cables released by WikiLeaks. Indeed, supporting these allegations, several other cables question the impact that Saudi Arabia possesses on the markets in the long term. Indeed, "[c]learly they can drive prices up, but we question whether they any longer have the power to drive prices down for a prolonged period".[198] This perceived inability to drive prices down will be well received by Tehran, reflecting the need for higher oil prices to meet domestic financial needs.

Yet, economic relations between Riyadh and Tehran have not always been of a belligerent nature. Indeed, the OPEC meeting in September 1993 witnessed Saudi Arabia cut production and reduce its market share in order to permit Iran to increase its oil production.[199] This period of economic goodwill coincided with improvements in relations between the two states, six years after the *Hajj* deaths. However, this period of cooperation was not to last, stemming from mutual suspicions over adherence to OPEC quotas and Saudi ties to the United States.[200] Further, given the size of respective oil reserves, the strategies employed by Saudi Arabia and Iran differ. Saudi Arabia "is a relatively low population, large-reserves producer, which means policy-makers need to secure long-term prospects for oil markets, but can afford to forgo immediate price maximisation"[201] not reaching its highest oil producing capacity; in contrast, given the size of the Iranian population, coupled with much smaller oil reserves, Iran "will therefore be relatively less interested in the very long-term future of the oil market".[202] Thus, Tehran feels compelled to press for higher prices in the short term,[203] a solution achievable through cutting production. However, these calls to cut production have been met with staunch resistance from those states with higher production levels, such as Saudi Arabia.[204] Given the sensitivity of regional economic dynamics, those responsible for oil policy within Saudi Arabia must "manoeuvre between their own domestic politico-economic needs, and the need to manage regional sensitivities".[205] The nature of economic relations between Saudi Arabia and Iran shows that, although cooperation is possible, the differing positions on the price of oil, combined with innate suspicions of the "other", the possibility for cooperation appears limited.

In addition to competition within OPEC, the notion of providing support for proselytizing groups across the MENA (Middle East and North Afrcia) region and into Asia has fostered an increasing level of competition between Saudi Arabia and Iran. Indeed, both states actively court geopolitical and ideological influence among neighbouring states.[206] Support for proselytizing groups will be discussed in greater detail in chapter six.

Characterising the Rivalry

The nature of the rivalry between Saudi Arabia and Iran oscillates between periods of antagonism and détente. Within this oscillation, Aarts and van Duijne suggest that the most prominent position is that of cautious pragmatism.[207] While many perceive that sectarian tensions within the ideological sphere define the rivalry, also accounting for many of the tensions within the Middle East, this perception avoids many other key dynamics. As Aarts and van Duijne argue, perhaps a more appropriate description would be that the sectarian *shapes* relations,[208] yet the importance of sectarian tensions must not be understated. There exists much suspicion over the extent to which Iran holds sway over Shi'i populations of the Middle East; however, "most [Shi'i populations] regard the Islamic Republic with a degree of spiritual and emotional affinity but not as an object of political emulation".[209] Indeed, in 2008 King Abdullah stated that the sectarian issue was a "matter of concern, not a matter of danger",[210] yet Saudi involvement within Bahrain may suggest otherwise. Through the success of the "Arab Street" foreign policy initiative, "Iran has acquired an appeal that has on occasion transcended sectarian differences",[211] an achievement both Saudi Arabia and Iran aspire to, in an attempt to achieve larger political goals.

Conclusions

While ideological competition has dramatically increased in the aftermath of the 1979 revolution, the nature of geopolitical competition has evolved from purely hegemonic competition to disputes concerning the extent of the influence of Washington throughout the region. Indeed, US presence and influence across the region has increased as a consequence of several events. Geopolitical competition has been complicated by Tehran's relationship with Washington, which was damaged initially by the removal of the Shah and then by the taking of US hostages in November 1979.[212] While Riyadh's relationship with Washington has not always been harmonious, diametrically opposed views as to the role of the United States in the region have proved damaging to relations between the two. The regional security environment has been further complicated by several proxy conflicts and fears concerning Tehran's pursuit of nuclear weapons.

These ideological and geopolitical spheres detail the nature of the rivalry between the two states; however, it is imperative to consider the internal dynamics of both Saudi Arabia and Iran to truly understand the nature of these two spheres. The myriad identities located within Saudi and Iranian borders pose internal security dilemmas within each state, the response to which shapes the nature of each sphere. Furthermore, the two spheres are not distinct entities and as such, while treated thus for analytical clarity, one must be aware of the possibility of seepage between the two.

3

HISTORY, POLITICS AND NARRATIVES OF STATE-BUILDING

As Fred Halliday suggests, the conflict between Arabs and Persians, and Gulf States, "is a product not so much of imperialist interference or of millennial and atavistic historical antagonisms, but of the two interrelated modern processes of state formation and the rise of nationalism".[1] Given Halliday's assertion, this chapter considers processes of state-building and the importance of narratives within each state. The process of state-building and the necessity of deriving legitimacy for new regimes often results in leaders referring to myths and tales that evoke nationalist sentiment, which, when coupled with Islamic rhetoric, complicates regional relations. In addition, analysis of these elements will facilitate awareness of normative structure, both for the rivalry, and for Saudis and Iranians.

The chapter begins with an examination of the formation and political structure of Saudi Arabia and Iran. In doing this, the chapter will stress the importance of narratives, both historical and religious, in the state-building processes of Saudi Arabia and Iran.

Saudi Arabia's Tribal Web

Saudi Arabia is the largest country in the Middle East,[2] located on the Arabian Peninsula, sharing borders with Iraq, Jordan, Yemen, Oman, the UAE, Qatar and Kuwait; Saudi Arabia also borders the Persian Gulf and Red Sea. The area of land contained within Saudi Arabia's borders is 2.149 million square kilometres,[3] split across four regions: Hijaz, Nejd, Hasa and Asir, which are split into 13 administrative provinces. The population of Saudi Arabia is 28,686,633, including 5,576,076 non-nationals, as of July 2009, 4.75 million of whom live in Riyadh.[4] The population of Saudi Arabia is heavily urbanised. Ninety per cent of the population are Arabs, while the remaining 10 per cent are Afro-Asian.[5] Islam is the faith of Saudi Arabia, enshrined in law. The two holy places of Islam, the *Kabaa* and *Al-Masjid al-Nabawi*, are located within Saudi Arabia, in Mecca and Medina, respectively.

State-Building on the Arabian Peninsula

Saudi Arabia is a nascent state, the current incarnation of which was achieved in 1932, posing problems for the creation of a national identity. This problem was addressed by Josep Nevo, who focusses on "the use of religion by the royal family to consolidate a Saudi national identity which in turn will constitute an additional attribute for the legitimacy of the ruling dynasty".[6] Nevo examines how the desired Saudi national identity falls under the jurisdiction of the House of Saud, which subscribes to a strict adherence of Wahhabi interpretations of Islam, which engenders legitimacy.

The state narrative of the Kingdom's history begins in the eighteenth century, a time of chaos akin to the Hobbesian state of nature.[7] The emergence of the first Saudi state (1744–1818) is introduced in Saudi literature as a "corrective mechanism bringing the *umma* to the right path".[8] The first Saudi state was ended by an Egyptian expedition, sanctioned by the Ottomans, aimed at curbing the growing power in Arabia.[9] The second Saudi state was born only six years after demise of the first, during which time the land formerly ruled by the Saudi-Wahhabi alliance had "returned to unbridled tribal rivalry and feuding".[10] The second Saudi Kingdom ended in 1887 and was characterised by internal feuding, tribal rivalries and civil war. The failure of these two state building projects demonstrates the difficulty of the process of state formation across the Arabian Peninsula, given disparate geographical settlements and the strength of tribal loyalties.

The twentieth century witnessed the emergence of many new states, shaped by the the throes of colonialism and the remnants of nineteenth-century nationalism. The Kingdom of Saudi Arabia is one of many Middle Eastern countries to have been brushed by colonial rule; indeed, the influence of Britain on the emergence of a unified state is one important factor in the development of the Saudi Arabian state. Post World War One, with the demise of the Ottoman Empire, two strong rulers emerged in the land of Arabia: Abdul Aziz ibn Abdul Rahman Al Saud – commonly known as Ibn Saud – and Sharif Husayn, in the regions of Najd and Hijaz, respectively. With British support, through the provision of weapons and subsidies, Ibn Saud was able to unite the four regions of Saudi Arabia.[11] Essential to the process of state formation was the *ikhwan*, a standing army comprised of tribesmen who converted to Wahhabism. The *ikhwan* helped facilitate the creation of the Saudi state, acting as a standing army for Ibn Saud.[12]

The creation of a Saudi Arabian state differs from the establishment of other states in the twentieth century that built upon popular nationalist movements. Thus, Ibn Saud faced serious problems, given that prior to the creation of the state the Arabian Peninsula was divided by strong regional and tribal differences that seemed to be polemic to ideas of national unity.[13] Ibn Saud's state was established through the use of force, which was perhaps necessary to achieve the desired goal of unification. Thus, as Madawi Al-Rasheed argues, "The twentieth century witnessed the emergence of a state imposed on people without a historical memory of unity or national heritage which would justify their inclusion in a single entity".[14]

However, perhaps criticism of the use of force as a tool to facilitate the unification of Saudi Arabia is an attempt to project Western norms upon the process of state formation in the early twentieth century and as such should be carefully considered. One way in which Ibn Saud sought to remove tribal differences was through a process of inter-tribal marriage; it is alleged that Ibn Saud married into 30 tribal families.[15] Accordingly, the emergence of the state of Saudi Arabia in

1932 is spoken of in terms of unification rather than of conquest, a distinction that is carefully made during the education process; indeed, narratives are essential for the state-building process within Saudi Arabia. Madawi Al-Rasheed highlights how pupils are denied knowledge "in pursuit of a grand narrative that celebrates 'stability' and 'modernisation' ",[16] demonstrating the extent of tensions within Saudi Arabia, particularly of legitimacy and of tensions between Wahhabism and the process of modernisation.

Political Structure

The Kingdom of Saudi Arabia is ruled by an absolute monarchy, alongside "a political system rooted in Islam's cherished traditions and rich culture"[17] and a legal system stemming from *Sharia* law. The second in line to the throne is given the office of Crown Prince, although problems regarding the issue of succession have been rife. According to Article 5 of the Basic Law of 1992,[18] rule passes to the sons of the founding King, Abd al-Aziz Bin Abd al-Rahman al-Faysal Al Saud, and to his son's sons, and so forth. However, given the large number of Ibn Saud's sons, there remain problems with succession within Saudi Arabia, so much so that King Abdullah created the Allegiance Council, which gives senior princes the capacity to choose future crown princes.[19] A further concern emanates from what has been termed the "Sudari Seven", or the seven sons of Ibn Saud from his marriage to Hassa bint Ahmed of the Sudari tribe. Within the number of Ibn Saud's sons, the Sudari Seven is the largest number of full brothers from the same mother. A concern within the upper echelons of the Al Saud is that these seven sons would act as a coherent unit, retaining power within their number.[20]

Government within Saudi Arabia is unicameral; the king receives support from a Council of Ministers, or Cabinet, appointed by and responsible to him. This Council of Ministers includes a prime minister (the king), deputy prime minister (the Crown Prince), 21 ministers with portfolio, seven ministers of state and various advisors.[21] The responsibility of the council includes "drafting and overseeing implementation of the internal, external, financial, economic, education and defense [sic.] policies as well as the general affairs of the State".[22]

Offering support to the Council of Ministers is the *Majlis as-Shura*, or consultative assembly: a body of (currently) 150 advisors.[23] These advisors are appointed by the king and serve a four-year term. The members of the *Majlis* occupy 12 committees that advise on all facets of Saudi life. Candidates for the *Majlis* must be Saudi nationals, over 30, and competent persons of recognized good character.[24] Political parties are non-existent in Saudi Arabia, with any organisations offering a political agenda declared illegal.

In an effort to promote reform, municipal elections were held in 2005, with males over 21 voting within 178 municipalities. However, these elections were non-partisan and only accounted for half the appointments. Reports suggested that women would be able to vote in the 2009 elections; however, these elections did not occur, although King Abdullah has stated that women will be able to vote in 2015.[25] The notion of political reform within the Kingdom is something of a taboo subject, unless broached by the regime itself. In 2005, three academics who petitioned the royal family to adhere to their promises on political reform were arrested.[26]

The Rentier State

Saudi Arabia is a prime example of a Rentier state, understood as a state that derives a large percentage of their GDP from the sale of indigenous natural resources. Rentier states receive income from external sources and, as a consequence, do not require taxation of their citizens. As Gregory Gause articulates, the "dominant interpretation is that the increased wealth of the general population, combined with the increased power of the state to bestow or withhold that wealth, has reduced demands for political representation and participation".[27] In short, citizens of Saudi Arabia pay no taxes but have no political representation.

The history of Saudi Arabia demonstrates how the Kingdom "is founded upon a patriarchal conception of the role of the ruler and the ruled: the regime is the source of prosperity and social welfare, in return for which the people implicitly leave the government to decide and carry out policies without consultation".[28]

Saudi Arabia is the largest producer of oil in the world, with petroleum exports valued at $283.21 billion;[29] however, with fears regarding the finite supply of oil and natural gas, concerns arises that "the role of the state as a universal provider of goods and services may have to be reduced".[30] This move could have severe repercussions for the internal security of the state, especially when coupled with the wealth of the ruling family and the transparent profligacy of hundreds of its members. Indeed, these concerns are especially acute, given the spate of protests across the Arab world in 2011 and the Al Saud's attempts to placate protesters by offering a package of welfare benefits totalling $36 billion,[31] with a further $94 billion to follow in the coming years.[32] Given Saudi oil reserves, the Kingdom plays an integral role within OPEC. To satisfy economic needs, Saudi Arabia requires oil prices to remain around $51 per barrel.[33] Vast oil reserves allow Riyadh to manage oil prices, in conjunction with OPEC, according to laws of demand and supply.

With the influx of oil money, the nature of Saudi Arabian civil society has changed, in particular through shifts in social relationships and demographics.[34] Given the increases in health services and the standard of living, there has been a corresponding increase in the size of the population. In addition, the number of students enrolled in education has increased tenfold over a 30-year period, from 547,000 to 5 million.[35] The educational issue is of interest when considering that the number of students studying at universities in the United States throughout the 1970s and 1980s was around 30,000, compared to around 6000 in the early twenty-first century.[36] These students are now studying at indigenous universities, both secular and Islamic, although the standard of teaching at the Islamic universities is of concern, especially so given the influence of "radical elements" present at certain institutions.[37] This combined increase in population and education, coupled with a large expatriate workforce, has caused problems of unemployment, with jobs for only one in three Saudi national high school graduates.[38] Indeed, it is estimated that 40 per cent of the Saudi youth population are currently unemployed.[39]

The extent of change fostered by the discovery of oil can be demonstrated by examining the huge range in revenue gained from the sale of oil. Between 1959 and 1970, revenues grew from $655 million to $1.2 billion. In 1973, this total stood at $4.34 billion, while one year later, total revenue was $22.5 billion. This figure peaked in 1981, at $108 billion, yet, in the ensuing six years, revenues dropped to between $16 billion and $18 billion.[40] The vast amount of money brought in through the sale of oil would dramatically impact upon Saudi Arabian society, as articulated by David Commins:

> The influx of oil wealth transformed the social landscape [...] Unskilled Saudis refused jobs that paid low wages for exhausting work. Few Saudis possessed the technical expertise to supervise and manage construction costs. Consequently foreigners flocked to the Kingdom to build roads, expand ports, erect buildings and staff the growing network of schools, clinics and hospitals.[41]

The pressure of absorbing this massive influx of money and a foreign workforce put undeniable strains upon both rulers and ruled, which can be seen initially within the employment sector; however, the changing demographic workforce also has obvious cultural ramifications within the Kingdom. Indeed, the influx of oil money has altered the narrative used in the state-building process, to some degree moving away from spreading the Islamic message, consequently creating tensions between the Al Saud and prominent Wahhabis.

The Islamic Narrative

Religion is at the heart of life in Saudi Arabia: "the Saudi constitution is the Qur'an, and the *Sharia* is the source of its laws".[42] Muslims located within Saudi Arabia predominantly subscribe to the (broad) Sunni branch of Islam, with a large majority adhering to Wahhabist values, although there are Shi'i Muslims located in the oil-rich Eastern Province of the country.

The architect of Wahhabism, Muhammad b. 'Abd al-Wahhab, was born in 1703, in a small Najd town of al-'Uyayna. Al-Wahhab spent a considerable amount of time in Medina, where he studied the work of Ibn Taymiyya,[43] who undeniably influenced al-Wahhab's work.

Both Taymiyya and al-Wahhab shared "a delight in polemics: [Taymiyya's] targets included Christianity; Shi'ism; {and} many practices and doctrines of the Sufis".[44] al-Wahhab proved to be a controversial figure, causing him to be driven out of several townships. Upon leaving al-Uyayna, al-Wahhab received an invitation to al-Dir'iyya, an oasis settlement, where he met Muhammad Ibn Saud. During the time al-Wahhab spent at al-Dir'iyya, the alliance between Wahhabism and Al Saud was formed, with Muhammad Ibn Saud agreeing to support al-Wahhab "against unbelief and idolatry",[45] on two conditions:

> First that he pledge to continue supporting Ibn Saud if their campaign to establish God's unity triumphed. Second, that Sheikh Muhammad approve of Ibn Saud's taxation of al-Dir'iyya's harvests. The reformer agreed to the first condition, but as for the second he replied that God might compensate the amir with booty and legitimate taxes greater than the taxes on the harvests.[46]

The alliance formed between al-Wahhab and Muhammad Ibn Saud remains intact today and was instrumental in aiding the process of state formation in the twentieth century. This alliance between religious zealot and political power endures to the present day; however, the journey to a unified Arabia was not without incident. During the formative years of the Saudi Arabian state, Wahhabis foresaw their doctrine playing an integral role. However, their aspirations for involvement within the fabric of the state were tempered by political considerations, which dictated the speed and entrenchment of Wahhabi norms within the Kingdom's structure.[47]

The success of the Wahhab-Saud alliance in uniting vast areas of Arabia was not to go unnoticed for long: the Ottoman Empire, sensing the emergence of a regional and ideological rival, set out to discredit the alliance, eventually resorting to military force. The nineteenth century proved to be one of turmoil, which spilled over into the unification process of the twentieth century. During the early years of the twentieth century, Ibn Saud faced a dilemma: "to absorb the Holy Cities in a way that reassured the Muslim world that a new Wahhabi regime would not disrupt the pilgrimage or disturb the large number of foreign Muslim residents. At the same time, he had to satisfy his Wahhabi constituency that idolatry would be stamped out".[48]

To this day, there exist tensions between the Al Saud dynasty and Wahhabism, along with tensions within Wahhabism, stemming from "dual characteristics of Wahhabism as a militant reform movement and as a state religion suggest an inherent contradiction".[49] This contradiction is furthered when considering the process of modernization occurring within the Kingdom. The emergence of "Western" lifestyles provoked a surge of opposition groups of a fundamentalist nature; as Joseph Kostiner notes, "the product of an affluent era".[50] These tensions are discussed in greater detail in chapter four.

Tensions within the Kingdom

Saudi Arabia is a land of contradiction, with strong tensions between Islamic authority and the transformations brought about by oil wealth. The Al Saud dynasty is decidedly concerned with ideological and military vulnerability and utilises Islam as a tool to secure its legitimacy. This is seen through the title of the monarch: "King (whoever), Protector of the Two Holy Places. The Custodian of the Two Holy Mosques". However, the use of such Islamic rhetoric is a double-edged sword, as stressed by Joseph Nevo and Madawi Al-Rasheed. The use of Islamic rhetoric seeks to enhance the Al Saud's (and Saudi Arabia's) position both domestically and internationally, but in referring to Islamic norms and ideals, leaves the regime open to criticism whenever this norm was violated.[51]

The profligacy of certain members of the Al Saud regime discredits attempts to portray the Kingdom as an Islamic state, leading to opponents suggesting that the Al Saud family is attempting to "establish a *Mulk*, a secular, ruler's estate, rather than an Islamic community [. . .] an antithesis to Islam, and their control of the holy places an unlawful practice (*bid'a*)".[52] Further undermining the legitimacy of the ruling family is the number of princes, which some estimates put as high as 10,000.[53] Indeed, this poses a further problem, namely of succession once the sons of Ibn Saud have died, with 80 princes having a claim to the throne;[54] the number of Saudi princes is said to double every 22 to 26 years.[55] Moreover, the "royal political and economic power has caused a substantial amount of jealousy and political friction within Saudi society".[56]

Through the alliance with the Wahhabi movement, the ruling family derives Islamic credibility, essential when considering the elusive nature of nationalist sentiment within Saudi Arabia. Within the Kingdom, tribal loyalty is important, with many possessing greater loyalty to the tribe than to the state. As such, official accounts of the development of Saudi Arabia stress the importance of loyalty to faith as opposed to tribal solidarity.

Demographically, the Kingdom is fractious, with younger generations of Saudis, lacking patriarchal leadership and any kind of youth culture, increasingly seduced by the trappings of the West. Technological developments such as the Internet, coupled with cultural phenomena ranging from fast food to pornography,[57] are leading to an internal dichotomy: the developments of the West against the fundamental teachings of Wahhabism. Indeed, "old bases of the Saudi regime's legitimacy have been eroded due to factors such as the elaboration and complication of society, the increasing infiltration of external ideas, the growing sophistication of the population, and burgeoning intelligentsia".[58] Thus, demographic changes coupled with an increasingly educated population result in the emergence of serious tensions within the kingdom.

The state has sought to eradicate these tensions, initially through the use of narratives, but also through seeking to stress the legitimacy of the regime. As such, the role of tribalism as a legitimising tool for the Al Saud is imperative within the Kingdom. One way that tribalism is used as a legitimising tool is through the institutionalisation of tribal values within the infrastructure of Saudi society. Another such use of tribalism in legitimising the Al Saud regime is tribal dress, which is often used in public appearances. Yet, given that tribes have the potential to pose threats to the security of the regime, detribalisation policies have also been perused. This apparent contradiction will be discussed at length within chapter five.

Additional sources of tension stem from the Kingdom's relationship with the United States, from whom it seeks to guarantee its security, despite an anti-Western attitude within the general population. In addition to the dichotomy within the Saudi population, the Al Saud finds itself torn between appeasing both internal actors, namely the Wahhabi *ulama* (legal scholars) and the United States. Further complicating matters is the ideological enmity inherent within both parties towards the other.[59]

The influx of oil money and ensuing process of modernisation clashed with the principles of Wahhabism. Thus, oil money, combined with the profligacy of the royal family, increased tensions inherent within the Kingdom, which violently manifested themselves in 1979. The siege of the Grand Mosque in Mecca in 1979 highlights the extent of tensions within Saudi Arabia, brought about by the clash between modernisation, oil money and Islam. The event demonstrated the atmosphere within Saudi Arabia during the 1970s: "The mosque siege was part and parcel of the material modernisation of the 1970s. It was a political awakening drawing on religious rhetoric that became more articulate under the sponsorship of religious centres of learning, education and literacy".[60]

In addition to tensions proliferating throughout the Kingdom, the Shi'i population, mainly located within the Eastern Province, became increasingly ostracised. Wahhabi doctrine brands Shi'i Muslims as heretics and, combined with the occupation of many Shi'a (a large percentage of whom worked menial jobs), this community was held in low regard. However, the revolution in Iran was to inject life into the Shi'i population of Saudi Arabia. As Fouad Ibrahim notes, the revolution of 1979 "invigorated the shattered spirit of the Shi'is in Saudi Arabia as well as the Shi'is elsewhere in the Muslim world [...providing] them with a sense of power and self-confidence".[61] However, it is important to note that the increasing politicisation of the Shi'a was not purely a consequence of the revolution in Iran, rather, one must also take into account the role played by modernisation and the increasing role of Wahhabi ideology within the state.[62]

Saudi Arabia and Regional Security

Saudi Arabian perceptions of regional security across the Gulf region and wider Middle East have initially been concerned with ensuring regime security. This is reflected in the main foreign policy goals of the regime, notably "to protect the country from foreign domination and/or invasion and to safeguard the domestic stability of the Al Saud regime".[63] Post 2003, it is perceived that the biggest state threat to regime security is resulting from burgeoning Iranian power, in particular the rise of the "Shi'i Crescent", which has resulted in a shift in power across the Middle East region. This, in turn, poses problems for the internal stability of the kingdom and the rule of the Al Saud, given the importance of Islam as a legitimising tool. Furthermore, as previously discussed, Iranian calculations within the "Arab Street" appear to be challenging Saudi Arabia's position across the Arab world, leaving the Al Saud with a dilemma over their response.

This fear as to increasing Iranian power can be seen within several states, notably Iraq, Bahrain and Syria. Riyadh is concerned at the burgeoning Iranian influence within Iraq. However, Saudi involvement in Iraq has only recently moved from mere concern towards a more proactive engagement,[64] which reflects concerns about Iranian gains in light of a US withdrawal. Fear about Iranian gains, and the potential for future gains, leads to a belief in Saudi Arabia that Iraq is a zero-sum game, and, as such, any Iranian gains must be limited. Furthermore, unlike Iran, Saudi Arabia has worked alongside the United States in Iraq, which again demonstrates the diametrically opposed views of Riyadh and Tehran as to the role of the United States in the region.

The perception of increasing Shi'i influence within Bahrain is seen by Riyadh as a sign of increasing Iranian influence, as articulated by the International Crisis Group: "Saudi Arabia purportedly is responding to dual fears: that the popular uprising could lead to a Shiite takeover, and a Shiite takeover would be tantamount to an Iranian one".[65] Indeed, these concerns are echoed across the GCC states, with numerous foreign ministers "deeply worried about continuing Iranian meddling".[66] However, while it is difficult to ascertain the extent of Iranian influence and, thus, the veracity of this perception is contested, the mere existence of this perception means that Saudi Arabia must behave as if this is the case. As such, Riyadh's actions within Bahrain have been based on the assumption that Tehran has provided support (in whatever guise) to the Shi'a of Bahrain, thus calculating that Saudi Arabian support is needed to secure the rule of the Al Khalifa. In contrast, the Syrian crisis has presented Saudi Arabia with an opportunity to reduce Iranian power within the Levant and, thus, further isolate Iran.

Iran's Ethnic Tinderbox

The Islamic Republic of Iran is located on the eastern flank of the Middle East, sharing borders with seven countries: Turkmenistan, Afghanistan and Pakistan to the east; and Azerbaijan, Armenia, Turkey and Iraq to the west; its borders also overlook the Persian Gulf, Gulf of Oman and Caspian Sea. Iranians claim these borders evolved naturally, rather than being imposed at the whim of colonial powers. Iran has an area of 1.648 million square kilometres,[67] consisting of 30 provinces, with each province governed locally; these provinces are further reduced to counties. The total population of Iran is 66,429,284 (a July 2009 estimate),[68] with 94.6 per cent of the population under the age of 65. This statistic is partially derived from the catastrophic events of the Iran–Iraq War, in which a generation of Iranians was killed. The population of Iran is heavily urbanised, with a dramatic increase in the number of people living in cities, from 27 per cent in 1950 to around 67 per cent in 2005.[69]

Iran is an ethnically diverse country; approximately half of its citizens are Persian and, given the existence of a plethora of other ethnicities, John Bradley has referred to Iranian society as an "ethnic tinderbox".[70] Indeed, Iran's ethnic jigsaw also contains Azeris, Kurds, Arabs, Turkmen, Baluchis and Lors. This collection of ethnic groupings has led some to suggest that labelling Iran as a "nation-state" is inappropriate[71] and that such a diverse mix of ethnicities is hazardous for the regime in Tehran, causing problems for internal stability.[72] Allegations of discrimination against minorities are rife. With the increasing importance of ethnic minorities in neighbouring countries, especially the involvement of Kurds and Turkmen in the Iraqi government, Iranian minorities feel they are deserving of improved living conditions and rights.[73] In addition to Iran's ethnic mosaic, there is also a degree of religious proliferation: Islam is the state religion, with 98 per cent of Iranians Muslim and 90 per cent adhering to Shi'i Islam.[74] Yet, in addition to these Muslims, there are also Zoroastrian, Jewish, Christian and Baha'i communities.[75] The impact of these ethnic and religious identities upon Iranian internal security is discussed in chapters 4 and 5.

Narratives and State-Building

The nature of Iranian identity is steeped in history; however, given the tempestuous nature of the twentieth century, stories and narratives are often referred to in order to derive a form of popular legitimacy. Farideh Farhi suggests that Iranian identity is "Janus-faced", building upon the idea of being the children of both Cyrus the Great and Mohammed.[76] As such, it is necessary to unpack Iranian history to discover the roots of this identity.

Persian history is comprised of various dynasties, the legacy of which shapes Iran today. Iranians perceive their state to be of a "natural disposition", that is, a state free from the whim of colonial powers. The history of the state dates back to approximately 700 BC, when the first Iranian state was established by the Mede tribe.[77] Paradox and contradiction are rife in Iran; as Michael Axworthy articulates, one of the most prominent paradoxes is that of image. The paradox of image is primarily located within semantics, stemming from history: Iran, in name alone, came into existence in 1935, replacing Persia as the name of the state used in official documents. The move from Persia to Iran has encouraged contradictory images, with Persia encouraging images of:

> myster[y], flirtatious women, sharp sabres, carpets with colours glowing like jewels, poetry and melodious music [...] Iran has a rather different image: frowning mullahs, black oil, women's blanched faces peering, not to their best advantage, from under black chadors; grim crowds burning flags, chanting "death to..."[78]

The idea of image is important within Iranian identity, given such polemic interpretations of Iran, Iranian perceptions of itself, and its role within the region.

Within Iranian history one of the more important figures is Cyrus the Great, a Persian prince claiming to be descended from the royal house of Persia. Cyrus established the Achaemenid dynasty in 549 and ruled an "empire that stretched from the Greek cities on the eastern coast of the Aegean to the banks of the river Indus – in extent perhaps the greatest empire the world had seen up to that time".[79] The reign of Cyrus is, to this day, held in high regard and referred to in order to foster a sense of national pride. This is firstly due to the level of glory brought upon Persia through Cyrus's military conquests and, secondly, for the level of toleration during Cyrus's rule, which included freedom of worship and the return of holy images of the gods to their rightful homes in various temples across Mesopotamia and Western Iran. The importance of Cyrus's rule can still be seen today, with Farideh Farhi speaking of a modern Iranian society, seeking its own identity through drawing from both Cyrus and Muhammad.[80]

Throughout the formative years of Persian life, the Sunni branch of Islam was the state religion. In 1501, the 14-year-old Safavid leader Esma'il, on the back of a military victory, proclaimed "Shi'ism as the new religion of his territories".[81] Although prior to 1501 there had been strong Shi'i elements, the epicentre of Shi'ism was southern Iraq. The move from a Sunni state to a Shi'i state would prove to have severe repercussions for both regional and internal stability over the coming centuries. An additional aspect of the Safavid dynasty concerns what Homa Omid terms the "westoxification of Shi'ism", which "turned red Shi'ism a revolutionary colour bestowed by the martyrs of the movement, to that of black Shi'ism of tears and sorrows".[82]

Competing Narratives: The Rise of Nationalism

With the demise of the Safavid dynasty, Persian notions of independence were challeneged by external actors: initially by the Ottoman Turks, followed, from the 1800s onwards, by British and Russian involvement in domestic politics. The role of Britain and Russia within Iran is reflected by Iranian references to their "northern" and "southern" neighbours,[83] and also demonstrated by the Anglo-Russian treaty of 1907, which divided up Iran into British and Russian spheres of economic and political influence. The role played by external actors in guiding the behaviour of Persia can be seen during World War One, in which Persia claimed neutrality; however, given the presence of large numbers of British and Russian troops within Persia,[84] these claims were somewhat vacuous.[85]

As Homa Katouzian articulates, Persia at this time featured "national disunity, political conflict, economic disruption and poverty, social insecurity, and administrative corruption and incompetence".[86] In 1921, Iran underwent a *coup d'état*, reflecting the dissatisfaction pervading the political environment, notably in the wake of "famine, foreign occupation, and the chaos of World War I".[87] Indeed, some estimates suggest that 25 per cent of the population had died since 1912 as a consequence of economic problems and famine.[88] The *coup* was undertaken by Reza Khan, a commander of the Cossack brigade, and the journalist Seyyid Zia Tabatabai, who operated with both the consent of British General Ironside[89] and the Shah of the time, Ahmad Shah. Ahmad Shah's support for Reza Khan's coup was reflected in orders for garrisons in Tehran not to offer resistance against the intruders,[90] which demonstrated both the weakness of the Qajar dynasty and a misguided belief that Khan would ensure the stability of his regime. The role of Britain within the *coup d'état* is uncertain, although suspicion can be traced back to the failure of the Anglo-Persian Agreement.[91]

Despite this suspicion of British involvement, both Reza Khan and his supporters sought to diminish the role of Britain and argued that the *coup d'état* was against London's interests.[92] Ali Ansari suggests that given British interests within the state post World War One, British involvement appears likely; however, it is uncertain as to whether this involvement came from Whitehall or "the energetic responses of local British military and diplomatic officials".[93] Ansari suggests that the role played by the British was in both offering logistical support and discouraging doubts in Whitehall about the *coup*.[94]

Reza Khan would play a key role within Persian politics during this period, as both Prime Minister and chief of the army. Khan was an ambitious man, demonstrated by renaming himself Reza Pahlavi in an attempt to foster increased nationalist support. Reza Pahlavi was crowned Shah of Iran in 1926 after the *Majlis* deposed Ahmad Shah while he was on holiday in Europe.[95] One of the most important aspects of Reza Pahlavi's reign occurred in 1935 and remains in place today: the order for foreign governments to change the name of Persia in official correspondence, to Iran, "the ancient name that had always been used by Iranians themselves".[96]

Succeeding Reza Shah was his son, Mohammed Reza Phalavi, who ruled from September 1941 to February 1979. The reign of Mohammed Reza Phalavi was tempestuous, marked by two abdications: the first in 1953, and the second in 1979. The 1953 abdication stemmed from increasing nationalist and anti-monarchical sentiment, along with the growing popularity of Dr. Mohammed Mossadeq.[97] Mossadeq's popularity grew through the process of nationalisation, in particular of the Anglo-Iranian Oil Company (AIOC).

The AIOC played a prominent role within Iran during this time, along with the British Imperial Bank of Persia, comprising what Ansari refers to as "the twin pillars on which British influence in Iran had been constructed in the twentieth century".[98] Perceptions of the AIOC were less than favourable within Iran, especially as it was common knowledge that the AIOC paid a greater amount of tax to the British Exchequer than they paid in royalties to the Iranian government.[99] Indeed, Iran initially only received 20 per cent of net profit,[100] although this marginally improved over time. This demonstrates the power of both Britain and the AIOC within Iran at the time. The dispute between Britain and Iran occurred over claims of ownership of the oil, with the British believing that ownership of the oil was theirs, as they had "discovered, exploited, refined, transported and marketed it",[101] regardless of its territorial location. In addition, anti-British sentiment increased through poor working conditions for Iranian workers at the AIOC.

The nationalisation of AIOC was not a smooth process; indeed, this accounted for the life of one prime minister, and the resignation of another.[102] Following from Hossein Ala, Mossadeq was nominated as Prime Minister. Mossadeq was a hugely popular politician within Iran, and his life had been dedicated to the cause of Iranian nationalism.[103] However, external perceptions of Mossadeq were less than favourable.

As Geoffrey Jones notes, the British Ambassador to Iran, Sir Francis Shepherd, spoke of Mossadeq in dispatches "as a 'lunatic' and characterised as being 'cunning and slippery,' with 'short and bandy legs' and 'a slight reek of opium'".[104]

On 15 May 1951, the AOIC was declared closed, with Mossadeq assuming control over the oil industry on behalf of the Iranian state.[105] The nationalisation process proved antagonistic to Britain, whose economy benefitted greatly from the favourable rates "negotiated" with Iran. Given the anti-British sentiment and poor working conditions, public sentiment was firmly behind the *Majlis* and Mossadeq in the nationalisation of the AIOC. Despite popular support within Iran over the nationalisation of the AIOC, externally the actions of Mossadeq proved cause for concern. In an effort to restore stability, the American Central Intelligence Agency (CIA), with support from the British Secret Intelligence Service (SIS), organised the removal of Mossadeq, providing an opportunity for the Shah to return to Tehran.[106] Yet, as Stephen Kinzer documents, the *coup d'état* was a far from smooth operation. However, the audacity and perseverance of the plotters should be noted, as demonstrated by the idea that "American had organized the upheaval in Iran, but Henderson [the US ambassador to Iran] was portraying them as its victims".[107] Mossadeq's guilt at the treatment of "guests" in Iran resulted in him immediately banning protests and ordering the police to end trouble in the streets; as Kinzer suggests, Mossadeq essentially disarmed himself.[108]

The involvement of the CIA and SIS solidified the notion that "everything that happened in Iranian politics was manipulated by a hidden foreign hand".[109] With the return of the Shah, Iranian society became corrupted by "power and fear",[110] coupled with an increase in vocal opposition to the Shah. Opposition to the Shah's rule was led by a *seyyed* (descendent of the Prophet), Ayatollah Rouhallah Khomeini. Khomeini began to speak out against the Shah's regime in the early 1960s, at which time he was banished, via Baghdad to Paris.

The Rise of Islam

Much has been written of the events leading to the revolution of 1979, yet two issues are worth reinforcing here: the heavy handedness of the Shah's military in crushing opposition forces, and the capacity to draw parallels with Hosein, Ali, and the martyrs of Shi'ism,[111] which provided additional ammunition for the Islamic opposition. The year prior to revolution began with governmental attempts to discredit Khomeini, which resulted in protests in Iran. These protests provoked severe responses from government forces, leading to several deaths, sparking a spiral of protests and additional deaths, and culminating in two atrocities. On 8 September, known as Black Friday, a crowd in Jaleh Square, Tehran, was gunned down after refusing to disperse from a protest. The tragedy of Black Friday was to occur again at the beginning of Moharram (the first month of the Islamic calendar), with 135 deaths in Qazuim, when tanks drove over protesters.[112]

The myriad deaths and protests culminated in a crowd of more than 1 million people turning out for Ashura celebrations.[113] Shortly after, on 16 January 1979, the Shah abdicated, this time not to be reinstated. On 1 February 1979, 3 million people welcomed Khomeini back to Tehran. The demise of the Pahlavi dynasty brought hope to those ostracised under the Shah of a reformation of social order, providing hope for political space.[114] Yet, despite the revolution drawing upon various facets of Iranian political and intellectual life, ranging from nationalism to Marxism, Khomeini was able to manipulate events to remove opposition to his ideal form of government, *velayat-e faqih*, in which "day-to-day government should be secular, but with ultimate power in the hands of a leader committed to Islamic government".[115] The revolution would have a dramatic impact upon regional relations. Indeed, a year after the revolution, Iran was at war with Iraq, partially as a consequence of Iraqi attempts to quash the revolution.

Rouhollah Khomeini died on 3 June 1989 and, although Iran lacked an obvious successor, Ayatollah Ali Khamenei was elevated to the position of Supreme Leader, despite not being a *marja' al-taqlid*, a high-ranking cleric who was a source of emulation.[116] The period from 1989 to the present day has seen Iran oscillating between aspirations for reform, particularly under the presidency of Mohammad Khatami, and an ardent desire to return to the Islamic ideals of 1979, especially under the presidency of Mahmoud Ahmadinejad. The elections of 2009 and the ensuing growth of protest movements highlight this tension between desires for reform and a return to Islamic principles.

Islamic Narratives and Political Structure

The Islamic Republic of Iran has become the most influential and vocal Shi'i state in the world,[117] despite many key sites for Shi'ism being located within Iraq. Elements of Shi'i thought are enshrined within the fabric of the Iranian state through the system of government. The political structure of the Islamic Republic is based upon the notion of *velayat-e faqih,* which enshrines and protects the political legitimacy of Khomeini's ideas. The principles of *velayat-e faqih* are expanded upon in Ayotollah Khomeini's work *Islamic Government: Regency of the Jurist.* Khomeini's work builds upon the premise that the Shari'a is the word of God and, thus, should regulate human conduct; as such, this is the only legitimate form of law. Given the primacy of theological thought, only *mojtaheds* (high ranking clerics) are able to rightly interpret and apply the Shari'a and, thus, rule, because of their training in Islamic theology and jurisprudence.

Power structures within Iran are comprised of formal and non-formal structures.[118] The formal power structures of the Iranian system of government initially appear incredibly complex, with nine different bodies, directly responsible to and for each other.

The Political Structure of Iran[119]

This system is split into two sections comprised of three directly elected bodies and six unelected bodies, with power currently built around the pillars of the Supreme Leader and president.[120] The most powerful office in Iran is that of the *Faqih*, or Supreme/Spiritual Leader: "constitutionally and practically the Leader's position remains the locus

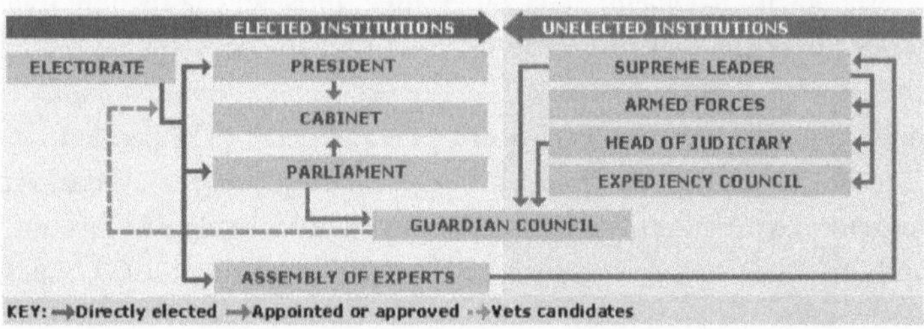

Source: 'How Iran is Ruled', BBC. Available from: http://news.bbc.co.uk/1/hi/world/middle_east/8051750.stm [Accessed 9 June 2009].

of power in the republic, around which are spun the other offices of the state".[121] The Supreme Leader is responsible for the appointment of several offices of state: the head of the judiciary, six members of the Guardian Council, commanders of the armed forces, Friday prayer leaders, and the heads of TV and radio.

The armed forces are comprised of the IRGC and regular forces; the IRGC is "the popular organ which has emerged from the core of the revolution, to protect it and its ideological purity and to act as the powerful arm of the Islamic revolution and protector of the oppressed the world over".[122] The commanders of both IRGC and regular forces are appointed by and answerable solely to the Supreme Leader. The Head of the Judiciary is responsible for maintenance of the Shari'a and is appointed by the Supreme Leader. It is pertinent to note the role played by the IRGC in securing the ideological security of the Islamic Republic. Initially created by Ayatollah Khomeini as an ideological guard for the newly created regime,[123] today the IRGC has "articulated a populist, authoritarian, and assertive vision for the Islamic Republic of Iran that they maintain is a more faithful reflection of the revolution's early ideals".[124] The importance of the IRGC within the Islamic Republic can be illustrated by the fact that many in the upper echelons of power in Iran have served within its ranks. Furthermore, under the presidency of Mahmoud Ahmadinejad, a veteran of the IRGC, fellow veterans have begun to play key roles within government and intelligence posts.[125] The prominent role played by the IRGC also results in a greater predilection with security and tougher stances on negotiation, both within the system and with external powers.[126] It is also important to note that falling under the control of the IRGC is a paramilitary organisation known as the *Basij*, a youthful force, emanating from rural regions and poorer areas of cities. In 1979, Khomeini called for the establishment of "an army of twenty million" to protect the newly formed Islamic Republic, which led to the creation of the *Basij*. The mission statement of the *Basij* is to "create the necessary capabilities in all individuals believing in the Constitution and the goals of the Islamic Republic to defend the country, the regime of the Islamic Republic, and aid people in cases of disasters and unexpected events".[127]As such, *Basijis* tend to be "ideologically motivated and deeply religious".[128] It is suggested that the *Basij* are responsible for internal security within the Islamic Republic,[129] as seen in the aftermath of the 2009 elections.

The head of the judiciary is also responsible for appointing six jurists to the Guardian Council (approved by the *Majlis*). The remaining members of the most influential body in Iran are six theologians appointed by the Supreme Leader. The members of this body are elected for six years in a staggered system, with half the members changing every three years. The Guardian Council vets candidates hoping to stand for president and the *Majlis*; it also has power of veto if it deems a bill passed by the *Majlis* is un-Islamic or unconstitutional. The final body is the Expediency Council, an advisory body appointed by the Supreme Leader that has supervisory powers over all branches of government, with particular focus upon arbitrating between the *Majlis* and Council of Guardians.[130]

The electorate is responsible for the final three offices of state, voting for the president, *Majlis* and Assembly of Experts, with those over the age of 18 eligible to vote (prior to 2007 the voting age in national elections had been 15). The president is elected for a term lasting four years and can only serve two consecutive terms. The office of the president is the highest elected office in the country, but is the second most powerful office, after the Supreme Leader.[131] The influence of the president is predominantly within aspects of domestic sphere, such as social, cultural and economic policies.[132] One must be aware that Ahmadinejad is the first non-cleric to become president, which has angered fellow conservatives.[133]

The president chooses the cabinet, although this is approved by the *Majlis*. The *Majlis* is constituted of 290 members, each of whom is elected every four years. The *Majlis* is responsible for the introduction of laws, with the power to summon, and impeach cabinet ministers and the president. The final elected body is the Assembly of Experts, which is responsible for appointing the Supreme Leader. The Assembly of Experts is based in Qom and is constituted solely by clerics.

In contrast, informal power structures tend to revolve around spheres of influence such as religious-political associations of the leadership elite or around revolutionary groups and security forces. As

Wilfred Butcha notes, informal power structures are autonomous and, while possessing ties to the president, are not controlled by him.[134] The development of informal power structures suggests an attempt to secure the Islamic nature of the state.

Iran and Regional Security

Iranian relations across the Middle East have been the source of much debate in recent years. Indeed, this debate questions the nature of Iranian regional aspirations post 2003, involvement in Iraq, Tehran's support for Shi'i groups across the region, nuclear ambitions and rhetoric towards Israel.

With the US-led invasion of Iraq in 2003, the removal of Saddam Hussein left a power vacuum within the Gulf. Prior to this, Iraq had arguably been the dominant power within the Gulf region, demonstrated by a belligerent attitude towards regional neighbours and the international community. Sensing this emerging vacuum Iran sought to lay claim to such power, thus engaging in geopolitical competition with Saudi Arabia for control over the Gulf region. Coupled with concerns over Iranian Shi'i expansionist policies that increased with the election of conservative president Mahmoud Ahmadinejad in 2005 (building upon both Islamic and nationalist narratives), there exist fears as to the power of Iran over both Gulf and wider Middle East regions.

In addition to the "Arab Spring" within Bahrain, highlighting the sectarian cleavages within the kingdom that present Tehran with the opportunity for increased involvement across the archipelago, Iran has historically laid territorial claim to Bahrain. Yet within Tehran's strategic calculations, there exists confusion as to how to behave towards Bahrain. One line of argument suggests that Iran has sought to improve its relations with members of the GCC, as demonstrated by Ahmadinejad's presence at the GCC meeting in Doha in 2007. However, at the same time, numerous prominent figures within the Iranian regime have offered inflammatory remarks that appear to be in stark contrast to advancing relations with the GCC. Indeed, in 2007, *Kayhan*, an Iranian newspaper with strong ties to Khamenei, published an editorial stating that it had seen "undeniable documents" indicating that "Bahrain was a part of Iran's territory until forty years ago".[135] Furthermore, the editorial rejected the notion that Bahraini independence from Iran was achieved in a legitimate manner. A second example of these remarks came in 2009, when Ali Akbar Nateq Nuri, a former speaker of the *Majlis* and head of the accountability bureau in the Supreme Leader's office, claimed that Iran possessed sovereignty over Bahrain,[136] also declaring that Bahrain had been "the fourteenth province of Iran until 1970".[137] The proximity of these two sources to the Supreme Leader suggests that this use of rhetoric was undertaken with the knowledge of Khamenei.

Iranian ambitions of increasing regional power can also be seen when examining Iran's role within Iraq. With the removal of Saddam Hussein, Iranian influence within Iraq has increased, given shared religious bonds and reflecting both ideological and geopolitical ambitions. Around 60 per cent of the Iraqi population subscribe to Shi'i Islam, which Iran has sought to control through working with numerous Shi'i political parties and militias. Michael Eisenstadt, Michael Knights and Ahmed Ali suggest that in addition to projecting Iranian influence, Tehran has sought to reduce US power in Iraq,[138] thus increasing tensions with Saudi Arabia, who were concerned as to the stability of Iraq post withdrawal.

This desire to reduce American power in Iraq again reflects Iranian concerns about the position of external powers, namely the United States, within the region. To this end, Iran has both the ability and desire to provide support for armed militias within Iraq.[139] In contrast to this hard power support, one should not overlook the soft power ties existing between Iran and elements of the Shi'i population within Iraq, which are predominantly based on shared religious values,[140] although also contain economic aspects. It is this soft power aspect that Eisenstadt, Knights and Ali suggest poses the greatest threat to Iraqi sovereignty.[141] However, despite this involvement, one should not discount the importance of nationalist sentiment within Iraq, or ethnic differences, which may threaten Iranian aspirations.

Supplementing Iran's regional ambitions is a longstanding alliance with the Shi'i organisation Hizballah (Party of God) in Lebanon. Many perceive Hizballah to be an Iranian (and Syrian) proxy and while there are certainly ties between Hizballah and both Iran and Syria, the nature of these ties is to some extent ambiguous.[142] Nevertheless, if one considers Article 3.16 of the Iranian constitution, which provides foreign policy guidance, one can see a "fraternal commitment to all Muslims, and unsparing support to the *mustad'afiin* of the world".[143] This article suggests a necessity to provide support for those oppressed, particularly Shi'i Muslims.

Ties with Hizballah transcend financial support and are firmly rooted within the ideological, stemming back to the creation of Hizballah in 1982. The emergence of Hizballah followed a "time of great foment, enthusiasm, and transition among the Shi'a of Lebanon",[144] stemming from both a desire to emulate the Iranian Revolution and the continued Israeli presence within Lebanon.[145] The formation of Hizballah owes much to both Iran and Syria, through the provision of funds and arms, although for Iran "the creation of Hizballah was a realization of the revolutionary state's zealous campaign to spread the message of the self-styled 'Islamic revolution'".[146] In the formative years of Hizballah, Iran also provided 1,500 members of the IRGC to train Hizballah fighters in the Bekaa Valley.[147] Transcending this sectarian inspired violence, Hizballah maintains a political arm and won 58 seats in the Lebanese parliament in the June 2009 elections.[148]

As noted in chapter two, the actions of Hizballah during the summer of 2006 were greatly beneficial to Iran. Indeed, as outlined in a 2009 Rand report, Hizballah "effectively bested the vaunted Israeli Defence Force",[149] which served to engender further support for Iran's "Arab Street" policy, purely by proxy. It is uncertain as to whether Hizballah launched the operation to capture Israeli soldiers with Tehran's permission,[150] or at their bequest; there are certainly some who believe this to be the case.[151] As Magnus Norell notes, Tehran was informed of Hizballah's action on 12 July 2006, the day war broke out, in accordance with agreements between the two actors that Iran would be informed of any future Hizballah action.[152] However, some such as Amos Harel and Avi Issacharoff hold that for Iran:

> the war between Israel and Hezbollah could have been premature. It exposed the extent of Hezbollah's Iran-assisted military

> deployment in Lebanon, which Tehran would have preferred to have used against Israel only at such as time as it (Tehran) gave the order: in the event of an American or Israeli attack on Iran's nuclear installations.[153]

This supports an argument made by Rola El Husseini, who suggests that while there are clear ideological ties between Hizballah and Iran, operational ties between the two are harder to ascertain.[154] Furthermore, ties between the two were criticised by former Hizballah Secretary General Subhi al-Tufeili, who accused Hizballah of becoming a "tool of Iran, and even its security service".[155] Despite this criticism and the severity of the Israeli response, perceptions of the conflict of the conflict still commonly refer to Hizballah's success as a resistance organisation, fostering a huge level of symbolic capital, from which Iran also gains.[156]

Through the outcome of the 2006 War, Hizballah laid bare an inherent dichotomy within Arab foreign policy: to support those who oppose Israel or to oppose Shi'i groups within the region; again creating space for Iran to exploit. Building upon competition within both ideological and geopolitical spheres is the use of rhetoric against several neighbouring states. In particular, one should consider Mahmoud Ahmadinejad's rhetoric towards Israel, which has included Holocaust denials:

> They have fabricated a legend under the name Massacre of the Jews, and they hold it higher than God himself, religion itself and the prophets themselves [...] If somebody in their country questions God, nobody says anything, but if somebody denies the myth of the massacre of Jews, the Zionist loudspeakers and the governments in the pay of Zionism will start to scream.[157]

Such rhetoric undeniably impacted upon the international community, leading to widespread condemnation. In turn, this rhetoric incensed Israel, leading many, both within Israel and the international community, to believe that Iran posed such a serious threat to the state of Israel that pre-emptive strikes are necessary to thwart the Iranian threat.[158] Indeed, this led some to suggest that Iran posed a threat to regional security as a whole, especially when taken in conjunction with perceived support for belligerent organisations operating within neighbouring states.

When these factors are taken together, it is understandable that uncertainty exists as to Iran's geopolitical intentions. Geopolitical and ideological designs over the region, coupled with support for Shi'i groups and perceived nuclear aspirations, have fostered a sense of trepidation across the region, fuelled by the rhetoric employed by Ahmadinejad.

Conclusions

Taken together, the factors outlined above comprise both structural and normative conditions within both Saudi Arabia and Iran. It considered the emergence of the state, political structure and tensions within the two states. Understanding state-building processes and the narratives involved, coupled with an awareness of history, helps facilitate comprehension of the normative values guiding behaviour within both states. Indeed, these narratives play a prominent role in shaping the nature of the regional environment and also in resolving internal tensions.

While discussing Saudi Arabia, the discourse built upon state formation and political structure, while also articulating the existence of tensions within the Kingdom. These include tensions between religious groups within the state, the role of the United States in providing security to the Al Saud and problems emanating from the use of Islam as a legitimising tool. While discussing Iran, the argument focussed on the importance of history, both Persian and Islamic, and the relationship between the two. In addition, the chapter expanded upon *velayat-e faqih* and political structure within the Islamic Republic. It discussed the importance of history in shaping a strong, nationalistic Persian identity, which remains of contemporary importance. The argument also demonstrated the role of soft power, both for Iranian involvement within Iraq and for ties between Hizballah and Iran.

Examination of these structural conditions facilitates awareness of the restrictions on behaviour, while also demonstrating the entrenchment of actors within certain normative environments. This is especially seen when considering the importance of Islam for both states. Given the importance of Islam, particularly used as a legitimising tool for regimes to resolve internal security dilemmas and to demonstrate external legitimacy and vitality, it is easy to see how moves by either Riyadh or Tehran within an Islamic sphere have ramifications for the legitimacy and security of the other. This demonstrates the existence of a soft power security dilemma guiding the rivalry, which, although rooted in the ideological sphere, has ramifications within the geopolitical sphere.

4

RELIGIOUS INCONGRUENCE

Standard assumptions of sovereignty, based upon the Westphalian model of 1648, assume congruence between nation and state, and that shared identities fall within the territorial boundaries of sovereign rule. Yet this is not always the case, especially within the Middle East. The persistent nature of the state-building process across the region meant that "when a new wave of state-building came along the states' boundaries were often radically different",[1] resulting in a mosaic of identities across the region. Further, the imposition of the contemporary state system was "at the expense of a pre-existing cultural unity deriving from centuries of rule by existing empires ruling in the name of the Islamic *umma*".[2] The assumption of congruence between nation and state is fallacious on two levels: both irredentist movements and trans-state identities have the capacity to separate the nation from the state, thus undermining sovereignty. Moreover, the spread of identities across borders can foster interstate conflict, border disputes or interference in another's domestic affairs in support of irredentist agendas. Thus, as Hinnebusch articulates, "because boundaries lacked the impenetrability or sanctity of the Westphalian system, with ideological influences and trans-state movements readily crossing state lines, each state was highly sensitive to and vulnerable to the actions of others".[3]

It is remiss to avoid those authors who posit a counter-argument to that of Hinnebusch, in particular, Martin Kramer. Kramer articulates how Middle Eastern states resisted pressures emanating from societal groups, notably Islamic groups, and "emerged hardened and strengthened by the test of its mettle".[4] Kramer argues that identity groups have not affected dramatic change; rather, that the state remains the final arbiter of power within the region. However, while this argument is compelling, it is important to stress that while not necessarily setting the trailblazing agenda envisioned by many scholars of the Middle East in the 1970s, identity groups retain an influence on state behaviour.

Thus, given the assumption of congruence between nation and state, trans-state identities have the capacity to undermine internal stability, which leaves regime security open to the whims of others, as demonstrated by the popularity of Pan-Arab and Pan-Islamist ideologies across the region. However, trans-state identities can also be used as legitimising tools, for both the internal and external identity groups. This is achieved through the processes of strategic framing and symbolic exchanges.

As such, the mosaic of identities across the Gulf region presents a unique challenge to ruling elites, providing tests of both an internal and external nature. The location of the threat determines the response, with threats at one level often requiring accessing resources at another.[5] Primarily, ruling elites are concerned with retaining domestic stability, as such, managing identity groups, particularly those with irredentist or trans-state agendas is imperative. Yet the retention of domestic stability has scope to impact upon relations with neighbouring states. Thus, identity groups play a key role in determining both domestic and foreign policy. Furthermore, the challenges posed by the various identity groups demonstrate how states are susceptible to the actions of others, in particular through the provision of support for groups operating within a state.

The Rise of Violence

Given an absence of political space and a perceived failure of legitimate action, identity groups may resort to illegitimate action, which can be understood as political violence. The resort to violence has been discussed by Ervin Staub and Daniel Bar-Tal, who suggest that structural conditions are important in attempting to explain the onset of violence between groups: "power arrangements and institutions, social conditions, cultural factors, and particularly psychological dynamics involving beliefs, values, feelings, and motivations shared by group members"[6] are inherent within the rise of tensions and the move to violence. It can thus be deduced that societies with limited political space and high levels of identity incongruence are more prone to violence.

It is held that conflicts between identities generally arise "over tangible matters involving territory, material resources, and access to opportunity, power and privilege";[7] however, in addition to these tangible factors, conflict may arise over "intangible issues or psychological forces such as values, ideals, identity, mistrust or perceived threat from the other".[8] When facing conflict over tangible matters, it is often the case that intangible factors are utilised to further conflict. This is especially true when a state is challenged by an identity group, regardless of whether that challenge is in a territorial or ideological sphere. Furthermore, given that conflicts occurring on what Bar-Tal calls the macro level[9] generally involve ethnic groups with shared characteristics, these conflicts include all members of society.[10] Indeed, the mix of identities and tensions between identities in both Saudi Arabia and Iran possess hallmarks of these tangible and intangible factors.

When considering the nature of conflict within societies, one must differentiate between tractable and intractable conflicts. Tractable conflicts are generally of a short-term nature, over lesser goals, and are perceived as solvable through negotiation. In contrast, as Bar-Tal notes, intractable conflicts are:

> over perceived important goals; they involve great animosity and vicious cycles of violence; are prolonged because neither side can win and therefore are perceived as unsolvable and self-perpetuating; at the same time both sides are not interested in compromising and resolving them in a peaceful way; in contrast, each side mobilizes society members to participate in them and is focusing only on own needs and goals.[11]

Given the belief that groups hold their goals to possess an "existential importance",[12] this belief can often position a group in immediate conflict with another group that also perceives its goals as possessing the same importance. Furthermore, the magnitude of issues such as territorial dispute, or ideological clashes, demonstrates the significance of such matters. The threat posed by such existential issues is especially relevant when discussing identity conflict within Iran.

Social conditions are frequently the starting point for the emergence of violence, although this is not always the case: "They frustrate important needs, which eventually may give rise to psychological and societal processes that begin an evolution towards mass violence".[13] However, as Bar-Tal articulates in a 2011 work, the mere perception of the goals of a group being in contradiction with another's goals has the capacity to induce conflict,[14] which suggests that social conditions need not necessarily be responsible for the emergence of violence. Difficult social conditions can be derived from economic hardships, political tensions and problems concerning basic needs, defined as security, food, shelter, a positive identity, and feelings of effectiveness or control. Thus, "[d]ifficult life conditions make people feel insecure, ineffective, and not in control, with their sense of self diminished".[15] As a consequence, these conditions appear to challenge what are conceived as basic rights by an individual. When basic rights appear contested, then individuals may begin the process of moving towards violence. Furthermore, difficult life conditions can foster shared psychological reactions, leading to greater group identification.

When an individual's life gets tougher, Staub and Bar-Tal suggest that an inevitable consequence is to turn to a group, in order to provide "an ideological movement for identity [. . . wherein] individuals elevate their group, initially by psychologically diminishing the other through devaluation, and ultimately harming the other".[16] As such, while ideas can initially manifest themselves in small groups, these groups have the capacity to evolve from protests to violent action. This shift from protest to violence then has the capacity to threaten interests and the security of an "other", thus provoking responses. The role of ideology is important when fostering a coherent group, as ideologies "establish commonality of perceptions, norms, and values, as well as foster interdependence and coordination of social activities".[17] Furthermore, the more vociferous the ideology, the more scope exists for a group to engage in violent action.

The process of fostering a group identity then has the capacity to define characteristics that do not belong to the group, thus differentiating between group identities. In order for there to be an other, there must be a sharp demarcation between the "us" and the "them", which identifies characteristics that do not belong to the group. Given the perceived existential importance of a group's goals and the zero-sum nature of competition, it appears that the use of violence is almost inevitable.[18] It is then possible to build upon this demarcation and engage in a process of devaluation of the other, which in turn makes the other an easier target for violence, explaining both the eruption of and continuation of conflict.[19] As such, "the other often comes to be seen as a mortal enemy and the identity of one's own group as partly defined by its enmity to the other",[20] again illustrating the zero-sum nature of this aspect of political violence.

When examining both Saudi Arabia and Iran, one can see the existence of numerous identities within each state that challenge either the ideological or territorial integrity of the state. As such, given the existence of identity incongruence, conflict between these internal identities is undeniable. Given that religion plays such a prominent role within each state, it is important to begin examination of the second stage of the analytical framework, of identities located both within and across Saudi Arabia and Iran, with religion. The place of religion within the fabric of each state is undeniable, notably stemming from the 1979 revolution and the emergence of an Iranian theocracy, coupled with the position of Wahhabism within the Saudi state. In addition, both Saudi Arabia and Iran have sought to export their Islamic beliefs across both Gulf and wider Middle East regions.

In understanding the role of religion within each state, principally the constitution of religious groups within Saudi Arabia and Iran, one must possess an understanding of the location of Shi'i and Sunni belief systems within the overarching Islamic narrative, as discussed in chapter two; moreover, it is essential to then locate Twelver Shi'ism and Wahhabism within Shi'i and Sunni Islamic doctrines, respectively. While considering the numerous religious identities, the argument shall be guided by several areas: firstly, a consideration of the numerous religious identities operating within each state; secondly, analysis of the challenge that each identity poses to the regime; and lastly, an examination of the response of the state to these identity groups.

Saudi Arabia

This section on religious identities within Saudi Arabia begins with discourse on Wahhabism, starting with a history of the movement, detailing theological origins, the relationship with the Al Saud, the location within the Kingdom, and the impact upon policy making. The argument then turns to Shi'i groups, with particular focus upon political space and capacity for action.

The most prominent religious group within Saudi Arabia is Wahhabism, an Islamic school of thought considered outside the four orthodox schools of Sunni thought. Wahhabism occupies a prominent place within the Kingdom as a result of the centuries old alliance between the Al Saud and Wahhabi clerics. While it is suggested by Stephen Schwartz that "no more than 40 per cent of the Saudi population are Wahhabi",[21] Wahhabi clerics hold a monopoly on religion and worship within the Kingdom, extending into all facets of the Saudi state. This includes the judicial, given adherence to Wahhabi interpretations of the Shari'a, which leaves no space for the *madhahib*.[22] Although many in Saudi Arabia adhere to Wahhabi norms in public, in private it is pertinent to question the extent to which Wahhabi values are practised. Given its institutionalisation through the state-building process, Wahhabism has become synonymous with Sunni Islam within Saudi Arabia, leaving little scope for clear distinction between the two, despite the rejection of Wahhabism by many Sunni scholars. As such, given the prominent position of Wahhabism within Saudi Arabia, this chapter shall focus upon the role of Wahhabism within the state, rather than considering the role of other Sunni strands of Islam, or Sufism.

Wahhabism

Wahhabism is an intellectually marginal movement, standing outside the four orthodox schools of Sunni thought. As Hamid Algar articulates, "Wahhabism is essentially a movement without pedigree; it came out of nowhere in the sense not only of emerging from the wastelands of Najd, but also its lack of substantial precedent in Islamic history".[23]

Scholars are divided when explaining the origins of al-Wahhab's religious beliefs, with some suggesting that these were formed through the experience of studying in Medina, advocating the revival of the *ahadith* and a desire to bring Sufi teachings in line with Islamic rule.[24] Others suggest that the time al-Wahhab spent in Basra shaped his beliefs, given that Basra had a strong Shi'i population (in contrast to the Sunni heartland of the Najd region). Furthermore, while at Basra, "he began public preaching against what he deemed illegitimate ritual innovations [. . .] and violations of man's duty to devote all worship to God alone".[25] Al-Wahhab's father was the *qadi* (judge ruling on the Shari'a) of al'Uyayna, and belonged to the Hanbali *madhab*.[26] Given this, it is possible to understand why people believe that the Wahhabi mission possesses a "Hanbali stamp",[27] or can be interpreted as a Sunni sect.

In the absence of Saudi oil patrons, the success of Wahhabism was not assured, stemming from the demographic and geographical situation in the Muslim world. According to Algar, the purpose of Wahhabism was to facilitate a return to the twin sources of Islam, namely the Qur'an and Sunna.[28] Although *The Book of God's Unity* houses Wahhabist thought, dealing with matters of theology and behaviour as a true Muslim, the work contains nothing on Islamic law.[29]

David Commins suggests that the most distinctive facet of Wahhabism is "the insistence that proclaiming, understanding and affirming that God is one do not suffice to make one a Muslim, but that one must also explicitly deny any other object of worship".[30] At the heart of al-Wahhab's teaching is a conviction that all actions should be to serve God along with a rejection of interpretations of Islam that could be perceived as illegitimate, such as "reverence given to dead saints as intercessors with God".[31]

In order for one to be considered Muslim, it is generally accepted that an acceptance of *shahada* "[t]here is no god but God, and Muhammad is the messenger of God",[32] however, this understanding of who is defined as a Muslim is rejected by Wahhabism. Wahhabis hold that in order to be Muslim, one must undertake worship in the correct form, demonstrating a belief in the oneness of God, desiring a return to the "pristine condition of the early days of the Islamic community".[33] This belief stems from the acknowledgement of Arab idolaters, living at the time of Muhammad, who held that "God was the Creator and the Lord of all creation, yet they were the Prophet's worst enemies".[34] As such, Wahhabis hold that there is a second aspect to a belief in God, which

> requires one to devote worship purely and exclusively to God. Any act or statement that indicates devotion to a being other than God is to associate another creature with God's power, and that is tantamount to idolatry (*shirk*).[35]

This separates Wahhabism from other schools of Islamic; however, there remain tensions within Wahhabism itself.

Tensions within Wahhabism

While the institutionalisation of Wahhabism within the Kingdom is undeniable, the supposition that Wahhabism is a coherent entity is infelicitous. Indeed, it is possible to demonstrate the existence of tensions inherent in Wahhabism, separating Wahhabis between those who possess loyalty to the Al Saud and those who still adhere to the traditional tenets of Wahhabism. Inherent within Wahhabi thought is the notion that the *ulama* should avoid the company of idolaters, a notion that would prove troublesome when allied with the Al Saud, who are held by many of the more conservative *ulama* to be guilty of idolatry. In addition, given the conflicting nature of nation-state and *umma*, the existence of tensions between "the exclusivity of Wahhabism and the imperatives of inclusionary nation making"[36] appears problematic. As a consequence, this creates tensions between Wahhabism and the Al Saud.

A second area of tension is outlined by Gwenn Okruhlik, who notes a distinction between the embodiment of Wahhabism within the state and Salafis, understood as believers within a Muslim community who seek to bypass the state appointed *ulama*, preferring direct links to the Qur'an.[37] Okruhlik develops this point further by suggesting that many within the Kingdom and within the wider Islamic *umma* question "the very idea of a single set of official interpreters".[38] This, in turn, challenges core beliefs of Wahhabi doctrine.

A third area of tension within Wahhabism occurs when considering the rise of fundamentalist Islamic movements within the Kingdom. Indeed, this is can be seen when considering the seizure of the Grand Mosque in 1979. During the pilgrimage season, Juhayaman ibn Muhammad al-Utaybi, with support from both Saudi and non-Saudi followers, seized the mosque. Al-Utaybi proclaimed his companion, Muhammad ibdn Abdullah al-Qahtani, the true *mahdi* (the one who guides).[39] The seizure of the mosque was undertaken in protest at the "moral laxity and degeneration of the Saudi rulers".[40]

The siege ended after two weeks with the killing of al-Qahtani and the capture of al-Utaybi and of 170 followers.[41] Although military action in the mosque is forbidden, legitimacy of action was derived from a *fatwa* issued by the *ulama*. The political message of the siege was hidden by claims concerning the new *mahdi* and the emergence of a theological debate on the characteristics of a *mahdi*.[42] Sherifa Zuhur suggests that al-Utaybi represented a "frustrated ultra-Wahhabism",[43] which again challenges the notion that one group can correctly interpret the Qur'an and demonstrates the tensions within Wahhabism.

Tensions between the Al Saud and Wahhabism

In addition to tensions found within Wahhabism, tensions can also be seen within the relationship between Wahhabism and the Al Saud. Indeed, it is during the process of state formation that Ibn Saud understood the need to "curb Wahhabism's xenophobic impulses".[44] While the Wahhabi-inspired *ikhwan* advocated the strict adherence to Wahhabi norms and beliefs, Ibn Saud was far more relaxed to issues such as smoking tobacco and worshiping at shrines.[45] Furthermore, while it is true that Wahhabism has traditionally acted as a legitimising tool for the regime, as Mohammed Ayoob and Hasan Kosebalaban correctly articulate, "some of its contemporary manifestations are intensely anti-status quo and have seriously threatened not only the legitimacy but also the very existence of the Saudi regime".[46]

The position of the Al Saud as the protectors of the two holy places in Islam created responsibilities for Muslims across all doctrinal beliefs, which, in turn, brought ideological disagreement with the Wahhabist *ulama*. Indeed, the Al Saud had to fulfill Islamic obligations to all Muslims while satisfying "the religious standards of [the] Wahhabi ulama".[47] Islamic tensions between the Al Saud and Wahhabist doctrine can be seen with regard to the presence of Shi'i Muslims on the *Hajj*, and with the Al Saud adhering to responsibilities emanating from the title of "Protector of the Holy Places of Islam" against the wishes of the Wahhabi *ulama*.

Yet tensions between the Al Saud and Wahhabist *ulama* are not restricted to the *Hajj*; rather, "[w]hilst Ibn Saud institutionalized Wahhabi authority, his relations with the ulama were complicated by his willingness to experiment with the trappings of modern nation-states and to adopt technical means that would buttress his power".[48] The mere engagement with the idea of a nation-state rather than the *umma* has increased tensions between the Al Saud and Wahhabi *ulama*. One such application of modern technology within the Kingdom was that of mass communication, held as essential for the creation of a coherent nation-state and the ensuing application and implementation of policy. Yet for the Wahhabist *ulama*, the employment of such techniques, particularly those that facilitated communication over long distances, "could only be the work of Satan-worship".[49] Despite these misgivings, the development of communication and transport would prove beneficial to the *ulama*, facilitating the proselytising of Wahhabi values.

Tensions also pervaded the realm of education, with the *ulama* rejecting the teaching of foreign languages, geography and art, casting these subjects as *bid'a*. In an effort to stem the tide of modernity and maintain the ideological purity of the Kingdom, the Wahhabi movement "would use its control over law, its influence on education and its moral legitimacy among a substantial portion of the population to hold fast against the tides of western-style modernity".[50] However, it is important to note that Ibn Saud embraced a programme of reforms advancing the education of women, despite the opposition of religious leaders and members of the royal family.[51]

In an attempt to reduce the threat posed by Wahhabism, Ibn Saud "suppressed the mission's most zealous current, employed non-Saudi Arabs as advisors and invited Americans to develop his land's resources".[52] The invitation of foreigners into the Kingdom angered the Wahhabi *ulama*, provoking much criticism. This criticism was especially vociferous following the Iraqi invasion of Kuwait in 1991, with the *ulama* accusing the Al Saud of betraying Islam, through inviting "infidel troops to occupy the land of the holy places".[53] Given the inaction of the Al Saud and Wahhabi *ulama*, Stephen Schwartz suggests that Wahhabism was "humiliated by the upstart Ba'athist ruler of Iraq".[54] But, despite this angering of the *ulama*, Wahhabi doctrine remained ensconced within the institutions of the state created by the Al Saud. Building on the entrenchment of Wahhabi values within institutions of the state, it is germane to note that these institutions often possess a proselytizing element. This notion of institutionalised proselytization is supported by David Commins, who suggests that "[c]ontrary to the expectation that incorporating Wahhabi ulama into a network of government institutions would diminish their influence, the ulama turned institutions into vehicles to entrench and even expand their sway".[55]

Commins describes the relationship between the Wahhabi *ulama* and the Al Saud as one of ebbs and flows, referring to "the resilience of Wahhabi ulama and their tenacious grip on the loyalty of broad segments of society".[56] Indeed, the fluidity of the relationship can be seen within legal discourse and the existence of two separate legal systems in the Kingdom. With both the Shari'a and a national legal system in place, authority and legitimacy have become much-debated issues, requiring the *ulama* and the ruling elite to negotiate and balance their respective interests.[57]

While it is possible to argue that Wahhabist doctrine guides the policy making of the Al Saud, it is perhaps more appropriate to suggest that Wahhabism is used to sanctify decisions, as opposed to influencing the decision-making process. As Clive Jones argues, the Supreme Committee of *Ulama*, constituted by regime appointed clerics and lawyers, "became the bastion of theological legitimation for policy decisions already taken by [former] King Fahd".[58]

The association with a fundamentalist religious movement would aid the process of state formation across the Arabian Peninsula; however, the alliance with Wahhabism would not protect the Al Saud from vehement criticism from Islamic sources. Indeed, "[h]aving opened the Kingdom's doors to broader Islamic revivalist trends, Saudi Arabia was not immune to further developments in these trends, most notably the rise of a militant stream commonly referred to as 'jihadist', or 'jihadi salafi'".[59] The rise of this militant stream can be best seen with the seizure of the Grand Mosque in Mecca, in the most dramatic manifestion of the tensions between those adhering to Wahhabist ideology and the regime.[60]

Given that the Kingdom is run in accordance with the Shari'a, it is argued by some that opposition to the state on Islamic grounds is meaningless.[61] Yet Wahhabist thought holds that idolatry is *bid'a*, as is association with those who commit idolatry. Thus, through association with the United States, the Al Saud are guilty of *bid'a*, therefore open to Islamic criticism. A development of this line of argument also posits Wahhabis as guilty of *bid'a*, given their association with the Al Saud.

Criticisms of Wahhabism

Within both Saudi Arabia and the international community, the relationship between the Al Saud and Wahhabism has evoked much criticism. The erosion of Wahhabi credibility within internal and external spheres occurred predominantly within four instances: firstly, the 1979 seizure of the Grand Mosque in Mecca; secondly, the Second Gulf War; thirdly, the attacks of 9/11; and fourthly, criticism of the Kingdom's human rights record. Indeed, these criticisms are levied at the Wahhabist *ulama* as well as at the ruling elite, given the prominence of Wahhabist doctrine within the Kingdom.

The seizure of the Grand Mosque in Mecca by Islamic fundamentalists was a violent manifestation of tensions within Saudi Arabia, resulting in part from pressures brought about by the process of modernisation, which facilitated greater transparency as to the behaviour of the Al Saud. The idea of Islamic fundamentalists seizing the Grand Mosque, which is protected by a ruling family operating with the support of the Wahhabi *ulama*, suggests a perceived erosion of the credibility of Wahhabism to internal actors.

The Second Gulf War was the second instance of Wahhabi credibility being eroded. King Fahd's inviting of US forces into Saudi Arabia, in an attempt to protect the Kingdom from the impending threat posed by Saddam Hussein's Iraqi incursion into Kuwait, demonstrated tensions within the Kingdom between those who supported the Al Saud and those who accused the Al Saud of idolatry and *bid'a*.

The third area in which Wahhabi credibility was eroded was the attacks of 9/11, after which it was revealed that 15 of the 19 hijackers were from Saudi Arabia,[62] moreover, that Saudi Arabia was a source of funds for Al Qai'da.[63] It is possible that such a large number of Saudi nationals were chosen by Al Qai'da to participate in the 9/11 attacks as a result of the relative ease in which Saudi nationals were able to obtain visas for the United States.[64] The revelation of such a strong Saudi contingent within the hijackers would erode much of the credibility of the Al Saud and the Wahhabi *ulama* internationally, despite cooperation with US investigators in the aftermath of the attacks.[65]

The fourth area concerns criticisms from human rights groups about attitudes to human rights within Saudi Arabia. In particular, this stems from the interpretation, and understanding, of the Shari'a, which is strictly enforced. An example of this can be seen with regard to the death of 14 girls at a school in Mecca. The school, Girls' Intermediate School Number Thirty One, caught fire, prompting the girls to flee the building. Present were the *mutawa* (religious police), who "forced girls who had escaped the burning building back into it, because, fleeing the flames, they had not fully covered up".[66] The behaviour of the *mutawa* in this instance alone has resulted in much condemnation.

Shi'i Muslims

The second most dominant religious identity group in Saudi Arabia is that of Shi'i Muslims, with a large number living in the Eastern Province of the Kingdom. It is believed that approximately 15 per cent of the Kingdom's population are Shi'a.[67] Historically, the Shi'i population within Saudi Arabia has been subject to persecution and disdain, the response to which has "moved between dissimulation, accommodation, attempted reconciliation, and terrorism".[68] Despite the increasing wealth of the Saudi state, the Shi'a did not benefit from developments in health and social services, and access to jobs was limited; moreover, Shi'i Muslims were banned from careers such as the army and education.[69]

The tensions between Wahhabis and the Shi'a are traced back to the nineteenth century, with the destruction of the tomb of Hosein at Karbala, along with those of the prophet's companions. This occurred as Wahhabis hold worship at tombs to be *shirk* (polytheism), thus posing conflict between Wahhabist and Shi'i thought. As previously noted, the defining premise of Wahhabism is that of *tawahid*, which appears incompatible with *shirk*. Further adding to tensions between Wahhabi and Shi'a in 1927, "the Wahhabi ulama published a fatwa calling upon the Shi'a to 'convert' to Islam".[70]

When examining the position of Shi'i Muslims in Saudi Arabia, it is imperative to stress the importance of the Iranian Revolution in 1979, from which it was argued that the Shi'a of the Kingdom comprised the *mustazefin*. It is important to note that Shi'i uprisings were not solely derived from the revolution in Iran,[71] but, rather, were galvanised by the events, resulting in seven days of violence in November 1979. During this time, protesters destroyed state property, burned a British bank, and held off 20,000 members of the Saudi security forces.[72] The uprisings continued, celebrating the first anniversary of Khomenei's return to Iran and also protesting against their status as second-class citizens within the Kingdom.[73] These uprisings were eventually crushed by the state. While Shi'i dissent abated at this time, the programme of civil disobedience and its catalyst only furthered suspicions of ties to Iran.

Wahhabi efforts to maintain the ideological sovereignty of Saudi Arabia have included placing limitations upon religious space by banning religious texts outside of Wahhabi doctrine. Shi'i organisations have thus experienced the banning, regular confiscation and burning of religious texts.[74] In addition to the confiscation of texts, several government clerics, notably Abdullah Ibn Jabreen, have called for *jihad* against the Shi'a, as a result of their practice of "bad faith".[75]

Shi'i Relations with the State

Joshua Teitelbaum suggests there are four areas governing the Al Saud's policy towards the Shi'a: Wahhabist ideology, pressure from and response to the Wahhabi *ulama*, the presence of the Shi'a in oil-rich areas, and the perceived Iranian connection.[76] In addition to the four areas posited by Teitelbaum, there is a fifth area guiding policy towards the Shi'a, notably the increasing power of Shi'i organisations across the region.

The first two areas have previously been discussed; the third area, the presence of the Shi'a in oil-rich areas, suggests demographic and economic concerns about the instability of key regions within the Kingdom. Indeed, Saudi Arabia's Shi'i population is primarily located within the key oil regions of the Kingdom, notably, the Eastern Province. Within the Eastern Province is a village called al-Awwamiyya, which has a long tradition of opposition to the state. As Toby Matthieson articulates:

> The village is not representative of the Shi'i population as a whole; it is famous, in fact, among Shi'a from elsewhere as a place where sentiment against the Saudi state is very strong and radical political strands are very popular. Many members of the Shi'i opposition movements come from this village and during the 1979 uprising, some activists claim, it was called the Islamic Republic of al-'Awwamiyya.[77]

The fear of secessionist agendas within the Kingdom, no matter how ephemeral, is a source of concern for the Al Saud. This concern manifests itself in a territorial sense, but also with regard to the location of oil reserves.

The fourth area articulated by Teitelbaum is the suspicion of Iranian interference within the Shi'i community. It is widely held across the region that the Shi'i population in Saudi Arabia is torn between loyalty to the Kingdom and loyalty to Iran, given the latter's position as the leader of the Shi'i world. Indeed, one Shi'i opposition group, Hizballah al-Hijaz, hold loyalty to Iran, accept the principles of *velayat-e faqih*, and are believed to have received financial support from Iran.[78] It has been alleged that Hizballah al-Hijaz are responsible for the bombing of the Khobar Towers residential complex in 1996, which killed 19 Americans, and wounded 372.[79]

The fifth area guiding the regime's response to the Shi'a builds upon suspicion of ties to Iran and considers a rise in Shi'i geopolitical power. The 2006 War in Lebanon, which increased the power of Hizballah, coupled with the kidnap of the Israeli soldier, Galit Shalid by Hamas,[80] had a dramatic impact upon the security of the Middle East. Indeed, the "ascendancy of the Shiites in Iraq and Lebanon has given rise to a feeling of empowerment amongst the Shiites of Saudi Arabia. They are proud of the accomplishments of their brethren".[81] Given the inherent guilt within Shi'i thought, such feelings of pride resonate well across the Shi'i world. The resulting increase in tensions between Saudi Arabia and Hizballah manifested themselves in hostility towards the Shi'a of Saudi Arabia.

The identification of Saudi Arabia's Shi'i population with Hizballah was problematic: "to identify with a Shiite movement, and, by implication, the Shiite state of Iran, ran counter to the normative Saudi ethos".[82] This suggests that, despite such anti-Shi'i rhetoric, the most important area of concern was located within the geopolitical sphere,and geopolitical competition in the Gulf with Iran.

The rising power of Shi'i groups in Iraq post 2003 fostered hope amongst the Saudi Shi'a for increases in their own political power and religious recognition. However, the Shi'i population in Saudi Arabia saw the need to explicitly express their allegiance to the regime. As such, a *fatwa* was issued, that:

> [D]emanded Shiite representation in Saudi-led international forums and charities, and asked the royal family to issue express support for dialogue between ulama of all the religious sects in

> the Kingdom. They were at pains to emphasize their loyalty, particularly at a time when they were accused of being more loyal to Iran than Saudi Arabia.[83]

The rise of Shi'i power in Iraq, coupled with the actions of Hizballah and the fingerprints of Iran over both, raised concerns among those in the ruling elite that there was a proselytizing agenda amongst Shi'i Muslims. Moreover, there existed a fear that this agenda was being manipulated by Tehran in a play for increased regional power. As such, the anti-Shi'i sentiment of Wahhabist zeal and the position of Wahhabism within the Kingdom left the ruling elites facing pressure to reduce the political space given to Shi'i groups within the Kingdom, reversing a trend of political, cultural and religious liberalisation. As a result, during December 2006, a *fatwa* was issued, signed by 38 radical Sunni members of the *ulama*, which offered support to Sunnis in Iraq. Despite this *fatwa* referring to Iraq, "it was strongly anti-Shiite in general, complaining about their un-Islamic practices",[84] and could be read as aimed at the Shi'a within Saudi Arabia.

The case of the Shi'a has also motivated Saudi Arabia's actions in Bahrain, viewed as a potential fifth column, open to Iranian influence. Indeed, this concern can be seen when considering the failed *coup d'état* attempt in Bahrain in 1981, which:

> would have established Khomeinism on the other side of the Gulf and would have had paramount importance in securing the sympathy of several hundred thousand native Saudi Shia living in the oases on the peninsula's eastern shore. Khomeini had been sending his propagandists on pilgrimage to Mecca since 1979 to challenge the legitimacy of Saudi control over the Holy Places; and when the Grand Mosque was attacked by Saudi dissidents in November 1979, Khomeini did not hesitate to accuse the Saudi authorities of acting against Islam by suppressing the riots within the sacred precincts.[85]

For the Al Saud, given the proximity (both geographically and ideologically) between the Shi'a of Saudi Arabia and Bahrain, the spate of uprisings within Bahrain are of great concern. This is especially pertinent when considering the potential ramifications for the stability of the Eastern Province, as Saudi Arabia has long feared the increasing Shi'i power of its own population. Thus, in offering support to the Al Khalifa regime against the Shi'i population of Bahrain, Riyadh is seeking to prevent the political empowerment of this community, fearful that "any political gains by Bahrain's Shiites will likewise be demanded by Saudi Shiites".[86] Moreover, the pressure placed on the Al Khalifa to resist calls for democratic reform can be traced back to Riyadh, again fearful at the consequences for its own Shi'i population. However, it is possible that the Saudi led GCC intervention has done more to incite Shi'i populations in both Saudi and Bahrain, in turn pushing these populations closer to Iran.

A Thawing in Relations?

Despite the aforementioned restrictions in religious space, as Teitelbaum articulates, Shi'i groups in the Kingdom are more than aware of the role played by the Al Saud in restraining the fanaticism of Wahhabism.[87] Building on this belief, there have been instances of dialogue between Shi'i representatives and state individuals. One such instance was the 1993 meetings between Tawfiq al-Shayf, an exiled Shi'i leader, and Saudi officials, including the King. These meetings were sought by Shi'i groups to express their demands and received by the Al Saud as both a means of closing down one form of opposition and preventing the emergence of alliances between opposition groups, regardless of ideological persuasion. Indeed, "compared to the tougher and potentially more dangerous demands of groups such as the CDLR, reaching a separate *modus vivendi* with the Shiite opposition was a small price to pay".[88] On the back of this dialogue, in 1993, several Shi'i opposition papers ceased publishing. In addition, the standard of living within Shi'i areas rose considerably; moreover, previously confiscated and banned Shi'i texts were returned. Most importantly, though, was the acceptance of five *madhahibb* within Saudi Arabia: the four of Sunni Islam, plus that of Shi'i Islam.[89] However, not all Shi'i groups accepted the concessions offered by the Al Saud, notably Hizballah al-Hijaz.

The 2005 municipal elections saw an increase in Shi'i representation, yet these successes engendered increased hostilities between the two sects. Alongside these tensions were further allegations that the Shi'a of Saudi Arabia possessed a stronger sense of loyalty to Iran than to the Kingdom. While such allegations were not new, the source of such allegations was, coming from former Egyptian President Hosni Mubarak,[90] again demonstrating the concern about the rising power of Iran across the region. Moreover, the lack of a state rebuttal of Mubarak's comments only furthered distrust of the Shi'i minority and increased Shi'i discontent within the Kingdom.

However, one must also question the importance of the events in Bahrain, notably how the Al Saud have sought to prevent reforms that would increase Shi'i power and political participation within Bahrain, given concerns that the Shi'i population within the Eastern Province would also demand these reforms. One must also consider the notion that in aiding the violent crushing of protests in Bahrain, Saudi Arabian legitimacy is diminishing, preventing a thawing in relations between the Shi'a of the Eastern Province and Riyadh.

Religious Violence in the Kingdom

Religious violence within Saudi Arabia can be split into Sunni and Shi'i violence, with motivations for violent behaviour differing in accordance with goals. Thomas Hegghammer examines the nature of Sunni Islamist violence within Saudi Arabia, questioning the emergence of a sustained programme of violence post 2003.[91] Hegghammer offers a synopsis of three paradigms dominating the existing literature, which possess the capacity to explain the emergence of Islamist violence in Saudi Arabia.[92] The first of these explanations uses an ideological approach, holding Islamist violence to be "a product of the religiosity of Saudi society or the 'inherent extremism' of the Wahhabi religious tradition".[93] The second explanation suggests that structural conditions are responsible for the rise in violence, as a consequence of constrictions placed upon agency. The third explanation suggests that Saudi Arabian Islamism should be considered as a social movement "whose ebbs and flows can be explained by the agency of, and resources available to, Islamist entrepreneurs".[94] However, all of these explanations fail to appreciate certain aspects of the Islamist movement and also make a fatally flawed assumption that Saudi Arabian Islamism can be grouped into a singular, coherent, entity.[95] Given the existence of numerous Sunni Islamist groups operating within Saudi Arabia, for the purpose of brevity, this argument shall predominantly be concerned with Al Qai'da, namely, Al Qai'da on the Arabian Peninsula (AQAP).

Al Qai'da

The Al Qai'da organisation emerged from the embers of the Soviet campaign in Afghanistan, during the 1980s splintering from *Maktab al-Khidimat,* which was originally formed by Abdullah Azzam. At its head was the Saudi national Osama bin Laden, who formed a group with the aim of overcoming the national and ethnic divides that had plagued the group of Islamic *mujahideen* and aspired to create "an 'international army' which would defend Muslims from oppression".[96] The Al Qai'da as perceived today was bolstered by the arrival of Ayman al-Zawahiri and members of the Egyptian Islamic Jihad in Afghanistan, following their release from prison for their involvement in the assassination of Anwar Sadat. Jason Burke suggests that the organisation that would become known as Al Qai'da was formed in 1988,[97] and would have the opportunity to defend Muslims from oppression only two years later, when Saddam Hossein invaded Kuwait. On the back of this invasion, bin Laden offered the use of his organisation to King Fahd, in an effort to offer an additional line of protection for Saudi Arabia from the threat posed by Hossein; an offer that was ultimately rebuffed in favour of using US forces. This rejection gave rise to hostility between Al Qai'da and the House of Saud.

The relationship between Al Qai'da and the Al Saud is more complicated than *prima facia* observations would suggest. Indeed, despite the vitriol directed towards the Al Saud for permitting US forces to enter the Kingdom, Saudi Arabia remains integral to Al Qai'da's cause. This is demonstrated on several levels: firstly, Al Qai'da's former leader, Osama bin Laden, was born in the Kingdom, as were 15 of the 19 9/11 hijackers.[98] Secondly, Saudi Arabia has long been a source of funds for Al Qai'da. Thirdly, the Wahhabist ideology of Saudi Arabia plays a key role in providing ideological guidance to Al Qai'da.[99] Furthermore, it is alleged that several members of the Al Saud family possess ties to Al Qai'da. Indeed, senior Saudi princes are "routinely accused of at the very least failing to prevent the funnelling of money from Saudi-based Islamic charities to terrorist organisations".[100]

Despite the level of support emanating from Saudi Arabia for Al Qai'da, existing predominantly at a grassroots level but also to some extent within the upper echelons of Saudi society, the Kingdom has not escaped the wrath of bin Laden and his followers. Indeed, one of Al Qai'da's most explicit areas of antagonism has revolved around the presence of US forces in the land of the two holy mosques. As Bruce Riedel and Bilal Saab correctly state, the war with Al Qai'da in Saudi Arabia, is over the "biggest stakes of all", notably the control of Islam's two holiest cities and the world's largest reserves of oil.[101]

Although Al Qai'da engaged in numerous acts of violence within Saudi Arabia during the 1990s, this violent agenda was postponed in 1998. This decision, although not explicitly stated, was referred to by *jihadi* ideologue Abu Bakr, who suggested that the Kingdom was not selected for change by the Al Qai'da high command,[102] along with former CIA director George Tenet, whose autobiography details that "prior to 9/11 [Bin Laden] had imposed a ban on attacks in Saudi Arabia".[103] It is suggested that the decision to postpone operations within Saudi Arabia was a consequence of the seizure of a consignment of missiles that were planned to be fired at the US consulate in Jeddah, coupled with the arrest of around 900 people.[104] However, as John Bradley observes, there are some who believe that the Al Saud paid off Al Qai'da to not launch operations against the regime.[105]

The return of Al Qai'da to Saudi Arabia was brought about by the fall of the Taliban regime, which meant that the value of Saudi Arabia as a source of both financial support and of recruits increased dramatically. This can be seen as a result of the logistical problems encountered by potential jihadis, notably as to where to train. Thus, "the Kingdom's value as a theatre of operations had increased because in 2002 jihadis were pursued less vigorously in Saudi Arabia than in most other countries in the region".[106] Post 2003, having witnessed the US invasion of Iraq and the return of Al Qai'da to Saudi Arabia, the Kingdom was engulfed in "the longest and most violent sustained internal struggle against the Saudi monarchy and establishment since the founding of the modern Saudi state".[107] This campaign began in May 2003, with a series of suicide car bombs across Riyadh.[108]

The manifestation of Al Qai'da within Saudi Arabia occurs predominantly under the guise of AQAP, an organisation originating in and currently based in Yemen.[109] The roots of AQAP in Saudi Arabia can be traced back to the late 1990s and the work of Yusuf al-Ayiri, who reported directly to Osama bin Laden.[110] Al-Ayiri amassed weapons and safe-houses and began to set up training camps across the Kingdom in the early 2000s. Although AQAP initially sought to operate within Saudi Arabia, as Hegghammer notes, "the declared purpose of the QAP [AQAP] campaign from the beginning was not primarily to topple the regime but to end what the militants perceived as the American military occupation of the Arabian Peninsula".[111]

In 2003, the Al Qai'da leadership ordered al-Ayiri to begin a campaign within the Kingdom,[112] against al-Ayiri's wishes, who argued that his mission was not ready. The successes of the Al Saud's security forces ultimately proved al-Ayiri correct, leading to the death of al-Ayiri and other prominent members of AQAP.[113] The deaths of these leaders resulted in a period of reconstruction for the organisation; however, AQAP became active again, following Umar Farouk Abdulmutallab's attempt to blow up a plane on Christmas Day 2009[114] and the discovery of explosive devices on board flights from Yemen.[115]

The propaganda magazine for AQAP, *Inspire*, which is written in English, seeks to spread the values of the organisation to the West, in the hope of recruiting future jihadis. One edition of *Inspire* details the arrest of Muhammad al-Mu'tiq, his wife and family in Buraydah, in February 2010. In criticising this event, *Inspire* portrays the Al Saud as "the stooges of the Jews and Christians [. . .] They do not have any respect for the sanctity of Muslim homes, and they do not respect Muslim honour. This act on behalf of al-Sa'ud [sic] is a proof of their lowness, meanness, and evil".[116] Within the same document is an interview with Shaykh Abu Basir, the head of AQAP, which documents the goals and scope of Al Qai'da operations. In addition, it also notes how since 1990:

> The youth of the Peninsula of Islam are defending their religion, their holy places and their land which their Messenger, peace be upon him, ordered to expel from it the disbelievers. They have executed a few operations against the Americans in and out of the Arabian Peninusla. The most famous are the Ulaya, al-Khobar, East Riyadh, USS Cole, Limburg, and the assassination of US soldiers in the island of Faylakah in Kuwait.[117]

When Basir was questioned on targeting Muhammad bin Nayif, the Saudi Arabian security chief and a senior member of the Al Saud, he gave the following response:

> [T]he targeting of Muhammad bin Nayif was part of our effort to purify the Arabian Peninsula from the traitors. He and his ilk are the ones who allowed the Americans to set base in the Peninsula of Islam [. . .] He is an American in the clothes of an Arab. If it wasn't for these traitors, the American airplanes wouldn't have bombed Iraq and Afghanistan from the airports of Kharj and Riyadh and others, and if it wasn't for them the Jews wouldn't have remained in Palestine for more than sixty years.[118]

Inspire facilitates the proliferation of a radical Salafist ideology to the Western world, demonstrating acknowledgement of key Pan-Islamist ideals in an attempt to increase support. *Inspire* also demonstrates the importance of Saudi Arabia within Al Qai'da's strategic goals. Such Pan-Islamist ideology has also been employed by the regime, which again demonstrates the incongruity in the regime's position towards Pan-Islamism.

The Shi'a

Religious violence has also originated from the Shi'i community. Despite their location within key strategic positions in the Kingdom, ideological disputes with the Wahhabist *ulama*, the perception of ties with Iran and the increase in Shi'i power across the Middle East has resulted in strong discrimination and oppression towards the Shi'i community. Indeed, ties with Iran have played a strong role in guiding Riyadh's policy towards the Shi'a. Furthermore, it is a commonly held assumption within Saudi Arabia that Shi'i movements are operating with the support, be that tacit, ideological, or financial, from Tehran, which facilitated the Khobar Tower bombings. However, Toby Matthieson suggests that it is impossible to ascertain the veracity of such claims.[119]

One of the most prominent Shi'i opposition groups, Hizballah al-Hijaz, is a "clerical based group aligned with Iran, modelling itself on Lebanese Hizbullah",[120] created in 1987. The application of the geographical region "Hijaz" in the name of the organisation serves to symbolise the whole of Arabia, while seeking to undermine the Al Saud. Shortly after their creation, Hizballah al-Hijaz issued a statement, articulating both their opposition to the Saudi elite and a long-term political goal, which was "the establishment of an Islamic Republic in the Arabian Peninsula after the Iranian model".[121] Ties between Hizballah al-Hijaz and Tehran have been alleged on numerous occasions, notably as a consequence of a shared religious vision. However, as Matthiesen quotes, "there is no doubt that our links [Hizballah al-Hijaz] with the Islamic Republic are very strong, because it [Iran] is a base for all the liberators and revolutionaries in the world",[122] which is in accordance with the revolutionary goals of Khomeini and his support for the *mustazefin* of the Muslim world.

While Hizballah al-Hijaz was responsible for numerous attacks within the Kingdom, the most severe was the bombing of the Khobar Towers in 1996, leading to the deaths of 19 Americans and injuries to a further 372. The ideological construction of Hizballah al-Hijaz permitted an attack on US soldiers in Saudi Arabia on the grounds of a desire to continue the struggle against the Al Saud and the supporters of the regime. While some, such as Hasan al-Safar, one of the leaders of the 1979 uprising, suggest that Hizballah al-Hijaz abandoned their revolutionary path,[123] this was refuted in a 2005 press communication stating that the goals of Hizballah al-Hijaz remain the downfall of the Al Saud, and "the military, economic and political liberation of our homeland (the Arabian Peninsula) from the American-Western Occupier".[124]

Iran

The Islamic Republic is dominated by Shi'i Islam, which has manifested itself within the political fabric of Iran in the form of *velayat-e faqih*. As previously noted, *velayat-e faqih* is transliterated as Regency of the Jurist, stressing the importance of a jurist who is responsible for the ideological direction of the Islamic Republic. While Shi'i Islam is the dominant religious group within Iran, there exist several other religious coteries. In accordance with Article 13 of the Iranian Constitution, however, only Zoroastrian, Jewish and Christian religious minorities are recognised by the state,[125] affording these religions some semblance of political space and protection from persecution. Yet there exist several other religious groups not officially recognised by the state. Despite the official recognition of several minorities, there exists persecution of both recognised minorities and those not officially recognised by the state. This section considers the religious constitution of Iran, beginning with the location of Shi'ism within the fabric of the Iranian state, then turning to the position of Sunni Muslims within Iran. The argument continues by locating official religious minorities within Iran, before considering the position of Baha'is.

Shi'i Muslims

As discussed earlier, the principle religious base of the Islamic Republic of Iran is Twelver Shi'ism, also known as Twelve *Imam* Shi'ism, adhered to by 89 per cent of the population.[126] The structure of the political system in Iran is to support and protect Shi'ism.[127] It is argued by Farid Mirbaghari that Shi'ism is by its very nature a political sect, stemming from the dispute over succession of Islamic *caliphs*.[128] The importance of Shi'ism within the Iranian political sphere can be seen with regard to the need for rulers to have legitimacy, which stems from questions concerning the legitimacy of the first three *caliphs*; indeed, ultimately, the Shah's inability to secure legitimacy for his rule ultimately proved costly.[129] Mirbaghari suggests there are four traits of Shi'ism that facilitate the politicisation of the doctrine. Of these four, the first two are especially relevant to the argument: *Usooliyoon*, a term that denotes the importance of adhering to Islamic principles[130] is used within Shi'i thought in order to "interpret religion in light of current circumstances".[131] Building on this, the second trait is that of *ijtihad*, which stresses the importance of policy makers listening to the *ulama* to maintain religious – and thus popular – support.[132]

Ayatollah Khomeini, the orchestrator of the Islamic Republic, posited a system of government, *velayat-e faqih*, which "formulated the theory of an Islamic state as the only legitimate government in Muslim communities".[133] Indeed, through theological sources, Khomeini sought to justify the need for an Islamic government in Iran.[134] This was the manifestation of a change in position for Khomeini, who in his 1943 work *Kashf al-Asrar* (Secrets Revealed), emphasized the need for a state, yet did not stipulate that this must be an Islamic state. Khomeini's logic builds upon the Prophet's behaviour, as located in the Sunna:

> The Sunna and path of the Prophet constitute a proof of the necessity for establishing government. First he himself established a government, as history testifies. He engaged in the implementation of laws, the establishment of the ordinances of Islam, and the administration of society [. . .] Second, he designated a ruler to succeed him, in accordance with divine command. If God Almighty, through the Prophet, designated a man who was to rule over a Muslim society after him, this is in itself an indication that government remains a necessity after the departure of the Prophet from this world.[135]

Traditional Shi'i *ulama* have posited two arguments for a Muslim state: Firstly, to protect the community from foreign invasions; and secondly, to provide order for the community.[136] Khomeini built upon these arguments, adding a third, "which made the existence of a secular and non-religious government impossible, namely for protection against the social and moral corruption of society".[137]

Given the endorsement of *velayat-e faqih*, the application of the Shari'a is not independent from the state. Indeed, the Shari'a is thus contained within the very essence of the state, serving as a beacon for the Islamic Republic's political agenda. In order to achieve this, a just ruler necessitates proper knowledge of Islamic jurisprudence.

Mohsen Milani posits an argument made by a member of the Assembly of Experts, Ayatollah Ali Akbar Ghorshi, who outlines how, because of *velayat-e faqih*, "government laws and decrees, are transformed as Allah's decrees, and obeying such decrees becomes religiously necessary".[138] This results in a position where disobeying governmental laws and decrees is tantamount to disobeying the laws and decrees of Allah, thus reducing scope for opposition to the regime.

While *velayat-e faqih* institutionalised Shi'i beliefs within the fabric of the Islamic Republic, the space for popular sovereignty within the political system derived from the people remains conspicuous by its absence. According to Khomeini, "Islamic government is a government of law. In this form of government sovereignty belongs to God alone and law is His decree and command".[139] Thus, the notion of popular sovereignty appears incompatible with *velayat-e faqih*, given that *velayat-e faqih* is the Government of Allah on Earth.[140]

Sunni Muslims

The second most-populated religious group within Iran are Sunnis, yet despite this, there is currently no Sunni mosque in Tehran.[141] Sunnis comprise approximately 10 cent of the population,[142] including numerous ethnicities,[143] notably Kurds, Baluchi and Turkmen. Post 1979, Sunnis faced a programme of persecution, articulated in 1997 by Dr. Hossein Khalighi, an exiled Iranian-Kurd of Sunni persuasion:

> We Muslim Sunni [sic] of Iran bear with daily insults ushered at us by the Shi'a clergy. They destroy our mosques to build and expand theirs, they humiliate our most sacred men and values in the officially controlled media, they encourage religious wars between Sunnis and Shi'as, they arrest, torture and kill Sunni Muftis and personalities, force Sunnis to convert to Shi'ism,

> forbid Sunni teaching in the schools in Sunni dominated areas, refer to Sunni *ulama* as apostates, and produce many volumes on Shi'ism while forbidding the printing of Sunni books.[144]

Given that across the region Sunnis are in the majority, often persecuting Shi'i minorities, and the history of ideological differences between the two sects, it is no surprise that such actions are reciprocated. It is felicitous to note that much discrimination of Sunnis occurs on grounds of ethnicity and as such, will be explored in much greater detail in chapter five.

Christians

Christianity within Iran can be traced back to the era of the Parthians, who ruled between 171 BC and 224 AD.[145] Approximately 90 per cent of Iran's 200,000 Christians possess ties to ethno-religious groups such as the Orthodox faith of Armenians and Assyrians. This majority conduct services in their own language and rarely engage in proselytization within Iranian society.[146] The absence of proselytizing, choosing instead to focus upon the private practice of religion, has meant that Christians of an Orthodox persuasion are afforded a degree of religious space.

In contrast with Orthodox Christians, the majority of the 10–15,000 Iranian Protestants are Evangelical, worship in Farsi and, as a consequence of their evangelical missionary history, seek out Muslim converts. Given this proselytization, persecution of Protestants increased dramatically throughout the 1990s, amidst charges of apostasy and insulting Islam.[147] The persecution of Protestants and human rights violations were outlined by Bishop Haik Hovsepian Mehr, former President of the Council of Evangelical Ministers of Iran and Secretary General of the Church of the Assemblies of God, who alleged that the regime was guilty of closing churches, beatings and intimidation.[148] In 1994, Bishop Mehr was stabbed to death; Iranian authorities placed the blame on an armed opposition group, the People's Mujahedin Organisation of Iran, and one of whose members, Farahnaz Anami, confessed to the murder. A Human Rights Watch report outlines a degree of suspicion regarding the murder, alleging that Anami had an accomplice, who to this day remains unaccounted for.[149] In addition to Mehr's death, the Human Rights Watch report details the deaths of two other prominent Protestants in Iran, again under suspicious circumstances, also noted by the Commission on Human Rights report.[150]

As such, one can conclude that if not attempting to proselytize, then religious coteries are permitted a degree of space to operate within. However, it is important to note that the restriction of political space to ethnic communities may have an impact upon the religious sphere, which can especially be seen with regard to Christian groups who worship in languages forbidden by the regime.

Jews

There are now approximately 25,000 Jews in Iran, yet prior to 1979, the Iranian Jewish community had nearly 75,000 members. The majority of this number fled following the revolution, fearing a persecution that appeared inevitable with Khomeini's new regime.[151] The existence of Jews in Iran predates that of Christians, dating back to the era of Cyrus the Great.[152] Jews possess political, religious and cultural space within the Islamic Republic, along with a representative in the *Majlis,* and are recognised as a religious minority within Iran. It is alleged that the imprisonment of Jews in Iran is a result of the suspicion of ties with Israel, again based upon ethnic ties rather than religious beliefs.

Zoroastrians

Zoroastrians[153] are the third officially recognised religious minority within the Islamic Republic, with approximately 10,000 followers. Historically, Zoroastrians had a place in the religious and political spheres in Iran, having been the official religion of three Persian empires prior to the arrival of Islam.[154] Zoroastrians have a representative in the *Majlis* and are treated in a similar manner to Orthodox Christians and Jews, possessing religious space as enshrined within the Iranian constitution. However, the Zoroastrian community have previously attempted to resolve their problems through dialogue with national authorities, rather than raising their human rights situation with the international community.[155] This suggests that the articulation of Zoroastrian human rights abuses to the international community could have negative ramifications for their situation internally.

The Baha'i

Outside of the three officially recognised religious minorities within Iran are the Baha'i, an offshoot of the religious movement Babism, a religious movement formed in Iran in the mid-nineteenth century, by Mirza Husayn-Ali, a self-declared prophet.[156] While the largest number of Baha'i are located within Iran, with the community totalling 300,000 members, the faith's headquarters is now based in Haifa, Israel. Baha'ism is a source of ideological contention for Muslims across the world, as it directly challenges several key beliefs of the Islamic faith, notably the premise that Muhammad is the final prophet, after whom there would be no further divine revelation.

Post 1979, Baha'ism was outlawed, a position reflected in the constitution, which "pointedly omitted Baha'ism from the list of recognised religions".[157] Baha'ism was omitted for three reasons: firstly, the Baha'i religion contradicts Islamic principles; secondly, Baha'is were punished for their position within the Shah's rule, with many Iranians believing Baha'is benefitted from a position of privilege under the Shah;[158] and thirdly, there exists suspicion regarding the motivation of the Baha'i community, with the perception that Baha'is are under the control of foreign agents. This suspicion is furthered by the spiritual home of Baha'is.[159] Indeed, "the Baha'is' association, in the minds of Iran's new leaders, with Iran's bitter history of foreign interference in its domestic affairs made them a target of suspicion",[160] a suspicion that is inherent within the Islamic Republic.

Due to this suspicion of Baha'is across Iran, the regime restricted Baha'i space on religious grounds. Moreover, in the immediate aftermath of the revolution, the regime executed "more than 200 adherents to the faith in the first six years of the revolution".[161] Furthermore, the Islamic Republic engaged in a programme of persecution against individual members of the Baha'i community, permitting little toleration of organised religious activities. Since 1983, "Baha'i assemblies have been banned, and participation in Baha'i activities, such as festivals or acts of worship in private homes is liable to prosecution".[162] As such, discrimination against the Baha'is is widespread. A Human Rights Watch report detailing the persecution of Baha'is demonstrates how discrimination occurs in all public spheres, reflected in the permanent dismissal from public office and governmental organisations for individuals found to be Baha'i.[163] Discrimination has pervaded civil society as a whole, with assets and private property confiscated, cemeteries raided, and no political or legal recourse.[164] Baha'is cannot vote and are excluded from all forms of representation; they "constitute legal and political non-persons, suffering total civil non-existence since 1979".[165] In a report carried out by the UN Special Rapporteur on the Question of Religious Intolerance in 1995, Tehran initially posited Baha'is as "a political sect historically linked to the Shah's regime",[166] whose persecution was attributed to the work of extremist groups with an anti-Baha'i agenda. However, the Special Rapporteur referred to documents such as the 1991 memorandum from the Supreme Revolutionary Cultural Council, which "clearly delineate[d] an official policy of persecution",[167] demonstrating the institutionalisation of discrimination within the Islamic Republic.

An Official Policy of Persecution?

Religious persecution does not solely fall on the Baha'is. All minorities are encouraged to convert to Shi'i Islam, as demonstrated by the inheritance law. If a child born into a religious minority family converts to Islam, all of the parents property and wealth is automatically given to him, at the expense of other siblings.[168] Furthermore, as noted in the Human Rights Watch report, while persecution and discrimination against Orthodox Christians, Jews and Zoroastrians is not widely reported, it is perhaps naive to hold that is does not occur.[169]

Moreover, it may be that those minorities who look to the international community for assistance are, in turn, subjecting themselves to increased suffering at the hands of the regime. While Baha'is and

Protestants have sought international protection and attempted to increase international awareness of their plight, Orthodox Christians, Jews and Zoroastrians have managed relations with the regime through dialogue. Moreover, those religious minorities with a history of proselytizing appear to suffer discrimination and persecution more than those minorities who remain within their religious, ethnic, and cultural borders. It can thus be deduced that the regime in Tehran is tolerant of religious groups who do not seek to undermine or challenge the Shi'i identity of the Islamic Republic.

Conclusions

The existence of religious identity incongruence within Saudi Arabia and Iran challenges the ideological sovereignty of each state. While both Saudi Arabia and Iran proclaim their dominance within the Islamic world as the leading Islamic state and bastion of Islamic values, the role of Islam within each state differs greatly.

While religion is perhaps not as engrained within the institutional fabric of Saudi Arabia as within Iran, there is no denying that Wahhabist zeal has a strong impact upon the rule of the Al Saud. The Al Saud uses Wahhabism and Islamic values as a way of both securing and increasing the legitimacy of their rule. However, the somewhat arbitrary use of *fatwas* has gone some way to undermine the Islamic credentials of both the government-endorsed *ulama* and the Al Saud regime. Further, in engaging in acts criticised by Wahhabist ideology as *bid'a*, the ruling elites are open to serious criticism from both Islamic fundamentalists and liberalists.

In contrast to opposition groups in Iran, which can be immediately portrayed as anti-Islamic, the Al Saud remains open to criticisms from an Islamic sphere. Indeed, despite the alliance with Wahhabism, which was hoped would circumvent Islamic opposition, the Al Saud is often criticised for its lack of religious piety and for engaging in the practice of *bid'a.* As such, reference to Islamic legitimacy seeks to remove Islamic criticisms.

Within Iran, the nature of *velayat-e faqih* and Ayatollah Khomeini's assertion that this form of government is the manifestation of Allah's government on Earth means that the impact of Shi'ism upon the policy making of the state is undeniable. The enshrinement of the Shari'a within the Iranian constitution solidifies Islam within the fabric of the state, supported by the checks and balances contained within the political construction of *velayat-e faqih*.

The idea that governmental laws and decrees are tantamount to the laws and decrees of Allah has the consequence that those organisations who oppose the state are portrayed as "un-Islamic", thus removing a level of criticism and positing an immediate response to anti-regime rhetoric. The ability to discredit such opposition is a useful tool at the regime's disposal. The very existence of other religious organisations within Iran, although protected by the constitution, appears to be nothing more than appeasement, easily circumvented if posing threats to the security of the Islamic Republic. Those religions with inherent proselytizing objectives appear most susceptible to persecution and a reduction in political and religious space. This appears to be a direct result of the *bid'a* nature of converting from Islam, and the notion that such proselytizing could pose a threat to the ideological sovereignty of the regime.

It can thus be seen that identity incongruence within the religious sphere challenges the ideological sovereignty of both Saudi Arabia and Iran. In addition, it is important to note the suspicion that both Saudi Arabia and Iran allay to the other, with focus upon the relationship that each state has with the respective minority contained within the other. Indeed, the suspicion towards the Shi'a within Saudi Arabia and the perception of an alliance with Iran has increased tensions between the two. This fear has been exacerbated by the events in Bahrain, where Riyadh has sought to secure the Al Khalifa regime and to prevent democratic reforms that would favour the Shi'a of Bahrain amidst concerns that these reforms would then be demanded by the Shi'a of Saudi Arabia. This shows how the ideological sphere feeds into the geopolitical sphere. Further, the perception of Saudi support for Sunnis with Iran has increased suspicion of the Al Saud within Iran. This perception can be coupled with a concern that both Saudi Arabia and Iran seek to export their interpretation of Islam beyond their borders, increasing legitimacy domestically and across the *umma*.

Yet, one must question whether this desire to proselytize is purely to export religious beliefs, or whether support for religious minorities across the region has a two-fold agenda: firstly, to assert dominance over the region and, secondly, to circumvent religious criticisms and unrest in the domestic environment by expelling vociferous opponents of the regime. In undertaking this agenda, states are, thus, also manipulating the internal security dilemmas of other states.

While it is undeniable that both Saudi Arabia and Iran, in the guise of Wahhabism and Twelver Shi'ism, seek to export their respective interpretations of Islam, there is a strong argument to be made that support for religious groups in other states is an attempt to draw attention away from domestic problems. The distinction between exporting and expelling religious groups occurs in greater detail in chapter six. However, regardless of intent, the consequences have a serious impact upon the external security dilemma.

5

ETHNO-TRIBAL INCONGRUENCE

Building upon the discussion of religious groups in chapter four, chapter five explores challenge to the state from ethnic and tribal groups. Saudi Arabia's ethnic population is predominantly comprised of ethno-tribal groups, although there does exist a large expatriate community comprising of workers from the eastern subcontinent, Africa and Western Europe. While there are many tribes located within the borders of Saudi Arabia, it is not possible to cover all tribes, especially given the processes of detribalisation employed by the Al Saud, so focus will be upon the major tribal groups. The chapter shall discuss the following themes: the formation of a national identity; an examination of major tribes currently located within Saudi Arabia; the importance of tribal values; a history of tribalism across the Arabian Peninsula, including the role played by tribes in the formation of the state; detribalisation policies; the impact of tribes upon domestic and foreign policy; and an examination of the expatriate community.

Building a Saudi Arabian Identity

At the turn of the twentieth century, within Saudi Arabia "the principle political unit was the tribe, decentralized and egalitarian in nature".[1] With the formation of the third state in 1932, Saudi Arabia underwent vast changes, both in terms of state-society relations and in terms of structure, notably the destruction of autonomous tribes. Given the tribal nature of society prior to 1932, such social changes proved necessary in order to facilitate the state-building process at a national level. Structural changes occurred through "bureaucratic expansion, occupational differentiation, sedentarisation of tribes, urbanization, demographic growth, and impressive rates of economic development".[2] Indeed, the existence of such decentralised and nomadic organisations posed difficulties to the notion of a coherent national identity. Attempts to foster a Saudi Arabian identity, according to Joseph Nevo, built upon a "strict observance of Islam and, of course, on loyalty to the House of Saud".[3] The Al Saud sought to create an environment wherein loyalty to the Al Saud is tantamount to loyalty to the state and, conversely, where opposition to the ruling family is taken to be opposition to the state.

The Tribes of Saudi Arabia

It is an oft-held assumption within Saudi Arabia that tribalism poses a "threat to integrity of the state and its ability to extract allegiance from its citizens",[4] particularly given a sense of divided loyalty between King and local Sheikh. However, before examining the role of tribes within the formation of Saudi Arabia, it is crucial to consider what is understood by the term "tribe". For Joseph Kostiner, the tribe is:

> a political unit that was identified or appeared in historiographical accounts as such. It consisted of a group of people who shared a common territorial base, true or mythological kinship ties, and a corporate existence. The members' political allegiance was to the tribe and in return they received physical and economic protection and social status.[5]

The concept of a tribe is not a recent construct; rather, the the tribe has historically provided organisational structure for social and political life in the Arabian Peninsula.[6] Building upon the aforementioned definition of tribalism is a caveat from Eleanor Doumato: "In the peninsula, a tribe is a group defined by perceived descent from a common male ancestor [...] Descent from one of two eponymous, Arab ancestors, Adnan or Qahtan".[7]

Historically, Saudi Arabia possessed no centralized state structure, with political organisation found in the socio-economic conditions of "pastoral nomadism, intercepted by smaller-scale urban and agricultural settlements".[8] Indeed, "[p]olitical microcosms revolved around tribal groups whose legitimacy rested on descent";[9] tribes whose legitimacy rests on descent are referred to as *qabila*.

Members of a *qabila* tribe, who claim higher status through purity of blood and origins, often "feel themselves superior to the non-tribal Khadiri, [. . .] who cannot claim such descent".[10] Indeed, these feelings of superiority result in marriage between members of *qabila* and *khadiri* tribes being frowned upon, given the consequences for the purity of blood.

It is widely accepted that there are two types of tribes: the *hatr* (sedentarised) and the nomadic, henceforth referred to as Bedouin, from the Arabic, *badawi*, meaning desert dweller. The Bedouin have experienced vast socio-economic and socio-political changes, through both the formation of the modern state and the economic transformation of Saudi Arabia, stemming from the discovery of oil. Indeed, these changes have occurred at home within the desert and also within new urban bases, in villages, towns and cities.[11]

Donald Cole, in an article discussing the location of the modern-day Bedouin, suggests that the evolution of the Bedouin has resulted in a move from a way of life to an identity, driven by heritage and culture.[12] This evolution occurred with the process of sedentarisation and settlement, moving from rearing livestock to agriculture. These changes were exacerbated by the speed of migration across Saudi Arabia between the 1950s and 1980s, and a reduction in Bedouin space, spanning administration of territory, "tribal legalities and the psycho-cultural implications".[13]

According to socio-economic indicators such as infant mortality, literacy and wealth, Bedouin in the 1950s were in the lower echelons of Arab societies across the region. As such, Bedouin life was not without difficulties; in particular, access to resources could prove problematic in times of drought or disease. This demonstrates the deficiency of pastoral nomadism, which is a result of "the unstable ecological conditions [along with] the vulnerability of animals",[14] which was previously overcome through theft of cattle. A key problem within this time was access to water.

Interestingly, despite the apparent demise of the Bedouin way of life and increasing sedentarisation of tribes across the Arabian Peninsula, Cole highlights the increased use of tribal names as surnames. The use of tribal surnames is important for individuals, in terms of social standing derived from tribal descent, couped with a historical Bedouin connection.[15] This Bedouin connection evokes a shared sense of common history and sub-culture, which has the capacity to cut across tribal boundaries.[16]

An important Bedouin tribe is the Shammar, led by the Al Rashid have played an important role in the history of the Arabian Peninsula. Indeed, the Al Rashid have historically posed a strong challenge to the Al Saud, destabalising the second Saudi state in 1891.[17] Several of Shammar lineages, the Al Rashid included, were semi-nomadic and mainted oasis gardens during parts of the year, while grazing animals in the desert during other parts.[18] It is suggested by Madawi Al-Rasheed that the Al Rashid possessed a political structure contingent solely upon tribal allegiances and descent, [19] lacking any religious ideology, in contrast to the Al Saud.[20] In addition to destabalising the second Saudi state in 1891, the Shammar and Al Rashid were opposed to the expansionist ideals of Ibn Saud and again offered resistance. However, unlike their ancestors, the Al Rashid of the early twentieth century were unsuccessful. As a consequence, when attempting to unite the tribes of Arabia, Ibn Saud and his descendents took several women from the Rashidi tribe as wives, which fostered "the development of kinship ties with the ruling group".[21] One of these marriages resulted in the birth of Abdullah, who would become the sixth king of Saudi Arabia.

The Role of Tribal Values

While tribal power diminished under Ibn Saud, tribal values remained and played an integral role within the state-building process. Indeed, "informal tribal practices loomed behind the bureaucratic procedures and institutions".[22] Institutional development, combined with certain other factors, including a centralisation of power in Riyadh, the growth of urban populations and an increase in the ease of travel also resulted in a diluting of tribal power. Alongside these developments, tribal leaders and chiefs became large landowners and consequently became upper class.[23] Conversely:

> many rank-and-file tribal members formed the bulk of the Saudi lower class [. . .] Devoid of sufficient skills, education, and income, tribal groups either settled in shacks on the outskirts of major cities or maintained a nomadic or agricultural life-style. The dissonance between their traditional ways and modernization led many to dissatisfaction with the new lavishness and Westernization, and they became alienated.[24]

The Al Saud's attempt to increase both legitimacy and support has led to the establishment of networks of support, associated with tribal leaders. It is through these networks that Kostiner suggests tribal values have the capacity to ease tensions between different levels of the state and have played a key role in the process of state building.

One such way this has been achieved is through the tribal *Majlis*, which has served as an unofficial forum for many. General sessions of the *Majlis* are said to last 40 minutes, with around 100 people present. A standard session of the *Majlis* contains a speech from the King on a specific issue, then those present are permitted to raise their concerns, often financially motivated, or to pledge their allegiance.[25] Despite the perception of some who hold that the *Majlis* is a form of democratic representation, this is incorrect. The ability to express views and opinions to a ruler is not tantamount to having an input into the decision-making process. Furthermore, the Wahhabi *ulama* perceive that sovereignty is derived from God, rather than understandings of popular sovereignty, which is derived from the people, making democracy appear incompatible with the Saudi political system.

An integral component of tribalism and of the Saudi state as a whole is that of *asabiyya*, "defined as zealous partisanship [. . .] party spirit, team spitit, espirit de corps [. . .] tribal solidarity, racialism, clannishness, tribalism".[26] The notion of *asabiyya* dates back to the work of Ibn Khaldun, which is incredibly important within tribal societies and the process of state building within these societies. As such, several passages from his work, *The Muqaddimah,* are worth quoting in full. When discussing security, Khaldun feels a collective can only be successful in their goals if the collective is a close-knit group, as this "strengthens their stamina and makes them feared, since everybody's affection for his family and group is more important".[27] If this is true with regard to protecting the homestead, he argues, "it is equally true with regard to every other human activity, such as prophecy, the establishment of royal authority, or propaganda".[28]

According to Khaldun, group feeling stems from blood ties, as found in the Qur'an and the words of the Prophet: "Learn as much of your pedigrees as is necessary to establish your ties of blood relationship".[29] The notion of pedigree implies closeness, derived from blood ties, which will eventually result in affection. However, the impact of *asabiyya* upon an established state appears less important. Indeed, after the firm establishment of a dynasty, Khaldun suggests that group feeling can be dispensed with on the grounds that "people find it difficult to submit to large dynastic (power) at the beginning, unless they are forced into submission by strong superiority".[30] For Khaldun, "royal authority results from superiority. Superiority results from group feeling. Only by God's help in establishing this religion do individual desires come together in agreement to press their claims, and hearts become united".[31]

Kostiner also stresses the importance and legacy of tribal values within the fabric of the Saudi Arabian state and in the state-building process: "they suited the patrimonial regime, which left the old social structure intact [. . .] In government decision making, informed tribal practices loomed behind the bureaucratic procedures and institutions".[32] Moreover, tribal customs and values have been emphasized as positive credentials both personally and socially.[33]

Thus, tribalism proved the bedrock of power, pointing "towards a tangible and ongoing role for tribal-kinship relations in contemporary, day–to-day sociopolitics".[34] Furthermore, tribal importance is reflected in the official title of the King, which possesses several aspects to develop loyalty: firstly, that of King; secondly, the protector of the Two Holy Places, to include that of the *shayk al-mashayikh*, or chief of the tribal chiefs.[35]

The Role of the Tribe in State-Building

The importance of tribalism in the formation of the third Saudi state cannot be denied. Through the use of force and an alliance with an Islamic ideology, "the Saudis created a state and prompted a 'general loyalty towards themselves as a kind of super tribe'".[36] Through tying tribal and religious ideologies together, Ibn Saud attempted to transcend localised tribal loyalties. Indeed, the success of the state-building process owed much to tribal imperatives. Yet, as Champion observes, it is remarkable that within such an entrenched tribal society, one tribe was able to exert control over the others.

During the formative years of the twentieth century, Saudi Arabian society remained in tribal groupings across the northern parts of the Arabian Peninsula, each of whom possessed a corporate life. This form of society was organised under the system of chieftaincy, which was based upon the notion of power sharing between tribes, urban populations and an urban-based ruler. This maintained both the autonomy of different regions and stability of state-tribe relations.[37] Tribes possessed a strong military power across the Peninsula, demonstrated by Kostiner's observation that tribal forces provided security for trade convoys and fought the enemies of the Al Saud, while expanding its territorial base.[38] In addition to a military role, tribal forces were seen as value leaders, often exporting these values during the process of military expansion.

However, during the consolidation period of state formation, it was necessary to address the burgeoning power of the tribes. Kostiner refers to the work of H. St John Philby, an advisor to Ibn Saud and former British emissary, who articulated how "Ibn Saud fully exploited the Wahhabi right to marry four women. By divorcing and remarrying frequently, he and his relatives were able to bind many tribes to the Saudi family".[39] One measure employed by Ibn Saud was that of strategic tribal inter-marriage, whereby key members of the Al Saud married women from rival tribes and families to foster support.[40] This process of inter-tribal marriage was undertaken in a manner that sought to foster dependency and marginalisation, and to break the internal cohesion of opposing tribes. The consequences of the process of inter-tribal marriage can be seen in present day Saudi Arabia, through the size of the ruling family.

One further way Ibn Saud sought to circumvent the challenge posed by tribal groups while utilising tribal support was the creation of the *ikhwan*, a standing army, who possessed three main qualities: traditional military prowess, religious fervour, and detachment from the restraints of positions of office. Indeed, "as pioneers, zealous proselytizers, and promoters of sedentarization, the *ikhwan* were also the centre of Saudi nonmilitary expansion".[41]

The *ikhwan* played an integral role within the formation of Saudi Arabia, expanding both territorial and ideological boundaries. The *ikhwan* were constituted of tribal groups, chosen by Ibn Saud, who were asked to abandon their Bedouin principles, convert to Islam and settle, in "special agricultural settlements created for them to lead a religiously inspired life",[42] called *hujar*. The ensuing description courtesy of John Habib serves to illustrate the *ikhwan* well:

> Those Bedouins who accepted the fundamentals of orthodox Islam of the Habali school as preached by Abdl Wahhab which their fathers and forefathers had forgotten or had perverted and who through the persuasion of the religious missionaries and with the material assistance of Adbl-Aziz abandoned their nomadic life in the Hirah which were built for them.[43]

The formation of the *ikhwan*, according to Kostiner, constituted a three-fold victory for Ibn Saud: neutralising inherent Bedouin aggression, harnessing a military prowess, and facilitating the proliferation of Wahhabi doctrine. Indeed, the *ikhwan* would serve to entrench both the religious and ideological beliefs of the Wahhabi *ulama* within the Najd region.[44]

Typical portraits of the *ikhwan* paint them as "bold fighters, fanatical and absolutely devoted to their country and to the spread of Wahhabi tenets [. . .] the *ikhwan* were expected to be warriors, farmers, and students of religion; they were not expected to play a role in politics and decision making".[45] The *ikhwan*, however, saw scope for evolution and improvement upon their previous position: "they were pioneers in sedentarization, zealous advocates of revivalism, and agitators for expansion [...and] played important roles in both expanding and consolidating functions, despite the looseness of their organisation".[46] Leaders of the movement perceived scope for political influence, transcending their role as a proselytizing tribal force. In addition to this, the development of a centralised infrastructure resulted in fears concerning the loss of tribal autonomy. The combination of ambition and fear would manifest itself in the *ikhwan* rebellion, subsequently crushed by the Al Saud, with British assistance, in 1929.[47]

Detribalisation Policies

Political organisation prior to the emergence of a centralised Saudi state was found in the socio-economic conditions of "pastoral nomadism, intercepted by smaller-scale urban and agricultural settlements".[48] Given the tribal distribution across Saudi Arabia in the early twentieth century, it would be difficult to refer to Saudi Arabia as a nation-state. Although one could define Saudi Arabia as a nation on the grounds of possessing a shared ethnicity or religion, this was undermined through the underpinnings of loyalty to the tribe. As such, as part of the state-building process it was necessary to break the power of tribal groups, through engaging in a process of detribalisation. The key aim of detribalisation policies was to achieve the "transformation of Saudi Arabia from a tribal polity to an established monarchical state",[49] in doing so achieving a secondary aim, namely reducing challenges to the regime emanating from tribal groups.

Policies of detribalisation aiming to strengthen the centralized nature of the state have a history stemming back to 1925, when Ibn Saud "abolished the exclusive rights of tribes in their own *diras* (territory)".[50] This was not a policy aimed at transferring ownership rights; rather, it was non-recognition by the state of the traditional power of tribal rulers over their own territories. Thus, the state intervened in areas that had traditionally been the domain of local tribal rule,[51] leading to an inability of tribal leaders to protect members of their own tribes or to manage resources located within communal areas. As outlined by Madawi Al-Rasheed and Loulouwa Al-Rasheed, this was a double-pronged attack on the tribes, consisting of both "overt confrontation and economic dependency".[52]

These detribalisation policies impacted upon social structure, especially social differentiation, as "the intervention of a centralized state alters the nature of the available resources and modes of access to them, thereby creating the possibility of wider inequalities".[53] Indeed, altering the availability of and access to resources would also reach into the realm of private property, which as Ugo Fabietti suggests, replaced the "traditional collective right of access to the land".[54] Fabietti details increases in inequality stemming from the emergence of a market for land; undeniably, these inequalities were further widened with the flowing of oil revenues.[55] Prior to oil revenues, finance was raised through custom dues, and dues levied on pilgrimages to Mecca,[56] demonstrating the importance of Islam within the early days of the Kingdom, while also cementing Ibn Saud's role as protector and regulator of the Holy Places. Further demonstrating the importance of religion within the Saudi state, Wahhabism undermined the autonomy of tribal leaders, which contributed to the state-building process, solidifying the rule of Ibn Saud in political, economic, social and military spheres.[57]

Gregory Gause suggests that the Al Saud employed three strategies to lessen dependence upon tribal loyalties: firstly, cultivating support from urban populations; secondly, fostering relations at the international level; and thirdly, utilising income from the sale of oil to shift the balance of power within the Kingdom.[58] There initially existed geographical restraints upon state authority within Saudi Arabia, as the geographical construction of the state facilitated tribal autonomy. As such, support from townsfolk proved important, both in ensuring the security of towns under the control of the Al Saud and in offering continued support in the face of fluid alliances with the tribes.

The second of Gause's strategies was to form alliances at the international level, and although Ibn Saud never entered into a formal protectorate treaty with Britain, it is undeniable that Saudi Arabia benefitted from relations with Britain. Indeed, the British played an important role, both helping Ibn Saud defeat his Al Rasheed tribal rivals (who received support from Ottoman rulers) and also to survive the economic crisis of the 1930s, when the global depression severely impacted on the revenues gained from the *Hajj*.[59]

The third way the Al Saud was able to retain power and control over the Arabian Peninsula was through use of oil reserves:

> Oil reserves [. . .] decisively shifted the balance of power away from tribal structures and towards the state. With oil money, the rulers ceased to rely upon local groupings – tribal or urban – for financial support. They now had money to give away, or better, to bargain for political loyalty and service. Tribal leaders were put on state payrolls, with generous regular salaries replacing the irregular and less lucrative subsidies of the past. Their ability to provide for their tribesmen has come to depend on the state, rather than their own and tribal resources. Tribal shayks have become salaried employees of the state.[60]

The last two sentences of this quote are especially relevant: through not being able to protect and provide for their tribesmen independently, the authority of tribal sheikhs was greatly reduced.

One can see the successes of detribalisation policies when considering the Rashidi tribe. In early twentieth-century Arabia, there existed two rival dynasties competing for power: one using Ibn Khaldun's concept of *asabiyya*, the other utilizing religious fervour. The rivalry between the two also included different political structures. The Rashidi political system was constituted by "political centralization, tribal loyalties, and a multi-resource economy consisting of pastoral nomadism, smaller-scale agriculture and trade".[61] After overcoming the challenge posed by the Al Rashid and killing the leaders, Ibn Saud "immediately announced himself the ruler of the town. Using Wahhabism to cast legitimacy over his leadership, he then endeavoured to spread his domination over most of the Arabian Peninsula".[62]

Once the Al Rashid dynasty was defeated, the tribe was marginalized and subjected to inter-tribal marriage in an attempt to foster a semblance of loyalty and ties between the two rival tribes. This marginalisation is still in existence; indeed, at times of crises, prominent members of the Al Rashid have been arrested, which has was seen in the aftermath of the assassination of King Faisal in 1975.[63]

Madawi Al-Rasheed outlines the process of marginalisation against her ancestors thus:

> Deprived of their confiscated wealth in Hail, the last Rashidi rulers were accommodated in homes in Riyadh. They received monthly food rations and provisions from Ibn Saud's treasury through his ministry of finance. The general rule was that these rations would cover the needs of each household without allowing for lavish entertainment and excessive socializing comparable to what had been experienced in Hail. Ibn Saud's policy was to limit the deposed rulers' ability to entertain large crowds who would be attracted by an overt display of generosity, a method most appropriate for building a leader's reputation in the cultural political context of Arabia.[64]

The process of marginalisation from the position of viable tribal leaders occurs as tribal leaders are neither able to reward loyalty, nor are they able to "compete with what the state and its hydrocarbon prince(s) can offer".[65] Indeed, as Gause articulates, while previously tribal leaders provided security for their members, "the state has now assumed that role".[66] Despite the marginalisation of the Al Rasheed, the state maintains recognition of the former status of the tribe, notably through public displays of respect in the *Majlis* and use of "special rhetoric that portrays and maintains their position as one of the status groups",[67] which also serves to restore dignity. Madawi Al-Rasheed and Loulouwa Al-Rasheed argue that, despite attempts at marginalisation, direct and excessive opposition of tribal leaders could prove detrimental to security and legitimacy, given the importance of tribal loyalty in the country; moreover, stating that the violation of tribal honour through humiliation is unacceptable.[68]

Yet, despite the attempts to reduce and remove threats posed by tribal groups, tribalism remains an important legitimising tool for the Al Saud. Indeed, public relations with tribal leaders occur in the

Majlis, where tribal traditions are clear.[69] Moreover, items of tribal dress, in particular the *thobe* and *kuffiya*, are often used to further the perception of most important tribal ruler within the Kingdom, again demonstrating the importance of tribal structures. This agenda strives to recapture aspects of life lost or in decline since the oil era, and also to "connect the political system with those cultural manifestations, as a way of asserting the authenticity of the monarchical-tribal form of these societies".[70] Furthermore, the ruling elites encourage subjects to perceive themselves as tribesmen as part of Champion's idea of a super-tribe, with the chain of loyalties culminating in the King,[71] in an attempt to foster national unity.

Expatriates in the Kingdom

The Kingdom of Saudi Arabia is home, either permanently or temporarily, to a large expatriate population. Although precise information is difficult to ascertain, it is possible to arrive at rough figures. Hassan Al-Husseini, an ex Saudi Aramco Senior Planning Consultant and writer, who claims to have seen Labour Ministry statistics, alleges that the number of expatriate workers in 2009 was 8.8 million.[72] This figure was 6 million in 1999, and 3 million in 1989; in comparison, Al-Husseini posits the number of male Saudis working in 2009 at 3 million.[73] Furthermore, over half of the expatriate number live in the two main cities of Saudi Arabia, Riyadh and Jeddah.[74] Expatriate workers can be segregated into three groups, according to language: Arabic, English, and other. Of this expatriate population, 6 million are Muslim, some of whom illegally stayed on the back of *Hajj* visits, 1.5 million are Christian, and 1.3 million are Hindu (or other).[75]

This expatriate population poses several problems for the Al Saud. Despite working in the state, all are disenfranchised. In addition, a large percentage of this number is from Asia, working in low-paid jobs. Stemming from this, there exists a concern that the presence of such a large number of non-Arab, and in 2.8 million cases, non-Muslim workforce will erode the cultural values and integrity of the state. This is especially a concern with regard to those expatriate workers within the childcare field.

Moreover, such a large expatriate presence may increase pressure on a Saudi workforce already buckling under the pressure of a demographic time bomb, reflected in rising unemployment and an increasingly educated population. As Mohammed Bosbait and Rodney Wilson outline, there have been great increases in the number of university students, although this education programme does not appear to be adequately equipping graduates for employment.[76] In addition, a large percentage of Saudi nationals are employed within the public sector. This stems from a reluctance of Saudi businessmen to hire their own nationals, "partly because Saudis have higher wage expectations and it is less flexible to employ permanent staff than expatriates on temporary contracts".[77] This, in turn, has the capacity to create bloated, inefficient bureaucracies.

Furthermore, the Saudi population is becoming increasingly aware of the economic challenges facing the Kingdom, with David Pollock detailing how within his research a "majority of urban citizens in this oil-rich country name inflation, unemployment, or poverty as Saudi Arabia's most important national priority".[78]

In light of the "Arab Spring" of 2011, the Al Saud were concerned that these economic challenges would result in uprisings across the Kingdom, much like as in other states in the region. In an effort to prevent this, King Abdullah offered a welfare package totalling some $36 billion.[79] As Madawi al-Rasheed suggests, this was a somewhat "transparent attempt to appease the burgeoning youth population and deflect it from the lure of revolution – [through offering] public-sector salary increases, unemployment benefits, and subsidies for housing, education, and culture".[80] One potential consequence of this is preventing the development and diversification of the private sphere of the Saudi economy, through encouraging a further reliance upon oil revenues. This appears to be preventing the regime's goals as set out in the Ninth Five-Year Plan,[81] which targets the highest growth in 30 years.[82]

Iran

This discourse locates the Persian, Azeri, Kurdish, Baluchi, Arab and Turkmen ethnic groupings within the Iranian state. Despite an awareness of the existence of various ethnic groups within Iran, exact knowledge of their populations remains uncertain, stemming from Tehran's reluctance to release demographic information. As such, the location of ethnic groups within Iran will be achieved through an examination of historical backgrounds, with particular focus upon language and religion,[83] an examination of respective positions within the state, and the impact upon both domestic and foreign policy. In addition to the aforementioned Persians, Azeris, Kurds, Baluchis, Arabs and Turkmen, there exist several more ethnic groups within Iran.[84] These groups also have the capacity to impact upon both domestic and foreign policy, yet for the purposes of brevity, the analysis shall not cover their respective positions within the Islamic Republic. The discussion shall consider the ethnic groupings within Iran, which necessitates an analysis of the importance of language, while also building upon the discussion of religion located within chapter four.

Building an Iranian Identity

Attempts to generate a national identity tend to evoke references to shared characteristics, reflected in the definition of ethnicity offered by Max Weber below:

> [T]hose human groups that entertain a subjective belief in their common descent because of similarities of physical type or of customs or both, or because of memories of colonization and migration; this belief must be important for group formation; furthermore it does not matter whether an objective blood relationship exists.[85]

Weber's definition allows those responsible for creating national identity to refer to shared characteristics, be they of a physical or abstract definition. In creating a national identity in Iran, the regime utilises two separate strands, nationalism and religion, again stressing that Iranians are the children of Cyrus the Great and Mohammed.

It is germane to note that while the 1979 revolution utilised rhetoric stressing the universal and borderless nature of the Islamic Revolution, members of the Shi'i community across the region are not considered Iranian, which perhaps gives weight to the notion that nationalist identity is more essential to the state building process than religion. Indeed, it appears that nationalist sentiment is now combined with Islamic goals in an attempt to engender a coherent national identity, within clearly defined territorial boundaries.[86]

Farideh Farhi suggests that there are different ways of articulating identity, either through language, religion, ethnicity or territory.[87] Of these, it can be argued that only the territorial articulation serves to encapsulate the entire Iranian population.[88] While Shi'ism is the dominant religion within the Islamic Republic, there exist several identity groupings that subscribe to both different facets of Islam and to different religions entirely. Further, while Persian (also referred to as Farsi) is the official language of the state, there exist several additional languages spoken within certain provinces.

The 1979 revolution, combined with the war with Iraq, led to an increase in what Farhi has termed "hyphenated Iranianism": a growth in the number of Iranians with a hybrid identity.[89] Yet, although many served their country in the Iran–Iraq War, and faithfully adhered to *velayat-e faqih*, not all of these "hyphenated Iranians" possess the rights that Persians do. However, the rights of ethnic groups, including minorities, are protected by the Iranian constitution; in particular, there exist provisions to safeguard expression, association and culture, yet these "are rendered impotent by clauses that give primacy to ambiguous Islamic interests".[90]

Persians

Persians are the dominant ethnic group within Iran, an Indo-Aryan race comprising approximately 50 per cent of the Iranian population.[91] The Persian identity contains an inherent dichotomy of identity, torn between being the children of Cyrus the Great and of Muhammad,[92] which demonstrates a dichotomy between nationalist and Islamic identities. In fostering an Iranian identity, facets of the Persian identity are utilised, reflecting the prevalence of Persian culture and history. The formulation of an Iranian identity initially occurs on two levels: firstly, using Persian ethnicity, taken to be language, culture, history and mythology; and secondly, using Persian language.

The nationalistic aspect of efforts to engender a national identity often draw heavily on an understanding and appreciation of Persian history, which helps foster a sense of more than 2,000 years of shared history.[93] The second attempt to demonstrate a shared identity is reflected in the official language of Iran being Persian, as recognised by Article 15 of the Iranian constitution.[94]

Persians occupy privileged positions within Iran, often residing in more affluent areas and, under both monarchy and Islamic Republic, are the main beneficiaries of governmental economic and social policies.[95] Building on the prominence of Persians within Iran, Persians are often engaged in the process of ethnic redistribution, a process discussed later in the chapter. Furthermore, state attempts to foster a national identity often recount Persian history and mythology, as reflected in references to Cyrus the Great.

Azeris

After Persians, Azeris constitute the largest ethnic group in Iran, with a population estimated to be somewhere between 15 and 20 million.[96] The Azeri population is predominantly located within the northwest of Iran, in the provinces of East Azerbaijan, West Azerbaijan and Ardabil, an area of Iran sometimes referred to as Southern Azerbaijan.[97] Azeris are predominantly Shi'a, thus possessing an affinity with the dominant Persian group. Azeris have played a prominent role within Iranian life, dating back to the Safavid Empire of the early sixteenth century. Iranian and Azeri histories have long been interlinked. Azerbaijan had previously been located within the borders of Persian empires until its incorporation into the Russian empire at the turn of the nineteenth century.[98] A series of treaties followed, which resulted in the cultural and geopolitical divide of Azerbaijan between Russia and Iran, with Russian-controlled areas becoming the Republic of Azerbaijan in 1991.[99]

Azeris are often considered as the most integrated of all ethnic groups within Iranian society. The importance of the role played by

Azeris be seen today as the current Supreme Leader, Ayatollah Ali Khamenei, is an ethnic Azeri. The Azeri language is spoken both in Azerbaijan and northwest Iran. However, Azeris are also subject of much prejudice within Iran, particularly from Persians, who view Azeris as the "muscle" of the Iranian economy, while perceiving themselves as the "brains". Indeed, this is reflected in the phrase "*torki khar*", the Turkish donkey,[100] which is directed at the Azeris.

Within the Azeri community, the main grievances against the regime in Tehran are a consequence of discrimination within the cultural sphere. Indeed, "Azaris {sic} complain that there is no Azari language instruction in schools for Azari children and no department of Azari literature in any Iranian university",[101] a point supported by Nasib Nassibli, who suggests that "Persian chauvinism" has sought to destroy the Azeri language.[102] Further, this restriction of cultural space has manifested itself in the Iranian media, in particular through a caricature depicting a cockroach speaking Azeri Turkish.[103] This caricature provoked rioting across the Azeri-dominated areas of Iran, particularly within the city of Tabriz.

Restrictions on space also are found within the political sphere, which can be seen in the case of Dr Muhammad Ali Chehregani, a candidate for Tabriz's seat in the 1996 elections for the *Majlis*. Dr Chehregani, a professor of linguistics at Tabriz University, based his campaign on issues of cultural discrimination, in particular of discrimination against Azeri culture. Dr Chehregani advocated the teaching of the Azeri language as a second language in Azeri areas, rather than Arabic, along with the recognition of Azeris as Iranian rather than Persian. This is a nuanced position advocating the adoption of a state identity, rather than an ethnic or national identity.[104] Indeed, while all Persians are Iranians, not all Iranians are Persians.

In the first round of voting, Dr Chehregani proved to be popular with the electorate, becoming one of the leading candidates. However, before the second round of voting, Dr Chehregani's name was removed from the ballot paper, resulting in large protests within Tabriz. The removal of Dr Chehregani's name was perhaps because of criticisms of the position of a Persian identity as tantamount to Iranian identity, and the apparent challenge to the nationalist narrative.

One must note the importance of Azeris, and also of Azerbaijan, with regard to the making of Iranian foreign policy. Azerbaijan is embroiled in two territorial disputes of a contradictory nature, in both of which Iran is heavily involved. First is the issue of Nagorno-Karabakh, an autonomous region of Azerbaijan, which is home to a large ethnic Armenian population. Given the location of ethnic Armenians within Azerbaijan, Armenia has laid claim to the Nagorno-Karabakh region, a claim Azerbaijan rejects on the grounds of "the sanctity of historic state borders and territorial integrity".[105] Second is the issue within what has been termed by some as Southern Azerbaijan, or Azeri populated provinces of northwest Iran. Azerbaijani irredentists argue that a split of North and South Azerbaijan is "a tragedy that split an ethnic group in half, and a wrong which must be corrected".[106] While these are obviously contradictory positions for some Azeris in Baku to hold, Tehran's policy towards both Azerbaijan and its own Azeri population is also convoluted. Despite religious ties between Iran and Azerbaijan, Iran sided with Christian Armenia in the dispute over the Nagorno-Karabakh region, regardless of the fact that most Iranian Azeris sided with Azerbaijan,[107] on grounds of both ethnic and religious affiliation. Tehran held this position in an attempt to maintain its own territorial integrity, which it holds as imperative for defining its national identity, while also engaging in a form of *real-politik*, countering Azeri gains through supporting Armenia.[108]

Kurds

The Kurds constitute a large ethnic group within Iran, located within the west and northwest of the country, also located within the Zagros Mountains. The Zagros Mountains are home to an ethnic group considered "the largest ethnic group in the world that occupies a geographically compact area and has no nation-state of its own".[109] Most Kurds are Sunni Muslims, an "aggravating factor in the Kurds' relations with the Shi'i central authorities in Iran".[110]

Kurds possess a strong military heritage,[111] stemming from centuries of conflict with neighbouring empires such as the Assyrians, Persians and Greeks.[112] Given the migration of a plethora of empires through the mountain range historically housing the Kurds, it is undeniable that certain cultural aspects must remain, notably facets of Persian language and Zoroastrian beliefs.[113]

Although the majority of Kurds are Sunni Muslims, there exist several other religious coteries within the Kurdish community, notably Christians, Jews and Zoroastrians.[114] Tribal ties play a prominent role in the organisation of Kurdish society, stemming from the lack of overarching authority, although these tribal ties are not clearly defined.[115] Some authors suggest that the nature of tribal life is derived from military organisation, stemming from centuries of fighting.[116] Despite a lack of definition of tribal ties, it is widely held that tribes are subdivided into clans, then further into families.[117] It is, however, worth noting that the Kurds are not a united ethnic group, despite transcending national boundaries. Although sharing common characteristics and ideals, there is no universal Kurdish language, and further undermining Kurdish unity are strong tribal ties that supersede loyalty to a larger transnational group.

Yet there do exist a variety of grievances that have proved to be rallying points for Kurdish dissent and resistance. These include issues in the social, economic, cultural and political spheres.[118] Kurdish resistance is notoriously vociferous within Turkey and Iraq, yet it is within Iran that the Kurds were able to establish an autonomous nation-state, albeit temporarily.[119] The demise of the Mahabad Republic forced members of the Democratic Party of Iranian Kurdistan (KDPI) to seek refuge, as a consequence of Tehran's quest to "suppress all traces of Kurdish national identity".[120]

Despite initially being supportive of the revolution of 1979 as a consequence of the Shah's penchant for crushing all forms of opposition, in particular from ethnic groups,[121] the Kurds continue to feel ostracized under the Islamic regime in Tehran. Indeed, post revolution, open conflict occurred between Kurdish factions, in particular the KDPI and security forces, notably the Revolutionary Guard. Tehran attempted to crush this manifestation of opposition through various means; one such method involved the use of revolutionary courts, the likes of which were chaired by Islamic judges of the ilk of Ayatollah Khalkhadi.[122]

In an attempt to reduce threats emanating from Kurdish areas, Tehran stationed large numbers of troops within Kurdish homelands, with some sources suggesting these numbers totalled 200,000.[123] Moreover, around 200 Kurdish villages were destroyed during the 1980s, with that number increasing dramatically during the early 1990s.[124]

Kurdish parties, opposed to the regime in Tehran, allege that the Islamic Republic is responsible for the deaths of numerous Kurds. Furthermore, the KDPI alleges that Iranian military units stationed within Kurdish areas have been known to force women into temporary marriage, a procedure tolerated within Shi'ism, but abhorred by Sunni Muslims.[125]

In addition to a military presence within Kurdish areas, Tehran has attempted to restrict the cultural space of the Kurds, highlighted by the careful censoring of the Centre for the Propagation of Kurdish Culture and Literature, and the imprisonment of prominent Kurdish academics.[126] This restriction spills into the political domain, with Kurdish candidates for the *Majlis* often rejected on grounds of prior allegiance with the KDPI.[127]

The Kurdish population within Iran poses several problems for Tehran, in particular challenging the territorial sovereignty of the state. While not all Kurds favour secession, or the creation of an autonomous Kurdish state, such sentiments do exist. Further, given the transnational presence of Kurds across the region, Iranian policy towards its Kurdish population must be strategically calculated so as not to fuel irredentist agendas. Moreover, the Kurdish issue complicates relations with those neighbouring states who also play home to Kurdish minorities. In addition, Iranian calculations must take into consideration the possibility that external actors may seek to support the Iranian Kurdish population, a strategy undertaken by Saddam Hussein during the First Gulf War.[128] It is believed by some in Iran that Saudi Arabia, other Gulf States and Israel are providing support to Kurdish movements, in an attempt to destabilise Iran.

Baluchis

Baluchis are a Sunni minority,[129] located in the Sistan-Baluchistan province in southeast Iran. The Sistan-Baluchistan province is one of key strategic value for Tehran, given that this province borders with Sunni Pakistan and Afghanistan with NATO (in particular US) forces residing within. Baluchis have long endured ethnic conflict with the Persian majority, stemming predominantly from a sectarian dispute. Baluchis are not as large an ethnic group as the Azeris or Kurds, totalling somewhere between 1.4 and 2.5 million,[130] but do posess the capacity to influence both domestic and foreign policy. Foreign policy concerns rest on irredentist claims to a Greater Baluchistan, comprised of elements of Iran and Pakistan,[131] while domestic policy concerns arise from desires for equality. Many Baluchis maintain strong tribal and familial ties with ethnic kin in Pakistan and Afghanistan. Baluchis within Iran predominantly speak Baluchi as a first language, rather than the official state language.

The Sistan-Baluchistan provice is one of the poorest in Iran, suffering from a lack of development and high unemployment.[132] Given the levels of insecurity within the province, it is alleged that a programme of forced relocation and ethnic redistribution is being undertaken within Sistan-Baluchistan. A Human Rights Watch report documents allegations from Baluchi sources as to how "a systematic plan has been put in motion by the authorities to pacify the region by changing the ethnic balance in major Baluchi cities".[133] This, it is suggested, has been achieved through the process of forced relocation of Baluchis and the offering of incentives for non-Baluchis to move into these areas. The idea of forced relocation demonstrates the concern that Tehran has over irredentist agendas and the importance placed on maintaining Iran's territorial integrity.

Baluchi areas are often subjected to violence; however, it is worth noting that political violence within Baluchi areas may overlap with criminal violence, emanating from ongoing smuggling activities within border areas.[134] Indeed, these criminal activities have impacted upon tensions both internally and externally. Internally, Behruz Khaliq suggests that tensions between Tehran and the Sistan-Baluchistan province demonstrate three fault lines within Iran: national-ethnic, Shi'i-Sunni, and centre-periphery.[135] Externally, tensions in Sistan-Baluchistan have complicated relations between Iran and Pakistan, and Iran and the United States, given the Iranian fear of external involvement within Iran.

Like that of the Azeris and Kurds, the discrimination of the Baluchis occurs within the cultural sphere, highlighted by the closing of three Baluchi-language publications that emerged from the embers of the revolution.[136] In addition to this, the teaching of Baluchi language and culture has been eradicated;[137] however, it is worth noting that the marginalisation of Baluchis predates the revolution and can be traced back to the time of the Shah.[138] It is accepted that apart from the presidency of Mohammad Khatami (1997–2005), Tehran has done very little to resolve ethnic problems.[139] As such, despite offering support for the revolution, along with other ethnic groups, the rights of Baluchis remain infringed upon.

Discrimination against Baluchis (and other minority groups) is facilitated by the practice of *gozinesh*,[140] which requires individuals to demonstrate allegiance to both Islam and the Islamic Republic. *Gozinesh* prevents equality within the fields of employment, both public and private sectors, and further education, on the grounds of prior political or religious affiliation. Under *gozinesh*, individuals are questioned as to their allegiance to both *velayat-e faqih*, and the Islamic Republic. Given that Baluchis are Sunni Muslims, they do not believe in the principles of *velayat-e faqih*, furthermore, given that *taqiyah*[141] is not deemed appropriate, Baluchis and other Sunni minorities are excluded from employment and education opportunities.

Given these instances of discrimination, several opposition groups have emerged, with one in particular offering a violent response to the state. Jundallah, translated as "Soldiers of God", is considered an insurgent organisation and, as of 2006, had around 1000 soldiers opposed to the regime in Tehran.[142] Jundallah's leader, Abdolmalek Rigi, was recently captured by Iranian forces, prompting allegations from Tehran about Rigi's ties to Mossad and the Central Intelligence Agency.[143]

Arabs

Arabs predominantly live within the Khuzestan province, which borders the Iraqi province of Basra and formerly comprised approximately 70 per cent of the 3 million[144] inhabitants of the province.

Khuzestan is the source of vast supplies of natural resources, including approximately 80 per cent of Iran's crude oil revenue, yet despite this remains one of the least developed provinces in Iran.[145] John Bradley outlines the dilapidation of the Khuzestan province since the war with Iraq, in particular detailing problems of drug addiction, sewage and absence of "decent" hotels.[146]

The majority of Arabs residing in Khuzestan are Shi'a, yet many are frustrated with their Persian rulers, partially due to ethnic differences, but also stemming from Khuzestan's impoverishment, in spite of the province's vast natural resources. In contrast, there exists a suspicion in Tehran that Arabs located within Khuzestan may have fostered strong ties with neighbouring states, on the grounds of shared ethnicity. During the Iran–Iraq War, one of Iraq's key strategic aims was to seize the oil fields of Khuzestan, and while many in Iran suspected that Arabs residing within the province would side with Iraq, this was not the case. While some Arabs sided with Iraq on grounds of proximity and shared ethnicity, a large percentage of Arabs within Khuzestan sided with Iran as a consequence of shared religious views.

Alam Saleh offers a historical account of tensions between Tehran and the Arabs of the Khuzestan province[147] in which he recounts how, despite the loyalty of the Khuzestan Arabs during the First Gulf War, Tehran remained suspicious of the region's population. Saleh's work suggests that, initially, the Arabs desired cultural space and equality, yet, given the manoeverings of the state, this changed to a desire for regional autonomy.[148] Tensions between the Arabs of Khuzestan and the regime would take on an international dynamic in April 1980 with the storming of the Iranian embassy in London. This was undertaken in an attempt to demonstrate to the international community the plight of Arabs in the region.[149]

However, tensions between Arabs and the regime possess a more contemporary element. Over the course of three days in April 2005, Khuzestan witnessed a spate of rioting, in which 20 people are alleged to have been killed and hundreds injured.[150] It is believed that the riots were triggered by a "forged" letter, attributed to former Iranian vice president Muhammad Ali Abtahi, which articulated a programme of ethnic redistribution across the region.[151]

Tehran has strong reason to be fearful over the future stability of Khuzestan, given that the region provides a large proportion of Iran's operating capital, accounting for 8–10 per cent of OPEC's total output.[152] Yet, despite this level of output from the region, it is believed that Tehran is reluctant to redistribute oil money back into Khuzestan, recently rejecting pleas for 1.5 per cent of total sums to be distributed.[153]

The Khuzestan province is also experiencing a programme of ethnic restructuring and integration, often resulting in the forced relocation of Arabs from the region. This process of ethnic redistribution has altered the demographics of the region, which currently has an Arab population of only 30 per cent,[154] again demonstrating the concern that the regime has about irredentist agendas.

Turkmen

The Turkmen are historically a nomadic race, spread amongst the border areas of three countries: Iran, Afghanistan and Turkmenistan (post 1991, historically the USSR). Turkmen are Sunni Muslims, who possess their own language, a Turkic language known as Turkmen. Within Iran, Turkmen live predominantly in the provinces of Golistan and North Khorasa, on the northeastern border shared with Turkmenistan and are estimated to total over 1 million people.[155]

Like other ethnic groups marginalized under the rule of the Shah, the Turkmen offered support for the Islamic Revolution, believing that once the Shah was removed they would be granted political and cultural freedom. However, as noted with regard to other ethnic groups, this liberalization of political and cultural space is yet to manifest itself.

As a consequence, again like other ethnic groups within the Islamic Republic, Turkmen are discriminated against through cultural and political marginalisation, on grounds of ethnicity, religion and language. The principle of *gozinesh* is also detrimental to Turkmen equality, which can especially be seen with regard to numbers of Turkmen continuing to higher education.[156]

It is alleged that the erosion of the Turkmen identity has occurred over a particularly short time: Azim Gorbanzadeh, a Turkmen doctor trained in the US, upon returning to his home town of Gonbad-e-Kavus, was shocked at the changes that had taken place.[157] Gorbanzadeh noted the increase in the use of Persian on signposts, shop names, even in conversation. In addition to the use of language, Gorbanzadeh recounts a shift in women's dress, from colourful traditional costume to the black robes and headscarf of Iran.[158] Supporting Gorbanzadeh's account of the changing nature of female dress, Saleh details how an uprising in 1983 resulted from state forces attempting to prevent Turkmen women from working on farms unveiled.[159]

Despite this, Iranian relations with Turkmenistan remain cordial and have been deemed "unbreakable" by Ahmadinejad.[160] These claims have followed the development of a second oil pipeline into Iran from Turkmenistan, further reducing Moscow's dominance within the energy sector.[161] In addition to the development of oil pipelines, the Atran-Gorgan railway project has been commissioned to link the two countries, at an estimated cost of $650 million.[162] However, despite this collaboration and the claims made by Ahmadinejad, the trans-national nature of the Turkmen and the ensuing support given to co-ethnic groups by Turkey poses challenges to the territorial integrity of the Iranian state.[163]

Irredentist Agendas?

From this, it appears as if Tehran faces serious challenges to its territorial borders. Yet, Farhi rejects the notion that irredentist agendas remain problematic within the Islamic Republic; rather, she suggests that the irredentist question should be rephrased as one looking at the ethnic challenge of equality within the state.[164] But, assuming this is the case, would irredentist concerns manifest themselves once more, given that equality for all ethnic groups within Iran does not exist? Moreover, regardless of existentialist debates concerning irredentist agendas, the mere perception of their existence is cause for concern in Tehran. Indeed, if one looks at the main ethnic groups within Iran, Azeris, Kurds, Baluchis, Arabs and Turkmen can all be argued to possess some degree of irredentist aspiration. Further, one should also consider the importance of cross-border ties between ethnic groups in Iran and neighbouring states, particularly given those that have a history of tense relations with Tehran, or those states containing US and other Western troops.[165]

One must also question why there has been a move towards ethnic and, thus, regional discrimination. Nayereh Tohidi suggests that there are three dominant reasons for this trend,[166] beginning with the changing geopolitical environment. The demise of the Soviet Union and the resultant emergence of the independent states of Azerbaijan and Turkmenistan, combined with the presence of US forces in neighbouring Afghanistan and Pakistan, has resulted in increased geopolitical pressure on Tehran. Moreover, the cross-border nature of identities within this region has affected regional dynamics, especially important to Iran. Secondly, what Tohidi terms "an uneven and overly centralised (mostly Tehran-centered) strategy of development in Iran" has resulted in the widening of the socio-economic gap between the centre and peripheries within Iran.[167] This policy can be seen with regard to the Khuzestan province and desires for the increased distribution of oil wealth within the province. Thirdly, Tohidi suggests that, despite protection of language within the constitution, this has not occurred in practice.

The irredentist challenge demonstrates the severity of the internal security dilemma for Tehran: the response to a group will reduce the security of either the ethnic group or of the state (in terms of territorial security) and may have implications for other groups in the state. Further, Tehran's response to ethnic groupings within its borders can also impact upon relations with its neighbours and, thus, upon regional security. Indeed, given the porous nature of the Middle East and transnational constitution of many ethnic groups, states are sensitive and vulnerable to the actions of others. Moreover, it is suggested that certain ethnic groups within Iran receive funding from oil-rich Arab neighbours and from their cross-border ethnic kin, exacerbating the severity of the internal security dilemma. Further, given allegations of interference within the domestic realm by external powers, this has the capacity to damage relations between Iran and its neighbours.

Ethnic Violence

The ethnic tinderbox of Iran has occasionally erupted, resulting in outbreaks of violence. Indeed, between 15 and 18 April 2005, anti-government riots in Khuzestan provoked a series of bombings that resulted in the deaths of 21 people.[168] In response to this, it is alleged that 50 Arabs were imprisoned and, according to Amnesty International, many of those arrested were executed.[169] These protests stemmed from the suggestion of ethnic redistribution, coupled with the separatist agenda of certain Arab–Iranians.[170] Aside from standard political violence, whatever the manifestation, recent events have revealed a move towards economic terrorism, which has seen the bombings of pipelines in Khuzestan, temporarily disrupting the supply of oil.[171] On the back of such violence, Ahmadinejad has been forced to cancel three visits to the region, on the grounds of fears for his security.[172]

Further adding to Tehran's problem posed by the Arabs of Khuzestan, Baluchis in the Sistan-Baluchistan province also resorted to political violence, predominantly undertaken by Jundallah, who state they have killed 400 Iranian soldiers.[173] Jundallah claims to be fighting on behalf of the Baluchi ethnic group, in both Iran and Pakistan, with a separatist agenda. Jundallah's typical *modus operandi* has involved bombing campaigns,[174] with the most recent attack occurring during the Shi'i festival of Ashura in 2010, which left an estimated 39 people dead.[175] Tehran has alleged that Jundallah possesses ties to Al Qai'da, along with various intelligence organisations, and is supported by the United States, the UK and/or Israel.[176] These allegations are a further attempt to create internal cohesion through portraying Iran as a victim of international conspiracies.

In addition to violence in Arab and Baluchi territories, protests have also occurred within Azeri and Kurdish territories. The May 2006 caricature depicting Azeris as cockroaches provoked demonstrations and protests. As a consequence of this perception, brought to the fore by the caricature, Azeris "feel insulted not only by the drawing but also by what is perceived by some as the economic and political marginalisation of non-Persians outside the capital".[177] The 2005 presidential election preceded an increase in the rough treatment of Kurds, demonstrated by the protests over the death of a young Kurd in Mahabad.[178] These demonstrations were brutally suppressed, leading to a further 20 deaths.

Kurdish opposition has manifested itself in the guise of three organisations, the KDP, the PKK and the PJAK.[179] The unwillingness of Tehran to open dialogue with Kurds about their position within the Islamic Republic has resulted in an "increase in militancy in some parts of Iranian Kurdistan, as exemplified by the actions of PJAK".[180] This can be demonstrated by allegations that PJAK were responsible for the death of an Iranian prosecutor in north-west Iran, in 2010.[181] Tehran is notably concerned about the irredentist tendencies of the Kurds, due to the legacy of Mahabad and of the strong Kurdish presence across the region.

The 2005 presidential election was followed by a promise that Ahmadinejad and his ministerial team would visit each of the provinces of the Islamic Republic, in an effort to respond to regional problems, many of which are ethnic in nature.[182] Yet, despite this promise, the goal was not achieved within his first year of office.[183] This dereliction to visit all provinces perhaps demonstrates both the insecurity of certain Iranian provinces[184] and the reluctance of Tehran to offer an adequate solution to its ethnic problem.

Conclusions

The ethno-tribal dimension of identity incongruence within Saudi Arabia and Iran differs greatly in each state, both in composition and in the response of the state in addressing threats posed by the incongruence. Indeed, even the nature of the threat posed by ethnic groups differs, ranging from irredentist groups in Iran to tribal groups contesting the legitimacy of the Al Saud. While in Saudi Arabia, tribal groups possess cultural and social space, but given the essence of the political structure within the Kingdom, do not possess much capacity for action, in Iran ethnic groups have limited political space, thus reducing their capacity for political action.

Although ethnic groups do not threaten the territorial integrity of the Saudi state, tribalism has the capacity to challenge the legitimacy of the Al Saud, as a consequence of a remaining sense of tribal loyalty, if not identity. In addition, while numerous tribal groups have been either marginalised or eradicated, values belonging to those tribes remain and have intermittently been encapsulated within the institutions of the state. Indeed, given the salience of these values prior to the creation of the state and their encapsulation within institutions, the circumvention and or destruction of the values appears problematic. Thus, it appears that there remains the potential for a strong undercurrent of opposition engrained within the fabric of the state.

Aside from a desire to create a unified, centralised state, a motivating factor in the Al Saud pursuing detribalisation policies was a concern that there were several tribes, notably the Rashidis and the Hashemites, who possessed greater claims of legitimacy than do the Al Saud. These tribes also possess strong ties to external states, as demonstrated by the Hashemites who have ruled Jordan, Iraq and Syria. Yet, there appears a dichotomy between policy and rhetoric employed by the Al Saud with regard to tribalism. Indeed, despite attempts to reduce threats posed by tribes, the Al Saud themselves employ tribal rhetoric to promote their own legitimacy. It is, however, possible to argue that the Al Saud are pursuing two distinctive tribal strategies, within the spheres of security and culture. Within a security strategy, the Al Saud sought to remove threats posed by rival tribal groupings, given the history of transient alliances and belligerence between tribes across the Peninsula. In comparison, within a cultural strategy, tribal values are celebrated, promoted and utilised as means of increasing the legitimacy of the ruling elites. As such, it is possible to separate the two potentially contradictory strategies, which has the capacity to move tribal issues from posing existential security problems, to weaving tribal groups within the fabric of the state and utilising their values as tools of legitimacy. Furthermore, it is possible that the move of tribalism from the security to cultural spheres is part of the state-building process within Saudi Arabia.

With the detribalisation policies of the Al Saud resulting in the dismantling of tribal groups, coupled with the income of oil wealth, Saudi Arabian civil society has been subjected to great inequalities. These inequalities, in turn, place great pressure on the state to respond.

In contrast to Saudi Arabia, it appears problematic to group ethnic identities within Iran under one unifying characteristic, especially given the apparent irredentist agendas of many of these groups. However, the general consensus for defining "Iranian-ness" is derived from ethnicity and language, building upon both Persian ethnicity and language.

While Persian is commonly used as the official language of Iran, as protected within the Iranian constitution, Azeris, Arabs, Kurds, Baluchis and Turkmen all possess their own language. These languages are primarily spoken within ethnic areas, as opposed to Persian. It is suggested that the decline of ethnic languages is a direct result of the prevalence of Persian within schools,[185] despite the protection of second languages within the Iranian constitution. The marginalisation of ethnic groups within Iran predominantly occurs within the political and cultural spheres. Both the process of ethnic redistribution and of *gozinesh* facilitates this discrimination.

While religion appears to offer a potential solution, the dichotomy between Sunni and Shi'a poses problems for unifying ethnic groups, without even considering those groups of Christian, Jewish and Zoroastrian persuasion. Yet, as previously noted, irredentist agendas mean that the territorial attempt to proscribe identity also remains problematic. Irredentist agendas of groups within Iran pose a serious threat to the Islamic Republic and, as such, the state has to act accordingly to deal with this threat. Such action has sought to restrict the autonomy and political space of ethnic groups across the state, while also attempting to engender a national identity, based upon a combination of Islamic and Persian history. This has an undeniable, immediate impact upon regional relations, with Tehran seeking to demonstrate the superiority of both Islamic beliefs and ethnic history. In addition, Ahmadinejad has employed rhetoric that has sought to create external others, adding to an increasingly complicated regional security environment.

6

THE RESPONSE OF THE STATE

When a state's sovereignty or survival appears contested or threatened, regimes will engage in practices to maintain security. However, these actions will be dependent upon the location and nature of the threat. Both Saudi Arabia and Iran have referred to narratives that seek to foster a sense of national unity, often building upon nationalist or Islamic history to evoke memories of unity and cohesion. However, in using such narratives, each state risks becoming increasingly embroiled in regional competition. Furthermore, regimes have sought to discredit opposition groups, often portraying them as un-Islamic, or anti-nationalistic.

Regimes have also sought to de-politicise the agendas of certain opposition groups, while seeking to crush other groups, perhaps as a consequence of the perceived level of threat to the regime. Ruling elites have also attempted to export and expel groups that have the capacity to undermine state legitimacy and stability.

The notion of de-politicisation, as discussed in chapter one, suggests that certain individuals are guilty of democratic apathy and, through this apathy, remove themselves from the democratic system. However, one can argue that de-politicisation is also a policy actively sought by regimes. Indeed, while not applicable to all identity groups, it is most certainly a tool in the arsenal of a ruling elite. Thus, de-politicisation can occur in several guises: firstly, through the increasing apathy of a group, as posited by Cavatorta; secondly, through the action of a regime in deliberately restricting political space, removing the possibility of an identity group engaging in legitimate forms of opposition; and thirdly, achieving the de-politicisation of a group through exporting or expelling the ideals and ideology of the identity group before it manifests itself as too much of an internal threat to the regime.[1]

The argument within chapter six is predominantly concerned with the second and third aspects of the de-politicisation argument, where identity groups wishing to continue participating with a political agenda are offered no alternative but to engage in forms of illegitimate interaction outside of the political system. In addition, inherent within both Iranian and Saudi Arabian religious doctrines is a proselytizing element, thus, the notion of exporting problems can have a two-fold benefit for the state. Assuming that the identity group to be exported is of a similar sectarian constitution as the ruling elite, not only can a potential threat be removed from the security calculus of a regime, but the threat can also be posited within the security calculations of a geopolitical rival. Alternatively, this group may facilitate a proselytizing agenda. Given this, it is imperative to consider the impact of exporting problematic identity groups upon regional security. This distinction between exporting and expelling opposition groups is subtle, yet important: a state may seek to export a group that maintains a level of popular support within a state, but that also poses a threat to the state. In contrast, a state may expel a group that poses what the regime perceives to be a severe threat to the ideological sovereignty of the state.

In addition, it is important to consider the importance of the provision of support for identity groups who subscribe to similar belief systems across the region. This support can often be given in an attempt to deflect attention from internal problems. As such, one can see both Saudi Arabia and Iran offering support for groups across the region in an attempt to deflect attention from internal problems, while also seeking to counter the potential gains made by the other state. Furthermore, the importance of geostrategic alliances has the capacity to transcend sectarian differences; indeed, one only has to look at the alleged Iranian support for Hamas in the Gaza strip to see that often sectarian differences are ignored in comparison with the perception of superior positioning within the geopolitical environment.

In addition, the reference to an "other" occurs at an external level as well as an internal level across the Gulf. Indeed, in an additional attempt to circumvent internal dissent within a state, both Saudi Arabia and Iran refer to the behaviour of external actors in an attempt to demonstrate internal unity, which destabilises the external environment.

Competing Islamic Narratives

In the aftermath of the Islamic Revolution in 1979, Saudi Arabia and Iran became embroiled in a spiralling flux of moves akin to Barnett's symbolic security dilemma. In seeking to demonstrate the legitimacy and vitality of post-revolutionary Iran, the narratives employed initially by Khomeini sought to both increase the legitimacy of the newly formed Islamic Republic and to create unity within the Islamic world:

> There is no difference between Muslims who speak different languages, for instance the Arabs and the Persians. It is very probable that such problems have been created by those who do not wish the Muslim countries to be united [. . .] They create the issues of nationalism, of pan-Iranianism, pan-Turkism, and such isms, which are contrary to Islamic doctrines. Their plan is to destroy Islam and Islamic philosophy.[2]

Indeed, Khomeini often suggested that nobody could defeat over 1 billion Muslims if they were united. In the aftermath of the revolution, Iran aspired to become a source of emulation and to hold a leadership position across the Islamic world, seeking to unite Muslims against the West, who were held responsible for the plight of Muslim states. The implementation of an Islamic government, coupled with a strong stance against Israel and support for the Palestinian cause, added to this growing emulation. However, despite striving for a united Islamic community, Khomeini reserved criticism for several leaders within the Middle East, in particular, the Al Saud.

Khomeini regarded the Al Saud as "corrupt and unworthy to be the guardians of Mecca and Medina"[3] and referred to them as "traitors to the two holy shrines".[4] This disdain for the Al Saud stemmed from a rejection that monarchy was an acceptable form of government within Islam, combined with the perceived impropriety of the Al Saud and ties with the West, notably the United States. Khomeini suggested that the behaviour of the Al Saud was not in accordance with Islamic traditions and principles, arguing that this behaviour was far more damning than any Iranian rhetoric.

> If we wanted to prove to the world that the Saudi Government, these vile and ungodly Saudis, are like daggers that have always pierced the heart of the Moslems from the back, we would not have been able to do it as well as has been demonstrated by these inept and spineless leaders of the Saudi Government.[5]

This rhetoric was supported by an apparent incitement to riot on the *Hajj* of 1987, calling for pilgrims to go from "holy *Hajj* to holy *jihad* by bathing yourselves in blood and martyrdom".[6] It is worth reiterating the suspicion that the pilgrims were predominantly affiliated to the Iranian regime. Furthermore, Khomeini sought to export his ideology internationally, seeking to oppose the West while offering support to the *mustazefin*:

> We will export our experiences to the whole world and present the outcome of our struggles against tyrants to those who are struggling along the path of God, without expecting the slightest reward. The result of this exportation will certainly result in the blooming of the buds of victory and independence and in the implementation of Islamic teachings among the enslaved Nations.[7]

This quote explains the roots of Iranian support for organisations such as Hizballah in Lebanon, along with support for Shi'i minorities across the region. It also demonstrates how Tehran positioned itself against many of the incumbent regimes in the region.

The alliance between the Al Saud and Wahhabism provides the Al Saud with Islamic legitimacy that circumvents a prior lack of tribal legitimacy and aided the state-building process. As such, any reference to Islamic leadership from Iran was (and remains) viewed as undermining the Al Saud's position within the Islamic world and necessitated a response from Riyadh. Saud Arabia sought to reduce the appeal of the revolution to Sunni Muslims by stressing the Shi'i nature of the revolution, reiterating the incompatibility of Shi'ism with both Wahhabi and Sunni thought. In addition, as Furtig notes, the revolution "was characterized as an upheaval of heretic Iranians who were trying to continue the previous policies of Iranian expansionism, but this time painted in Islamic colours".[8]

Prior to the *Hajj* of 1987, King Fahd directed a speech towards the Iranians in which he attacked the "hypocrites and pretenders who are using Islam to undermine and destabalise other countries".[9] Fahd warned that attempts to demonstrate on the *Hajj* that would create an atmosphere of "chaos and upset the peace" could not be tolerated.[10]

This spiralling rhetoric possessed a personal aspect: after Khomeini's suggestion that the Al Saud were infidels, Saudi rhetoric responded claiming that Khomeini was Hitler and the Iranian leadership were compared to Nazis.[11] The Al Saud sought to demonstrate their own Islamic credentials through the change in title of the King to Protector of the two holy places, thus removing impious parallels with God. Supplementing this was a strategy that sought to suggest Khomeini himself was creating parallels with God, through banners on the *Hajj* that stated "God is Great, Khomeini is Great; We obey Khomeini", along with watches worn by his supporters that were inscribed with the "Call of Khomeini".[12]

Khomeini's vitriol against the Al Saud was also found in his will, read by Khamenei in June 1989. In Khomeini's will, he stated that Muslims "should curse tyrants, including the Saudi royal family, these traitors to God's great shrine, may God's curse and that of his prophets and angels be upon them".[13] Khomeini also referred to the King Fahd as a "traitor to God" and to Wahhabism as a "superstitious faith".[14]

While Iran initially sought to downplay the sectarian split within Islam, the Al Saud have regularly employed anti-Shi'i rhetoric, incensing both Iran and its own Shi'i population. In the aftermath of the revolution, several Wahhabi clerics issued *fatwas* against Shi'i Muslims. Abdul-Aziz Bin Baz, the Kingdom's leading cleric, denounced the Shi'a as apostates, while Abdullah ibn Jibrin, a prominent Wahhabi scholar, also branded the Shi'a as apostates and sanctioned the killing of members of the Shi'i community.[15] These messages are contained within Wahhabi literature taught within schools.

While anti-Al Saud rhetoric has diminished slightly under Khamenei, who has sought to pursue a more pragmatic approach to relations with Saudi Arabia, there still remain instances of rhetoric criticising the Al Saud. For instance, in the 1990s, Khamenei referred to the Al Saud as "evil".[16] While there appeared to be moves towards *rapprochement* under the presidencies of Rafsanjani and Khatami, Ahmadinejad's tenure as president has seen a rise in belligerent rhetoric, although this is predominantly focussed upon gaining legitimacy in the "Arab Street" and creating a sense of unity against external others. Recent Islamic statements have sought to make a distinction between Wahhabi and Sunni Islam, along with the distinction between regime and non-regime clerics in Saudi Arabia.[17] However, Iranian support for Shi'i groups across the region, coupled with allegations and perceptions of the emergence of a "Shi'i Crescent", has increased sectarian tensions.

Saudi Arabia

Within Saudi Arabia, there are several areas of dissent that have manifested themselves in forms of illegitimate opposition to the state. As previously discussed, ethnic problems within Saudi Arabia are limited and tribal opposition has been circumvented through de-tribalisation policies; as such, much of the opposition has a sectarian aspect. The nature of Wahhabism is anti-Shi'a, which has often been reflected in the policy of the Al Saud. These policies have resulted in the build-up of strong anti-regime sentiment amongst the Shi'i population of Saudi Arabia. This anti-regime sentiment has manifested itself on several occasions in the form of violent opposition to the Al Saud. Moreover, the profligacy of certain members of the Al Saud family has further incensed opposition groups within the Kingdom. As a recent

US cable released by the WikiLeaks organisation highlights, although alcohol is banned within the Kingdom, it is readily available under the protection of members of the royal family.[18]

In a damning indictment of the House of Saud, Said K. Aburish offers an invective criticism of the ruling family, many of whom, he suggests "have hoarded huge sums of money and [...] have demonstrated an insensitive determination to maintain their lifestyles at a lavish level, regardless of the effect on their peoples".[19] Further, Aburish suggests that "[n]othing is being done or even planned to stop the process of deterioration in the internal equilibrium of the country",[20] demonstrating a predisposition towards self interest. Indeed, one of the most incriminating of Aburish's allegations concerns Prince Muhammad Abu Sharain, translated into English as Muhammad Twin-Evil,[21] who had his grand-daughter, Princess Mishaal, and her lover executed, documented in the film *Death of a Princess*.[22]

In addition to criticism from Aburish, the Al Saud has faced staunch criticism from within its Wahhabi supporters, who have been vocal of the profligacy of the ruling elite and of their alliance with the United States. This criticism has become conspicuous since the seizure of the Grand Mosque in 1979 and the attacks of 9/11. Furthermore, radical Sunni terrorist organisations such as Al Qai'da have been transparently vocal in their criticisms of the regime, coupling such criticisms with terrorist action within the Kingdom. Given these tensions, the use of narratives to demonstrate the unity of the Kingdom and the legitimacy of the Al Saud's rule is an important strategy.

The Use of Narratives

The Al Saud have sought to export Wahhabi values across the Middle East and into Central Asia in an attempt to increase Saudi legitimacy (both internally and externally) and placate aspects of the Wahhabi *ulama*. An added bi-product of this is to reduce scope for Iranian gains across the region. Given this strategy, it is necessary to consider the impact of exporting values upon internal stability and legitimacy, the level of support for regional groups and furthermore, upon regional security.

The idea of exporting Islamic values is not a recent phenomenan. Indeed, with the decline in oil prices during the 1980s, the Al Saud sought to deflect internal criticisms and opposition by promoting populist Pan-Islamism domestically by praising the Afghan jihad in official media, while also providing support to Saudi nationals who wanted to fight in Afghanistan.[23] This support for Pan-Islamist movements spread to Bosnia, which proved an important theatre of action, wherein, the:

> Saudi state tried both to compensate for its problems at home and to outdo its competitors abroad by providing a level of financial and military assistance to the Bosnian Muslims that was completely out of proportion with the size of the conflict or the previous ties between the Kingdom and Muslims in the Balkans.[24]

Indeed, the level of financial support for Muslims in the Balkans over the course of five years between 1992 and 1997 outstrips the level of financial support for Palestinians over 15 years, two to one.[25] However, the support for Pan-Islamist movements was undermined by the continued presence of US troops within the Kingdom.

The notion of exporting Wahhabi values appears to have transcended a region-centric position and has moved into Central Asia. In particular, the states within which Wahhabi goals have been exported to include Chechnya, Uzbekistan, the Phillipines and Kashmir. Stephen Swartz illustrates the spread of Wahhabi goals into Asia, where arms and money flowed to Wahhabi leaders and the Pashtuns.[26] In addition, Swartz illustrates how the *jihad* in Afghanistan provided an opportunity for the Al Saud to remove restless Wahhabi youths from within the Kingdom, sending them to martyrdom abroad.[27] Further, the combination of manpower, in the form of radical youths and financial support, suggests that in addition to purely exporting internal problems, the Al Saud sought to both proselytize their Wahhabi agenda and also demonstrate support for Sunni causes across the wider MENA region.

However, it is imperative to note that the Soviet invasion of Afghanistan and ensuing growth of resistance proved useful to

Saudi Arabia in offering an additional buffer to the ideological vision of Ayatollah Khomeini post 1979. Indeed, this idea of an ideological buffer can be noted with regard to the increase in Saudi spending in Iraq, as an attempt to counter the rising influence of Iran.

Moreover, it is important to mention the recent discovery of Wahhabist doctrine being taught in Islamic schools in the UK, which has further stressed the proliferation of Wahhabi values outside of the region.[28] Despite this discovery, one must question whether the exportation of Wahhabi values to the UK was the enactment of regime policy, or if radical groups already exiled were spreading their ideological views. Indeed, knowledge of the case of Wahhabi textbooks in Islamic schools in the UK was vehemently denied by Prince Muhammad bin Nawaf, the Saudi ambassador to the United Kingdom and Republic of Ireland.[29]

De-Politicisation

The Al Saud's policy towards violence in the Kingdom can be split into two categories: policies that seek to pre-empt violent actions and policies that seek to punish, or prevent, further action. The first category is two-fold and can be explained in either an attempt to export the ideology of the state, or to expel troublesome groups from the Kingdom.[30] The second category of policies responds to violent action and seeks to prevent such organisations from committing further violent action targeted at both organisations and individual members of organisations.

While exporting a state's ideology is incorporated in the use of narratives, a second aspect of this strategy builds upon expelling groups from the Kingdom. A prime example of this strategy can be seen with regard to the Committee for the Defence of the Legitimate Rights (CDLR). Clive Jones notes the emergence of the CDLR, who confronted human rights abuses in the Kingdom, called for the reform of the Saudi Arabian judicial system[31] and for a stop to "societal decay".[32] The CDLR was created by a group of six prominent Saudi academics who posited a manifesto that was signed by 109 members of the Najdi *ulama*. Integral within the message of the CDLR was an allegation that the Kingdom was not in compliance with the Shari'a, alongside a "wide-ranging critique of the economic, social and political development of Saudi Arabia since the end of the Gulf crisis".[33] This allegation stemmed from the perceived breakdown of the social contract within the Kingdom. While perceived by many in the West to be critical of the Al Saud, and thus more liberal, caution is required; indeed, the CDLR called for a more fundamental implantation of the Shari'a. As Jones articulates, the response of the state to the CDLR revealed a "fist within a velvet glove",[34] with attacks upon its theological basis courtesy of the Wahhabi *ulama*. On the back of a *fatwa* condemning the CDLR, the Al Saud banned the organisation and arrested both members and sympathisers. As a consequence, the CDLR would relocate to London in April 1994.

The second strategy employed by the Al Saud is concerned with responses to violent action and aims to prevent further acts of violence. The regime has sought to crush any organisation that possesses scope for revolt, with severe repercussions upon individuals and groups responsible for threatening the regime. This can be demonstrated by looking at the Al Saud's response to the seizure of the Grand Mosque in 1979 and the riots in the Eastern Province, which both posed serious threats to the regime. The response to the seizure of the Grand Mosque by Juhayman al-Utaybi was, much like the response to the CDLR, contingent upon an *ulama* issued *fatwa*, necessary given the importance of the Grand Mosque. The *fatwa* legitimised the use of force against al-Utaybi within the sacred shrine. Of those engaged in the seizure of the Grand Mosque, 177 were killed during fighting with security forces and 170 were captured, 63 of whom, al-Utaybi included, were executed.[35] A similarly strong response from the state crushed the *intifada* in the Eastern Province of the Kingdom. In response to the *intifada*, the state sent 20,000 members of the National Guard to the province, resulting in the deaths of 20 people and injuries to over a hundred more.[36]

When addressing the threat posed by Al Qai'da, the regime has employed a multi-faceted approach. While security forces have regularly engaged in gun battles with Al Qai'da operatives, there have been several other key aspects to the regime's policy. The media has been utilised to increase awareness of key Al Qai'da operatives within the Kingdom and an ideological response has sought to "paint the al Qaeda menace as a perversion of Islam and to rally the Wahhabi establishment against the threat".[37] The use of clerics has sought to discredit the movement in the minds of both the general population and also of prisoners who were subject to a deradicalisation programme that included re-education and rehabilitation, to "turn captured terrorists into peaceful citizens".[38] In facilitating these re-education and rehabilitation efforts, special camps were created, wherein pro-regime clerics sought to engage in ideological discussions and persuade them of "the errors in supporting al Qaeda".[39]

The regime's response to Hizballah al-Hijaz, initially after a spate of bombs at the Sadaf petrochemical plant in Jubayl, was the arrest and public execution of four members of the organisation,[40] a move that was again supported by a *fatwa* issued by the *ulama*. Moreover, in the aftermath of the Khobar Towers bombing, hundreds of Islamists were arrested, both Sunni and Shi'a.[41] Amongst these arrests were nearly all of those who had affiliations with Hizballah al-Hijaz, thus having a dramatic impact upon operational capability.

Manipulation of Internal Security Dilemmas and Support for Regional Groups

Given the nature of the internal security dilemma in Iran, Saudi Arabia has seen scope to manipulate the dilemma within the Islamic Republic, which is greatly feared by Tehran. The existence of shared ethnic and religious kinsmen in Iran has presented the Al Saud with an opportunity to provide ideological and logistical support to opposition groups, such as Arabs, Kurds and Baluchis.

In interviews conducted for a 2009 RAND report, Saudi analysts told researchers that Iran's internal security dilemma[42] "could be useful leverage to the Kingdom. But so far we haven't exploited this".[43] The RAND report also details Saudi Arabian support for Wahhabi elements in Iran;[44] however, anecdotal evidence suggests that this support may also be provided to Sunni groups in an effort to undermine the religious and territorial values of the Islamic Republic.[45]

This can be seen in Arab, Kurd and Baluchi areas, given shared ethnic and religious ties, combined with economic investment in the area, often in concert with Pakistan.[46]

A direct consequence of the concern of increasing Iranian influence within Iraq has been for Saudi Arabia to become more involved with Sunni organisations within Iraq, including Al Qai'da, through the provision of *jihadis*, ideological and financial support, although the degree to which this is a regime policy is questionable.[47] The increase in funding to Sunni groups in Iraq[48] can be seen as an attempt to deflect attention away from internal discontent; moreover, this involvement within Iraq can also be viewed as an attempt to prevent further gains made by Iran, which, given geopolitical concerns, appears the more persuasive argument. The increased involvement of Saudi Arabia within Iraq demonstrates an attempt to harness a cause that has the potential to deflect away from internal dissent, yet there remains the problem of the impact of returning *jihadis* from Iraq,[49] which is perceived as tantamount to the problem faced with the return of those engaged in *jihad* in Afghanistan and Bosnia.

Saudi Arabia's behaviour in the aftermath of the "Arab Spring" has contained a serious contradiction. While both seeking to ensure its own internal stability and that of its allies, Riyadh has predominantly sought to prevent the emergence of uprisings across the region. This has most notably involved offering support for the Al Khalifa in Bahrain, both economically and militarily. However, support has also been offered to opposition groups in Syria, who seek to overthrow the Assad regime, which demonstrates a clear a contradiction in Riyadh's policy of preserving the status-quo. Although, given Tehran's ties to the Assad regime, this supports the notion that geopolitical considerations outweigh ideological considerations.[50]

Given the Al Saud's support for various groups across the region, it is important to consider the ensuing perception of Saudi behaviour within the Middle East. While Iran is undoubtably hyper-sensitive about the external involvement and manipulation of internal security dilemmas, stemming from both the severity of the dilemmas and the legacy of interference within state narratives, Riyadh's involvement in Iraq, Bahrain and Syria is increasing Iranian concerns. Indeed, Iranian calculations of Saudi Arabian involvement in these three spheres has exacerbated the perception that Saudi Arabia is "meddling" in the Islamic Republic's internal security dilemma.

Regional Security

The effect of exporting Wahhabi values across the region has had an undeniable impact upon regional security. Indeed, a desire to spread Wahhabi values has often resulted in competition with others attempting to spread their own ideological values, notably Iran. In addition, offering support to certain groups within the region has complicated the regional security environment.

The ideological threats faced by Saudi Arabia have resulted in Riyadh engaging in a delicate balancing act, notably with regard to its domestic stability. In addition, Saudi Arabia's regional security environment poses challenges to Riyadh, given that it is flanked by the dominant Shi'i power in the world at its east and by a state engaged in a process of postwar reconstruction to its north. Indeed, the rising influence of Iran within Iraq has proved to be of great concern, leading to increased Saudi involvement within Iraq, competition with Iranian-sponsored organisations and an increase in sectarian violence in Iraq. It could thus be argued that Iraq is now a battleground for a proxy war of ideological constitution, between Sunni agents, operating with the support of Saudi Arabia, and Shi'i agents, operating with the support of Iran. However, the Al Saud's policy is somewhat precarious, given the prominence of Al Qai'da within Saudi Arabia. Thus, it appears that Riyadh is engaged in a delicate balancing act between the burgeoning influence of Iran across the region, and between the dangers posed by Al Qai'da. Indeed, there exists much concern towards the threat posed by those fighting in Iraq who could turn their attentions to the Al Saud upon their return.

The case of Bahrain and ensuing proxy conflict has demonstrated how the regime in Riyadh has sought to preserve the sectarian status quo within the region. Saudi Arabia acted decisively to counter the perception of Iranian gains, which seeks to prevent increasing Iranian power and to prevent growing unrest amongst the Shi'a of Saudi Arabia who may feel empowered by Shi'i gains within Bahrain.

In addition to Iraq and Bahrain acting as a proxy battleground for sectarian differences, one can look further afield from the Gulf to consider the Saudi response to Hizballah, in Lebanon. In a leaked US diplomatic cable, it emerged that the Saudi foreign minister, Prince Saud al-Faisal, felt that an Arab force was required to counter the threat posed by Hizballah. Furthermore, this was supplemented by a belief that within the context of Iranian advances, the Lebanese front would be far easier to win.[51]

Iran

It is suggested that opposition groups who engage in political violence within Iran can be categorised in one of two ways, stemming from the nature of the opposition. The first categorisation of opposition groups can be understood as a group that poses a threat to the ideological construction of the Islamic Republic.[52] The second categorisation can be understood as a group that poses a threat to the territorial integrity of Iran. As noted in chapter five, many of the ethnic groupings within Iran possess trans-state ties, and thus have kinship with the population of neighbouring states. Indeed, John Bradley suggests that ethnic groups within Iran are inspired by the "gains of their ethnic brothers in neighbouring states".[53] Given the trans-state essence of ethnic groups, there exists a strong fear within the Islamic Republic of the possibility of irredentist agendas amongst its ethnic population, which poses a threat to the territorial integrity of the state. The nature of the threat, be it to the territorial integrity or to the ideological sovereignty, will determine the nature of the state's response.

Given the Islamic Republic's ethnic constitution and concerns about the irredentist agendas of certain groups, the regime's policy towards opposition groups has sometimes appeared draconian, often resulting in a restriction of political and cultural space. Further, similar action has been taken by the state towards groups with sectarian agendas. As a result, these groups have faced existential questions as to their political, cultural and religious roles, as well as their mere survival. The response of the various opposition groups has differed greatly to persecution by the regime. The argument will discuss the response of the state to such opposition groups before ending the section with an examination of the impact of exporting hard and soft power upon the regional security environment.

The Use of Narratives

Iranian rhetoric has sought to foster narratives of external interference and to create notions of othering. While Tehran has not denied the existence of ethnic tensions within the Islamic Republic, official spokesmen have sought to depict these tensions as a result of foreign interference.

Ideological threats are overcome through reference to *velayat-e faqih* and theological legitimacy, given that loyalty to the revolution equates to loyalty to the Islamic Republic and God. As such, the practice of one being a good Muslim equates to being a loyal citizen of Iran. Shi'i bonds between the regime and several of its ethnic groups are emphasised in an effort to foster a stronger sense of national unity. Although, this strategy could further marginalise those ethnic groups who are neither Persian nor Shi'a.

Narratives have also been used to circumvent internal security dilemmas. As such, threats to territorial integrity have often been framed within the context of foreign interference, be they emanating from "alien forces", "foreign agents", "the identity-less" or those paid off by foreign powers.[54] Given the history of external influence within Iran, framing threats within the context of foreign interference is not problematic.[55] This notion of foreign interference has transcended the political realm and has manifested itself firmly within Iranian culture. One needs only to look at the seminal work of Iraj Pezeshkzad, *My Uncle Napoleon*,[56] to see this. In *My Uncle Napoleon*, the protagonist (Uncle Napoleon) is perennially concerned about, and suspicious of, imperialist (particularly British) agendas within Iran.

Building on this suspicion, state rhetoric speaks of the impact of external actors on internal stability, moreover, of:

> the conspiracies of foreign countries. From the acts of terrorism against innocent people in [provinces] such as Sistan [-Baluchistan]

> to the incidents in Khuzestan. [The Tabriz unrest] also seems to be part of this chain [of events].[57]

In an attempt to demonstrate national unity, the interior minister reminded Arabs in Khuzestan of their loyalty and heroic defence of the Iranian state during the course of the Iran–Iraq War.[58] In response to tensions within Khuzestan, Tehran initially sought to accuse foreign agents for being involved in "fanning the riots".[59] Those foreign powers accused were listed in the following order: British groups, or those associated with Great Britain; Zionist; US, or allied to the US; exiled opposition group Mujahedin-e Khalq; Pan-Arabists or Ba'athists; Royalists.[60] The reference to Pan-Arabism and Ba'athist ideology was an attempt to evoke memories of the Iran–Iraq War and the catastrophic impact upon a generation of Iranians. Indeed, references to foreign powers and Ba'athist ideology would serve to demonstrate a degree of cohesion within Iran against a foreign "other". In addition, the accusation of the involvement of foreign powers gives added credence to the value of *velayat-e faqih*, which was set up to prevent the on-going involvement of foreign powers in Iranian affairs.[61] Such statements were also made in support of Azeris, particularly through reference to their patriotism and historical role within Iran.[62]

In an effort to counter the threat posed by Azeris in undermining regime stability and legitimacy, Tehran has sought to portray Azeri nationalist sentiment as the action of Turkish spies or separatists, again supporting the belief that foreign agents are involved within Iran.[63] This was highlighted by the arrest of 29 "Turkish spies" in Western Azerbaijan Province, in April 1996; moreover, in March 1997, 50 more alleged Turkish spies were detained. Indeed, this period of time saw riots across Tabriz in protest at Tehran's discriminative policies.

Further, Tehran attempted to demonstrate the ties between state-sponsored Iranian nationalism and religious tenets of the revolution. Indeed, the "plasticity of semantics and symbolism is daily moulded and remoulded in a fashion that allows Iranian nationalism to be Islamist and Islamism to be Iranian nationalism".[64] As such, ties to the

Iranian state and also to Shi'i Islam are stressed, in an effort to demonstrate the existence of a coherent Iranian nation-state, as opposed to an Iranian state of several nations. This can be demonstrated by the employment of rhetoric by Tehran that attempted to demonstrate unity within the state:

> The threat is symbolically portrayed as a contamination, intrusion and violation of the territorial integrity, homeland sanctity and the "family" of a multi-ethnic Iranian nation, and the antidote and defence is patriotic solidarity and unity on the revolutionary path.[65]

In addition to attempting to portray unity and coherence within Iran, the ruling elite have played "on nationalistic registers well known to most Iranians, that is, the feeling of being exposed throughout history to foreign powers and their selfish interests".[66] Moreover, Tehran has employed assimilation policies that have sought to unify Iranians under a Persian identity, notably through a restriction in the political space of various ethnic groups.[67]

A second strategy of creating unity is the use rhetoric in the foreign policy sphere. In this regard, the target for much of Ahmadinejad's belligerent rhetoric has been Israel, with the Iranian president issuing calls for Israel to be wiped off the map, alongside issuing Holocaust denials.[68]

During the World Without Zionism conference, Ahmadinejad "called for Israel to be 'wiped off the map' and said a new wave of Palestinian attacks will destroy the Jewish state".[69] Problems concerning translation arose, leading some to believe that Ahmadinejad's remarks were a call to genocide,[70] whereas others held that his remarks were calling for an open referendum within a single state shared by Israelis and Palestinians.[71] Nonetheless, the international community responded with almost universal condemnation of Ahmadinejad's remarks.[72]

Two months later Ahmadinejad cast doubts upon the veracity of the Holocaust:

> They have invented a myth that Jews were massacred [...] The West has given more significance to the myth of the genocide

> of the Jews, [...it] deals very severely with those who deny this myth but does not do anything to those who deny God, religion, and the prophet. If you have burned the Jews, why don't you give a piece of Europe, the United States, Canada or Alaska to Israel? [...] Our question is, if you have committed this huge crime, why should the innocent nation of Palestine pay for this crime?"[73]

These comments were again met with international condemnation.[74]

Building upon antagonistic rhetoric used towards Israel, Ahmadinejad has also sought to attack America, provoking US, UK, and other European delegations to walk out of a meeting of the UN General Assembly in response to comments made by Ahmadinejad alleging the complicity of certain segments within the US government in orchestrating the 9/11 terrorist attacks.[75] While one should not necessarily take Ahmadinejad's comments as anything beyond bombastic statesmanship employing nationalist sentiement, the mere existence of such comments – directed both towards the United States and to Israel – clouds Iranian relations with the international system.

The Response of the State

In attempting to reduce the violence of opposition groups, Tehran has responded to the threats in several ways, which can be explained by examining the specific area of antagonism and the category the opposition group falls into, be that challenging the ideological sovereignty or territorial integrity of the state. While the use of force is a standard tactic, as Barry Buzan notes, the prolonged use of force is not sustainable when ethnic tensions are as prominent as they are in Iran. Indeed, the continued use of force has the capacity to widen divisions between identity groups and the state.[76]

Certain protocols guiding behaviour during protests emerged, which attempted to set out the parameters for legitimate protest. As such, loyalty towards the state ideology remains an important aspect when considering the sanctioned limits of behaviour and thought.[77] Moreover, "as pitting those committed to *nezam*, 'the order' [...] against those who are not committed and can variously be branded counter-revolutionaries (*zed-e enqelab*), hypocrites (*monafeq*) or those 'at war with God' (*mohareb*)".[78] Government statements demonstrated how acceptable protesters confront unacceptable protesters, with the differentiation occurring on grounds of offering support for both the territorial integrity and ideological composition of Iran.

In an effort to provide some semblance of scope for legitimate protest, while reducing both the credibility and potential threat posed by the protest, politicians reminded protesters of the possibility of their cause being manipulated. During an Azeri protest, the state reminded protesters of the "possibility of their legitimate cause being hi-jacked during the unrest by foreign agents and proponents of 'Pan-Turkism', which in official terminology equals separatism".[79]

An underlying fear governing the regime's response to the demonstrations across Iran has been the potential for increased irredentist and secessionist tendencies, thus eroding the territorial integrity of the Islamic Republic. This fear was especially important within Khuzestan, which had the potential to deprive Tehran "of its most valuable source of income as well as a part of the country that many Iranians see as a cradle of their culture and civilisation".[80] In addition to the heavy security presence in ethnic regions, demonstrating the highly securitised approach that Tehran has employed in response to ethnic aspects of the internal security dilemma, the state sought to stress, wherever possible, the shared ethno-religious bonds across the Islamic Republic.

It can thus be argued that responses to threats posed by irredentist and secessionist groups seek to foster a coherent identity, whereas the response to threats to the ideological sovereignty of the Islamic Republic seek to remove space to protest. Moreover, in an effort to maintain the ideological sovereignty of the Islamic Republic, it is possible that Tehran has employed a foreign policy that attempts to facilitate the spread of Khomeini's ideological goals, while also uniting an ethnically divided state, and prevent the emergence of opposition groups.

External Violence

The revolution of 1979 prompted a spate of action by the regime in Tehran that sought to ensure the survival of the Islamic Republic.

Given the tactics employed by the regime, both in ridding itself of threats and attempting to spread the ideological goals of the revolution, the regime often appears complicit in violent action. This can be seen stemming from the *fatwa* issued by Khomeini against Salaman Rushdie, for his depiction of Muhammad in *The Satanic Verses*,[81] which ushered in a more vociferous policy against dissidents, including targeted assassinations.[82] One such incident saw the death of four Iranian Kurds in Berlin that was investigated by a German court, which, during the process, "implicated the highest levels of the Iranian government and indicted the minister of intelligence, Ali Fallahian, for his role".[83]

As Gary Sick notes:

> Numerous assassinations of enemies abroad in the late 1980s and 1990s were widely and persuasively attributed to Iranian official sponsorship, and Iran was accused of sponsoring operations by other militant organisations, such as the Argentinean bombings of 1992 and 1994 and the 1996 bombing, attributed to Hizballah organisations in Lebanon and Saudi Arabia.[84]

Despite this, Iranian officials have previously condemned the state use of targeted killing and of terrorist tactics. In a CNN interview, Muhammad Khatami, while occupying the office of the president, rejected allegations of terrorism:

> We believe in the holy Quran that says: slaying of one innocent person is tantamount to the slaying of all humanity. How could such a religion, and those who claim to be its followers, get involved in the assassination of innocent individuals and the slaughter of innocent human beings? We categorically reject all these allegations. [...] Terrorism should be condemned in all its forms and manifestations; assassins must be condemned. Terrorism is useless anyway and we condemn it categorically. [...] At the same time, supporting peoples who fight for the liberation of their land is not, in my opinion, supporting terrorism. It is, in fact, supporting those who are engaged in combating state terrorism.[85]

Furthermore, when this line of questioning continued, Khatami responded with the following: "Any form of killing of innocent men and women who are not involved in confrontations is terrorism it must be condemned, and we, in our term, condemn every form of it in the world".[86] This condemnation of terrorist action appears somewhat incongruous when considering the provision of support for Hizballah, either in Lebanon or in Saudi Arabia.[87] When this incongruity is taken with Tehran's actions in the aftermath of the "Arab Spring", an apparent hypocrisy emerges.

Manipulation of Internal Security Dilemmas and Support for Regional Groups

Given the existence of shared religious ties, Iran possesses scope to manipulate internal security dilemmas across the Middle East. In particular, the increasingly troublesome internal security dilemmas in Saudi Arabia and Bahrain appear to have Iranian "fingerprints" on them. However, the extent of Iranian involvement in either Saudi Arabia or Bahrain is difficult to ascertain.

Given the location of oil reserves in the Eastern Province of Saudi Arabia, the stability of the province is of great concern for the Al Saud. Shared religious ties, coupled with the legacy of fears that the Shi'a of Saudi Arabia are an Iranian fifth column, increased the perception of Iranian involvement in manipulating Saudi Arabia's internal security dilemma. When this support is coupled with Iranian support for Shi'i groups in Bahrain, namely the IFLB and Shi'i protesters in the "Arab Spring", one can reach the conclusion that Iran is seeking to manipulate Shi'i-driven internal security dilemmas across the region.

The provision of support for radical organisations across the region has led some to allege Iranian involvement in the June 1996 bombing of the US military base at Al-Khobar,[88] which led to the deaths of 19 US servicemen and the wounding of a further 372. A Department of Justice (DOJ) report published in 2001 identified Hizballah al-Hijaz "as responsible for carrying out the attack and asserted that Iran had 'inspired, supported, and directed' Hizballah organisations in Saudi Arabia, Lebanon, Kuwait, and Bahrain since the early 1980s".[89]

However, despite this allegation, evidence demonstrating contact between Iran and Hizballah al-Hijaz was found only to display links in 1993 and 1994; no evidence existed for 1995 or 1996. These charges were levied with confidence, with claims that the only charges included were those that were believed to hold up in court.

In 2003, a car bombing in Riyadh killed 35 people, including the nine people responsible for the attack. Those responsible were Saudi militants acting under the direction of Al Qai'da. Much like the aftermath of the Khobar Towers bombing, the United States alleged Iranian complicity, although not in offering operational assistance, rather, that Iran was sheltering "senior Al Qai'da operatives who may have been involved in planning the attack".[90]

Despite the perception of ties between Iran and Al Qai'da, the veracity of such claims is open to question. Whilst the eastern border of Iran is alleged to be home to many members of Al Qai'da, it must be stressed that this border area is not secure, and whilst members of Al Qai'da may be present in the region, it may be more relevant to suggest that members of Al Qai'da are there without explicit support from Tehran, or, with support from organisations such as Jundallah. Moreover, despite the common assumption that "my enemy's enemy is my friend", the ideological differences between the regime in Tehran and Al Qai'da are pointed; a radical fundamentalist Sunni organisation and the manifestation of fundamentalist Shi'ism in government do not appear to be ideologies that sit well together.

This belief of Iranian complicity in regional insecurity can also be seen in the aftermath of the "Arab Spring" in Bahrain. Allegations of Iranian involvement in the uprisings in Bahrain have also thus far been unsubstantiated, although clerical ties between Bahrain and Iran are undeniable. Furthermore, ties between Tehran and the IFLB suggest the proximity between Bahraini opposition groups and aspects of the Iranian regime.[91] In addition to this, rhetoric emanating from Tehran has alluded to providing support for opposition groups across the region; however, Iranian support for the Assad regime suggests a hypocrisy with regard to Iranian behaviour in the aftermath of the "Arab Spring". It is, however, difficult to ascertain both the level of support provided to opposition groups in Saudi Arabia and Bahrain or to the Assad regime.

Regional Security

It is argued by Ali Rahigh-Aghsan and Peter Viggo Jakobsen that the rising power of Iran can be described in terms of hard and soft power,[92] with the rise of soft power occurring as a consequence of a changing religious and ideological balance of power across the region. The manifestation of such a changing balance of power has seen increasing Shi'i dominance across Iraq and Lebanon, along with increasing demands for Shi'i political participation.

The exporting of Iranian values through the provision of support, both financial and ideological, for organisations across the region, notably in Iraq, Lebanon and Bahrain, has further solidified Iran's position within the Middle East. Iranian soft power appears to have capitalised upon successes within its "Arab Street" policy. However, it is important to remember that whilst Shi'i power is rising and while there remains little doubt as to the provision of Iranian support to these groups, it may be that the nature of *velayat-e faqih* appears to prohibit stronger ties with Iran. This can be demonstrated by the inability of the revolution to permeate fully across the Middle East and into Central Asia and the Caucasus.[93] The legacy of ethnic tensions between Arab and Persian may also prohibit the emergence of strong ties with Iran, which can be seen in Iraq and Bahrain. Further, Rahigh-Aghsan and Jakobsen suggest that the increasing power of Shi'i populations across the region may result in sectarian tensions within Shi'ism itself, demonstrated by the increasing power of Shi'ism within Iraq.[94]

Iran has also offererd support to several of the "Arab Spring" protests in an attempt to increase its legitimacy across the "Arab Street". Iranian rhetoric has attempted to portray the emergence of Islamic groups in "Arab Spring" as a consequence of the 1979 revolution.[95] However, hypocrisy stemming from the lack of support for opposition groups in Syria, given ties between Tehran and Damascus, may undermine this position and add weight to the suggestion that geopolitical considerations are more important than ideological consideration.

This increasing soft power is often supported by hard power, as demonstrated by Iranian support for Hizballah in Lebanon. Building upon the notion of hard power, it is possible that increased hard power potential, perhaps through a quest for nuclear weapons, would cement Iran as the dominant power in the region. However, one must remember that the origins of the Iranian nuclear programme stem back to the time of the Shah and are not a product of the revolution, the leaders of which, at various times, have condemned nuclear weapons as being "un-Islamic".[96]

Conclusions

While differing slightly in response to opposition groups within each state, both Saudi Arabia and Iran have responded strongly. Although the nature of challenges has differed across the Gulf, challenges have generally threatened the construction of each state, be that in the guise of territorial integrity or ideological sovereignty. An internal security dilemma emerges when a regime chooses to responsd to the group. Given the trans-state characteristics of certain groups, the responses to these groups increase tensions in the external security environment.

Given the internal dynamics of Saudi Arabia and Iran, attempts to foster both increased cohesion and legitimacy and to circumvent challenges to the territorial integrity or ideological sovereignty of the state have been approached in two main ways. The first way was to seek to increase legitimacy and cohesion through referring to narratives, spreading ideological values and positing themselves as against an "other". The nature of the regimes in Saudi Arabia and Iran has provided scope for the exporting of ideological values. As such, both Riyadh and Tehran have sought to spread their interpretation of Islam, often bringing proselytizing agendas into conflict with one another. The second way attempted to shape the nature of internal challenges, through reducing political space for opposition groups and responding to these challenges in ways that would reduce the capacity for future operations.

The importance of Islam and ensuing use of Islamic narratives and rhetoric by both Saudi Arabia and Iran has increased tensions between the two. Indeed, attempts to demonstrate Islamic legitimacy by either Saudi Arabia or Iran have resulted in the other responding with their own rhetoric. In an effort to solidify the Islamic Republic's new status,

Khomeini launched a campaign of rhetoric against the Al Saud, seeking to move Islamic legitimacy from Saudi Arabia to Iran. Riyadh's response rejected the legitimacy of Khomeini and sought to establish a sectarian schism between the two states.

The Al Saud have responded clinically to violence within the Kingdom, initially through gaining *fatwas* to legitimise action, before seeking to remove all aspects of an organisation that may pose a threat to the stability of the state. Organisations threatening the ideological sovereignty of the Kingdom were disbanded and exported, whereas organisations that engage in violence were swiftly crushed. Exporting organisations has a two-fold impact, notably reducing internal tensions but also serving to act as an ideological buffer to Iranian expansions. The idea of legitimacy is important for the Al Saud, given the criticisms levied against the ruling elite and the challenge posed by Iran; as such, the need for *fatwas* legitimising action is indispensible. However, it is fundamental to consider the perceived legitimacy of the Al Saud, given both the alliance with the United States and the attitudes towards the House of Saud on the back of announcements concerning the profligacy of many members of the ruling family.

Iranian leaders have expressed concern as to the maintenance of territorial and ideological soveriengty amidst fears of the erosion of territorial integrity through irredentist or secessionist movements, and ideological sovereignty through competing religious doctrines. Tehran has sought to circumvent challenges to the territorial integrity of the state by highlighting the shared values of Iranian-ness, and Islam; however, as the threat posed by a specific group increases, the state has routinely engaged in a practice of reducing space, occurring within the political, religious and cultural spheres. While a degree of protest is permitted, this must occur in the correct guise, notably demonstrating loyalty to the regime. Furthermore, it is held that to disobey *velayat-e faqih* is to go against God.

In addition to reducing the space of a group, Tehran has also engaged in a policy of blaming external actors for inciting trouble within the Islamic Republic, which can especially be seen with regard to the Azeri protests and Arab riots. The notion of laying blame for dissent at the door of an external actor further stresses the sense of internal cohesion against the external "other". It is possible to hold that threats to the ideological sovereignty of the Islamic Republic are offered less scope for manoeuvre. Given this, threats to the territorial integrity of the state that also pose a threat to the ideological construction of the regime are dealt with in an increasingly severe manner.

The provision of support for regional groups and manipulation of other internal security dilemmas in other states by both Riyadh and Tehran has complicated regional relations, facilitating an increase in sectarian competition. Furthermore, the development of sectarian competition in proxy zones such as Iraq, Lebanon, Bahrain and Syria has facilitated the manifestation of a greater level of geopolitical competition between Saudi Arabia and Iran, demonstrating the importance of ideology within the geopolitical sphere. However, the contradictory positions taken by both states in the aftermath of the "Arab Spring" suggests that, while ideological concerns play an important role in determining the nature of the rivalry, geopolitical concerns play a more integral role in decision-making processes.

7

INTERNAL-EXTERNAL SECURITY DILEMMAS

As argued throughout the book, there exists identity incongruence within both Saudi Arabia and Iran. The severity of this incongruence has manifested itself in internal security dilemmas, between ethnic, tribal, religious and state identities, but also at an external level, with these identities often being in conflict with identities in neighbouring states. In addition to this internal identity incongruence, there exists an external identity incongruence, occurring between the state identities of Saudi Arabia, as an Arab Wahhabi (Sunni) state and Iran, as a Persian Shi'i state. As such, the regimes in Riyadh and Tehran have faced a delicate balancing act, seeking to preserve territorial integrity, ideological sovereignty, domestic and international legitimacy, and regime security. The notion of legitimacy is especially important to a regime, given the severity of pressures that both Saudi Arabia and Iran have to deal with, from both theocratic cores and the international community.

The resolution of internal security dilemmas has created an external security dilemma between Saudi Arabia and Iran, driven by soft power concerns. Within this chapter, the argument considers the the impact of the internal-external security dilemma in shaping the nature of the rivalry. In understanding the impact of the internal security dilemma upon the rivalry between Saudi Arabia and Iran, it is necessary to briefly revisit the internal dynamics of each state.

Revisiting Internal Dynamics

Saudi Arabia has not faced the same degree of identity incongruence as Iran; thus, the internal security dilemma within the kingdom is less severe. Indeed, the internal construction of the Saudi Arabian state reflects far more the nature of a coherent natural state than that of Iran, as reflected both in terms of ethnicity and religion. Nevertheless, Saudi Arabia still possesses internal challenges, as reflected by a fractious relationship with the Shi'i community, tribal pressures, and tensions emanating from the relationship between the Al Saud and Wahhabi *ulama*.

Efforts to create a national identity are fostered by building upon a combination of loyalty to the ruling family and an adherence to Islamic principles. As previously outlined, the Al Saud have fostered a position whereby opposition to the regime is portrayed as un-Islamic. Given this, much of the criticism from the Al Saud has occurred on the grounds that the Al Saud themselves are engaged in un-Islamic acts. The role of the United States prompts a large degree of criticism within the Kingdom, which builds upon the premise that the Al Saud are guilty of *bid'a*.

Opposition groups within Saudi Arabia have little political space within which to operate and, as such, these groups tend to coalesce around religious ideologies. While certain tribal identities may possess stronger claims of legitimacy than the Al Saud, these tribal groups are subjected to further limitations to their space. In times of extreme crisis, these tribal groups are also subjected to internment.

In contrast with Saudi Arabia, Iran faces a large degree of identity incongruence. The revolution of 1979 brought religious issues to the fore within Iranian politics. Previously, identity was based predominantly upon nationalist sentiment, however, post 1979, national identity became synonymous with a Shi'i Islamic identity. Indeed, this was coupled with the use of Persian nationalism, permitting reference to a rich tapestry of history that would supplement Islamic discourse on identity. However, in engaging in a narrow process of identity formation, numerous identity groups remain outside this process.

As noted in chapter four, there exist five religious identities in addition to the state identity, notably Sunni Muslims, Christians, Zoroastrians, Jews and Baluchi. Of these, only Zoroastrians, Jews and Christians are recognised as minorities by the Iranian constitution. Despite this recognition, all religious minorities are encouraged to convert to Shi'i Islam; indeed, the existence of religious minorities to some degree challenges the ideological fabric of the state. When considering ethnic groups, one can look at Arabs, Azeri, Baluchi, Kurds and Turkmen who are not included in Persian–Iranian identity. In addition, these five ethnic groups also possess, to some extent, an irredentist agenda, thus posing threats to the territorial integrity of the state.

As such, it is easy to see the level of identity incongruence existing within Iran. In 1979, identity incongruence was initially lessened, stemming from hope engendered by revolution, although many groups did not receive political and cultural space. Attempts to reduce the level of identity incongruence have predominantly involved restricting political space available to those groups who challenge the regime, in an effort to promote the national identity. This process is then at the expense of other identities within the state. Despite the existence of these threats, the Islamic Republic has retained both its ideological sovereignty and territorial integrity.

Regional Security

Regional security is driven by both soft and hard power. While considering soft power, the use of rhetoric by Mahmoud Ahmadinejad aimed at the "Arab Street" demonstrates the importance of soft power. Yet, the use of this rhetoric has often posited Iran in direct ideological competition with Saudi Arabia and other Arab states who feel threatened by Ahmadinejad's attempts to speak, as Barnett suggests, to the population of a neighbour, rather than to the leaders.

States then seek to maintain internal stability, while reducing the threat posed by external ideologies. Hinnebusch holds that efforts to maintain stability through consolidation have increased tensions within the region. This supports the idea at the heart of the Incongruence

Dilemma, wherein the resolution of internal security dilemmas results in an external security dilemma driven by soft power. Furthermore, the use of "Arab Street" rhetoric and attempts to engage with Arab portfolios is also seen as an attempt to foster internal stability and although emanating from soft power considerations, has the capacity to lead to hard power calculations. Take for instance, the burgeoning Iranian power across the region, which led King Abdullah to urge the United States to "cut off the head of the snake".[1]

The argument within this chapter shall consider the two main areas of competition that comprise the rivalry, the ideological and geopolitical. Given this, the chapter will consider the impact of identity incongruence both within and across Saudi Arabia and Iran upon each sphere.

Ideological Competition

Prior to the revolution of 1979, Saudi Arabia and Iran maintained a relationship that, although not characterised as belligerent, possessed certain characteristics that made a strong alliance unlikely. Despite both Riyadh and Tehran possessing some degree of ties to Washington, alongside "parallel security concerns and no religious leadership rivalry",[2] the relationship was unable to move beyond "a stiff cordiality".[3] The events of 1979 in Iran, however, created numerous spheres of competition. While prior to the revolution, competition between Saudi Arabia and Iran occurred within the guise of ethnic tensions between Arab and Persian, the events 1979 would lead to a marked increase in sectarian differences. Much rhetoric emanated from Tehran, condemning the Al Saud's position within the Islamic world and criticising them for un-Islamic conduct. Building upon the increase in sectarian differences, tensions increased on the grounds of attempts to export the ideological goals of the revolution, which, in turn, increased tensions with Saudi Arabia, who also sought to export ideological goals.

As expanded upon in chapter two, the nature of ideological competition between Saudi Arabia and Iran is located within four areas. Given the spread of ideological competition, the argument shall consider each area in turn, offering an outline of the evolution of ideological competition post 1979.

Ethnic Tensions

As discussed in chapter two, tensions between Persians and Arabs can be derived from centuries of intertwined histories, including a history of conquest achieved by both Arab and Persian armies; these tensions complicated relations between Saudi Arabia and Iran prior to 1979. The legacy of this tension remains and can be seen in Iraq and Bahrain.

Yet, while considering direct competition between Arab and Persian identities, it appears remiss to assume that such competition exists inherently between the two states. Indeed, one can look at the mélange of ethnic identities located within Iran and also the myriad tribal identities in Saudi Arabia to reject this premise. Thus, as a consequence, utilising a Persian identity to unite a state that also is home to Arabs, Azeris, Baluchi, Kurds and Turkmen, appears problematic. However, it appears that Tehran has sought to unite their population through the combination of nationalistic and religious sentiment, as demonstrated by the rhetoric of Mahmoud Ahmadinejad,[4] coupled with Iran's behaviour across the region. Indeed, as Shahram Chubin states, "Power and military strength thus ensure the regime's survival".[5] Building upon this, one can deduce that Iran's behaviour in the Gulf region and wider Middle East, in part, seeks to circumvent internal identity incongruence.

While Saudi Arabia does not suffer the same ethnicity problems as Iran, as discussed in chapter five, tribal loyalties have the capacity to undermine the legitimacy of the ruling family, but also serve as one of their strongest sources of legitimacy. However, the position of tribalism as both a threat to, and a bastion of, legitimacy, arguably causes problems for the Al Saud. Again, the Al Saud's behaviour across the Gulf, Middle East and into Asia can be viewed as an attempt to placate identity groups and foster increased internal cohesion. However, despite the ethnic and tribal mélanges in both Saudi Arabia and Iran, it appears that competition between Saudi Arabia and Iran on ethnic grounds is limited.

Sectarian Issues and the Revolution of 1979

The revolution of 1979 brought religion to the forefront of Middle Eastern politics, filling a space left by the demise of Pan-Arabism.

With the rise of Pan-Islamism, ruling elites across the region sought to demonstrate their Islamic credentials; however, this Islamic discourse across the Middle East was dominated by Saudi Arabia and Iran.

Prior to the events of 1979, Saudi Arabia and Iran were not overtly engaged in sectarian competition. Although Iran maintained a Shi'i identity, the role played by religion within the state was minimal. In contrast, religion was used as a legitimising tool within Saudi Arabia, in an attempt to maintain the ideological sovereignty and legitimacy of the Al Saud.

The revolution of 1979 brought sectarian tensions to the fore, demonstrating the differences between Sunni and Shi'a in a vociferous manner, despite the initial goals of Khomeini to avoid sectarian differences. As outlined in chapter four, Sunni and Shi'i interpretations of Islam differ over several issues, in particular with regard to interpretations of succession. The intricacies of each interpretation have helped to guide the behaviour of both states within the political sphere.

Sectarian tensions between the two were exacerbated by the *Hajj* deaths in 1987,[6] on the back of which diplomatic ties between Saudi Arabia and Iran were severed. This diplomatic crisis highlights the importance of the *Hajj* to both Saudi Arabia and Iran. Furthermore, Saudi Arabia derives much of its external legitimacy from its custodianship of the holy mosques, with one responsibility of this position involving offering protection to all who partake in the *Hajj*. Iranian protests occurring during the *Hajj* increased Saudi Arabian fears concerning Iran's attempts to undermine the legitimacy of the Al Saud within the Islamic world.

A key aspect of Iranian foreign policy in the early years of the revolution was the provision of support for the *mustazefin* across the Islamic world. One such manifestation of the process of offering support for the *mustazefin* was to offer support for Shi'i organisations within Saudi Arabia. Given this, organisations such as Hizballah al-Hijaz received support from Iran, which facilitated a spate of violence that challenged the internal status quo within the Kingdom.[7] Furthermore, Iranian support also went to Kuwaiti Shi'a, who were responsible for explosions near the Grand Mosque in Mecca in 1989,[8] and Bahraini opposition groups. However, it is important to stress that several of these groups possess closer ideological ties with Shi'i clerics in Iraq, such as Grand Ayatollah Sistani, rather than Iran.[9]

Competing Islamic Narratives and Exporting Ideological Goals

The importance of Islam within each state necessitates responses when Islamic rhetoric is used by the other, resulting in a spiralling flux of rhetoric in the aftermath of the revolution. While Iran initially sought to downplay sectarian differences within the Islamic world, Saudi Arabia saw scope to reduce the influence of Iran by stressing the Shi'i nature of the revolution and articulating incompatibility with Wahhabi and Sunni strands of Islamic thought. Iranian rhetoric was predominantly directed at the Al Saud, alleging corruption, impropriety and being traitors to Islam. The Al Saud responded by attempting to portray Khomeini's own impious parallels with God.

Both Saudi Arabia and Iran have sought to export their ideological beliefs across the Muslim world. While the drive to export ideological goals initially was located within the Middle East, this competition spread east into Asia, with both states heavily involved in funding Islamic organisations across the continent.

The nature of *velayat-e faqih* lent itself towards a proselytizing agenda, seeking to transcend the Shi'i world and to pit a "populist Islam of the 'oppressed' (*mustazefin*) against the 'oppressors' (*mustakbarin*), namely conservative, establishment Islam".[10] As such, in attempting to provide support for the *mustazefin*, Iran would provide support for Shi'i groups across the world. This provision of support included offering financial and ideological support for Shi'i organisations within Saudi Arabia, Bahrain, Lebanon and Iraq, further inflaming tensions between Riyadh and Tehran. However, it is important to note that this support was not always accepted, given the ethnic differences between Arab and Persian.

With the growing power of Iran across the region, Saudi Arabia sought to build on existing policies of exporting their own interpretation of Islam, stemming back to the previous decade. The exporting of Wahhabi ideology was furthered as a means to counter the increasing threat posed by Tehran, to expand on their ideological support and to resolve internal problems. With the two states holding positions as the dominant Islamic nations, it is undeniable that Saudi Arabia felt the need to counter gains made by Iran; indeed, it can be argued that within the Islamic world, the competition between Saudi Arabia and Iran (on purely sectarian grounds) can be viewed as a zero-sum game.

The Impact upon Legitimacy

Post 1979, both Saudi Arabia and Iran used religion as a tool to legitimise their respective regimes. Through exporting interpretations of Islam across the Middle East and into Central Asia, both Riyadh and Tehran sought to achieve two goals: firstly, to solidify their position within the Islamic world; and secondly, to expand their sphere of ideological influence. However, Riyadh also sought to achieve a third goal, notably, to use expansionist Islam as a tool to remove the challenge posed internally by revisionist groups.

The rhetoric employed by Khomeini in the aftermath of the revolution sought to increase the legitimacy of the newly formed Islamic Republic and also demonstrate the fallacy of Saudi Arabia's position within the Islamic world. In employing this rhetoric, the Al Saud's legitimacy within the Islamic world was challenged, necessitating a response from the ruling family to solidify their position within the Islamic *umma*. However, in engaging in religious discourse with Iran, the Al Saud opened themselves up to religious criticisms from within the Kingdom, as highlighted by Joseph Nevo and Madawi Al-Rasheed, who suggest that the use of Islam as a legitimising tool is a double-edged sword. Indeed, posturing and symbolic moves as to the possession of Islamic legitimacy also opened the Al Saud to internal criticisms from Wahhabis, who criticised the *bid'a* nature of the ruling family, along with organisations such as Al Qai'da.

As such, one can see the nature of ideological exchanges between Riyadh and Tehran as tantamount to Barnett's notion of symbolic exchanges and strategic framing. Thus, while not directly attempting to communicate with the leaders of respective states, instead focussing upon the *umma*, Saudi Arabia and Iran are engaged in a normative competition, given the entrenchment of both states within the norms of the Islamic world. However, dominance and control is sought through a process of strategic framing and symbolic exchanges.

The Impact upon the Rivalry

The events of 1979 had an undeniable impact upon the rivalry, and nowhere was this felt more than in the area of ideological competition. Through bringing sectarian issues to the fore, Iran sought to challenge the Islamic dominance of Saudi Arabia, both within the Middle East region and the wider Islamic world. As such, the impact of increasing sectarian tensions has caused change in the rivalry, leading to increasingly vitriolic relations. However, in addition, the emergence of increasing sectarian tensions at a state level has the capacity to increase identity incongruence internally.

Iranian identity incongruence has posed serious challenges to the ideological construction of the regime in Tehran. These challenges have coupled the ideological challenge with a threat to the territorial integrity of the regime. In an attempt to respond to the Islamic challenge posed by Iran, the Al Saud attempted to solidify their position within the Islamic world, which, in turn, opened the Al Saud to internal challenges to their legitimacy, as highlighted by Nevo's double-edged sword.

Given these consequences, it is undeniable that change has occurred within the ideological sphere, with Iran laying claim to Saudi Arabia's dominance within the Islamic world. Moreover, the increase in Islamic rhetoric has brought opposing interpretations of Islam to the fore in both Saudi Arabia and Iran, thus increasing incongruence on religious grounds within each state.

Geopolitical Competition

Historically, Gulf security was dominated by Iran and Iraq; however, the events of 2003 dramatically changed the security environment, creating space for Saudi Arabia to operate within, and for Iran to increase its power. With the removal of a belligerent Iraq from the region, both Saudi Arabia and Iran saw the demise of an existential threat to their security, although the presence of the United States within Iraq altered security calculations for both states.

The myriad conflicts besetting the region have undeniably shaped the nature of regional security, yet, in addition to these hard conflicts, there are several other areas determining the regional security environment. Arguably the most pressing is that of the Iranian nuclear programme, regardless of the veracity of such claims; however, there is an argument to suggest that for Sunni states, burgeoning Shi'i power is the most pressing concern. In addition, Iranian involvement in what have typically been perceived as Arab portfolios has fostered an atmosphere of uncertainty as to Tehran's intentions within Saudi Arabia and across both Gulf and wider Middle East regions.

As Chubin and Tripp articulate, post-revolutionary Iran "left a trail of devastation in its regional relations, littered with spontaneous utterances and unfettered intervention in neighbouring states",[11] which highlights the geopolitical changes brought about by the revolution. These changing regional relations impacted upon Saudi Arabia's regional policy, forcing the Al Saud to respond to the ideological changes brought about by the events of 1979.

Given Iranian desires to export the ideological goals of the revolution, and Saudi Arabia's attempts to increase legitimacy for both internal and external identity groups through the provision of support for organisations across the region, tensions between Riyadh and Tehran increased on the back of ideological competition. As such, these ideological tensions manifested themselves within geopolitical competition between the two.

History of Conflict

The Middle East has been beset by conflict since the creation of the state of Israel in 1948. While in years following 1948 the vast majority of state-state conflicts involved Israel, since 1979, most of the state-state conflicts have involved states located within the Gulf region. Indeed, the Gulf has been witness to three major conflicts since the revolution of 1979. With the removal of Saddam Hussein in 2003, there emerged a vacuum over which Saudi Arabia and Iran engaged in competition. As discussed within chapters two and six, it appears that Iraq developed into a proxy war occurring on sectarian grounds, given Iranian support for Shi'i organisations and Saudi Arabian support for Sunni organisations. This, in turn, raises further concerns as to the nature of Gulf security, with the two major powers competing within the sovereign territory of what was formerly the third dominant power in the region.

However, in addition to this interstate conflict, there exist a plethora of conflicts that have occurred between states and non-state actors, both externally, across borders, and internally, within borders. These recent conflicts have often possessed the "fingerprints" of either Iran or Saudi Arabia upon them, as can be seen with regard to the 2006 War between Israel and Hizballah, the events in Bahrain in 2011, the violence in Syria and the ongoing sectarian conflict in Iraq.

The Role of the United States

Prior to the revolution of 1979, Saudi Arabia and Iran maintained relations with the United States, with Washington aiming to create an alliance between the two. In the aftermath of 1979, Iranian-US relations were left in tatters, leaving the United States to form a stronger alliance with Saudi Arabia. As discussed in chapter two, the United States is seen in diametrically opposed ways by Saudi Arabia and Iran, with the former perceiving the United States to be a source of security, while the latter holds the United States to be detrimental to regional security. In addition to this distinction, the role of the United States creates tensions within Saudi Arabia, notably between the Al Saud and the Wahhabi *ulama*.

The Iranian Nuclear Issue

One of the main areas of antagonism between Saudi Arabia and Iran, and Iran and the international community as a whole is that of the perceived Iranian nuclear programme. As noted previously, the roots of the Iranian nuclear programme were located in the time of the Shah; however, it is important to note that Tehran rejects claims that it is seeking nuclear weapons. Regardless of the veracity of these claims, the mere perception that such a programme exists leads many to behave as if a nuclear programme was in existence.[12] As such, Saudi Arabia and the international community must proceed under the assumption that Iran is developing a nuclear weapons programme, immediately increasing geopolitical tensions within the Gulf region.

Saudi Arabia is especially concerned about the prospect of a nuclear Iran, which can be illustrated by the emergence of diplomatic material, released through WikiLeaks, alluding to the Al Saud's desire for the Iranian threat to be quashed. The comments from Dennis Ross, alleging that Saudi Arabia will get nuclear weapons if Iran does, adds weight to fears that Iran's nuclear ambition would trigger a spate of nuclear proliferation across the region.

Fears of Tehran's nuclear programme increase as relations between the two worsen, notably with the election of Mahmoud Ahmadinejad to the office of president in 2005. In an effort to counter the increase in Iranian threats, the balance of power has shifted within the region. Indeed, numerous Arab states have suggested the potential for collusion on the back of an Iranian nuclear weapons programme.

The "Arab Street"

A further complication of geopolitical relations is Tehran's attempts to lay claim to issues that have typically comprised Arab portfolios, that is, issues that are generally used to increase the legitimacy of rulers across the Arab world. This policy attempts to speak to Arab populations, rather than directly to Arab leaders. As articulated previously, the main Arab portfolios are focussed around the Palestinian issue and opposition to the West, and are typically played out within the Levant and the Arab–Israeli conflict.

The argument in chapter two questioned whether Iranian involvement within Arab spheres was an attempt to demonstrate influence across the region or an attempt to end Tehran's isolation from the rest of the region. Given the nature of competition between Iran and the Arab states, and the bellicose rhetoric used in an attempt to undermine Saudi Arabia and other Arab rulers, the notion that Tehran is purely attempting to foster Iranian inclusion across the region is infelicitous.

The first component of Iran's "Arab Street" policy, the Israel-Palestine issue, had long since been a key source of Saudi Arabia's domestic and regional legitimacy, with the Al Saud historically providing vociferous opposition to Israel. Moreover, offering rhetorical support for the Palestinians had long since been a key legitimising tool for Arab rulers across the region, regardless of an inclination, or lack thereof, to support that rhetoric with action. In addition, the second component within the "Arab Street" policy has witnessed increasing involvement within the Levant, notably as Tehran possesses strong ties to Hizballah. Increasing Iranian involvement within the Levant achieved two goals: firstly, increasing the Iranian presence across the region; and secondly, demonstrating the impotency of Saudi Arabia's attempts to oppose Israel efficiently. Furthermore, Iranian support for Hizballah in Lebanon posed problems internally for the Al Saud, who were in a dilemma with regard to offering support for Hizballah, who, despite their opposition to Israel and popular support within the Kingdom, maintain a vociferous Shi'i identity. However, with Iranian involvement within the Israel-Palestine arena and a thawing in relations between Saudi Arabia and Israel, it appears that the balance of power may be shifting.

Spill-Over from Ideological Competition

Given the competing nature of ideological competition, it is logical that this competition will spread into geopolitical competition, stemming from the expansionist nature of *velayat-e faqih* and the Al Saud's attempts to secure its position within the Islamic world. This proliferation of ideological competition into geopolitical competition can be seen in several areas, notably with the support offered by Iran for Hizballah in Lebanon, leading to increasing competition, given Saudi Arabia's support for Hamas.[13] Furthermore, the second manifestation of the proliferation from ideological to geopolitical competition concerns the provision of financial support for Islamic schools and seminaries across the region, with this financial support transcending the immediate Gulf and Middle East regions, spreading into Asia.[14]

The overspill from ideological competition, taken in conjunction with Iranian attempts to harness the support of the "Arab Street", can be seen to have dramatically increased geopolitical tensions within the rivalry. Prime examples of the manifestation of ideological tensions in geopolitical competition can be found in Iraq post 2003, in Bahrain and in Syria.

The Case of Bahrain

The involvement, either actual or perceived, of Saudi Arabia and Iran in Bahrain has severe implications for the security of the Gulf region and wider Middle East. While the roots of this proxy conflict are ideological, the geopolitical importance of the archipelago cannot be understated.[15] Saudi Arabian and GCC concerns about Iranian interference within Bahrain can predominantly be traced back to the revolution of 1979 and Khomeini's desire to export the revolution, although territorial claims to Bahrain existed before this time. Indeed, Shahram Chubin articulated this suspicion of Iranian intentions:

> They need reassurance, too, of the acceptance by Tehran of the principle of non-interference, a primary principle for any regional arrangement in their view. The Saudi government is cautious and believes that the onus is on Iran to prove its genuineness.[16]

Since 1992, Iranian action across the region has fuelled Saudi suspicions about Tehran's intentions.

The perception that protecting the Al Khalifa regime in Manama is a red line for Saudi Arabia has caused direct military intervention within Bahrain, under the guise of a GCC protection force. Bahrain can also be viewed through the lens of the "Arab Street", with both Riyadh and Tehran competing for legitimacy across the region. While the Al Saud have sought to preserve the Al Khalifa, Tehran's tacit support for opposition groups, many of whom are calling for the overthrowing of the monarchy, has increased tensions between the two states.

Internal dynamics within both Saudi Arabia and Iran have also added increased motivation for both Riyadh and Tehran to act in Bahrain. Riyadh is concerned at the increasing power of the Shi'a in Bahrain, and the potential consequences of this increase upon the Shi'a of Saudi Arabia's Eastern Province. In contrast, Tehran is concerned at the impact upon the ideological legitimacy of *velayat-e faqih* if support is not provided for oppressed coreligionists alongside a legacy of nationalist claims to Bahrain.

In light of the beliefs of Shi'ism and *velayat-e faqih*, namely the provision of support for the *mustazefin* of the Muslim world, it is alleged that Iran was increasingly involved in the protests occurring in Bahrain. This belief, coupled with the red line for Riyadh, provided justification for the Saudi intervention within Bahrain. However, as argued by the International Crisis Group report of 2011, "the intervention likely achieved precisely the opposite of what it intended",[17] increasing sympathy towards Iran from the Shi'i populations of Saudi Arabia, Bahrain and possibly also Kuwait. Moreover, in strategic calculations, Tehran can claim victory regardless of the veracity of claims of action within Bahrain on the grounds that sectarian tensions are increasing, within both Bahrain and Saudi Arabia. This is supported by Simon Henderson, who suggests that Iran has embarked on a larger, strategic game, "avoiding direct involvement for now and leaving its coreligionists to be bludgeoned by Bahrain's security forces".[18] Furthermore, sectarian tensions can be said to have been increased across the Middle East region as a whole, with condemnation of the presence of GCC troops in Bahrain from Hizballah's General Secretary Hassan Nasrallah and Iraqi Prime Minister Nouri al-Maliki. However, by failing to act decisively in the provision of support for the Shi'a of Bahrain, there is an argument to suggest that Iran has lost legitimacy within the Muslim world. Moreover, by selectively offering support to protesters across the Middle East during the "Arab Spring", while supporting the regime in the case of Syria, Tehran is in danger of further diminishing its legitimacy across the region.

The case of Bahrain also illustrates the debate over the provision of security within the Persian Gulf. Bahrain shares similar beliefs to Saudi Arabia with regard to the role of external actors, namely the role played by the United States. The Al Khalifa have sought to secure their security through an alliance with the United States, leading to a long-standing US naval presence in Bahrain.[19] However, the alliance with the United States and presence of the US navy's 5th fleet in Bahrain has been used as a leverage against the Al Khalifa by various Shi'i opposition groups, namely the February 14 Freedom Movement, who suggest that the Al Khalifa have allowed the US presence against the wishes of the "brave people of Bahrain".[20] The presence of the United States in Bahrain further adds to Iran's chagrin about the reliance of numerous Gulf states on external actors for security.

Economic Competition

The final aspect of geopolitical competition is that of economic competition. Economic competition was characterised by competition occurring predominantly within OPEC, over the sale of both oil and natural gas. Indeed, this is reflected by competing positions over the price of oil, given internal factors in Iran, resulting in Tehran requiring oil prices to remain around $91 per barrel. Indeed, these internal factors partially emanate from the impact of UN sanctions as a consequence of suspicion regarding the Iranian nuclear programme.

Furthermore, a second area of economic competition can be seen in the provision of financial support to organisations across the region; these organisations include those who possess an ideological affinity with either Iran or Saudi Arabia, or those who can be taken to fall within the geopolitical ambitions of either Tehran or Riyadh.

The Impact of Identity Incongruence

The impact of identity incongruence can clearly be seen with regard to increasing geopolitical tensions between Saudi Arabia and Iran. An obvious area wherein the impact of identity incongruence can be seen is by examining ideas of territorial integrity and congruence between the nation and the state, particularly with regard to Iran. While Saudi Arabia does not appear to suffer challenges to its territorial integrity, indeed, appearing tantamount to a nation-state, Iran faces numerous serious challenges from within.

Iranian geopolitical calculations are guided by concerns over the territorial integrity of the state, which demonstrates the importance of identity incongruence within Iran. As outlined in chapter five, the ethnic mélange in Iran contains six main ethnic groups, with four of those groups (Arabs, Azeris, Baluchis and Kurds) vociferously demanding secession from the Iranian state. These irredentist agendas have an obvious impact upon Tehran's relations with neighbouring states. Indeed, in the conflict between Muslim Azerbaijan and Christian Armenia, Iran sided with Armenia in an attempt to counter irredentist claims posed by Azerbaijan to what has commonly been referred to as "Southern Azerbaijan", or northwestern Iran.

In contrast, Saudi Arabia is not subject to such pressure from identity incongruence upon geopolitical considerations. As previously noted, Saudi Arabia's territorial integrity means that foreign policy calculations do not rest upon the need to placate identity groups within the Kingdom that possess irredentist agendas.

While it appears that the rivalry can be understood in sectarian terms, it is perhaps more important to describe sectarian competition as feeding into geopolitical competition. Indeed, it appears that sectarian competition can foster an increase in geopolitical tensions, with ideological proliferation impacting upon geopolitical stability. Furthermore, these sectarian issues feed into geopolitical concerns, as demonstrated by the Iranian nuclear programm, and attempts to increase support across the Arab world. Moreover, nuclear fears and increased involvement in Arab portfolios are of increasing concern given the ideological persuasion of each state.

The Impact upon the Rivalry

Geopolitical competition between Saudi Arabia and Iran has also evolved since 1979. In addition to ideological competition spreading into the geopolitical sphere, Iranian nuclear aspirations and attempts to be involved in what have typically been seen as Arab issues have increased levels of distrust between Riyadh and Tehran. Nuclear fears have increased Saudi Arabia's fears as to Iranian motives; moreover, Iranian involvement in Arab portfolios has fostered increasing competition between Saudi Arabia and Iran over geopolitical aspirations.

The nature of Iraq post 2003 provides scope for the manifestation of a proxy conflict, while also enabling both Saudi Arabia and Iran to export various groups that may have threatened the ideological construction of regimes in Riyadh and Tehran. The nature of the relationship is shaped in part by the ideological construction of the regime in power. This can be seen through the shift in power within Iran, notably post 2005 and the election of Mahmoud Ahmadinejad. In addition, one can look at the events in Bahrain in March 2011 to see this competition manifest itself further, with Iran supporting the Shi'i protesters, and Saudi Arabia supporting the ruling elite.

Conclusions

Throughout the course of this book, the severity of identity incongruence within Saudi Arabia and Iran has manifested itself in the form of an internal-external security dilemma. While the impact of identity incongruence differs greatly across the two areas of competition, the idea that identity incongruence has impacted upon the rivalry is undeniable. Firstly, there exists incongruence between the identities possessed by Saudi Arabia and Iran. Secondly, there exists incongruence internal to both Saudi Arabia and Iran. It is this second incongruence that constitutes the crux of this work, the response to which constitutes an internal security dilemma, which in turn led to an external security dilemma in the form of soft power.

Saudi Arabia has faced a transparent conflict between identities, as reflected by tensions between the state and its Shi'i population. In addition to the Shi'i challenge, the main threat posed to the Al Saud is in the form of ideological challenges to their rule. As such, one can see this concern manifest itself in policies seeking to portray the Islamic credentials of the ruling elite, often at the expense of its Shi'i community.

Iran faces identity incongruence on grounds of numerous ethnic identity groups existing within the fabric of the Islamic Republic. These ethnic identity groups also have a religious dimension, which has the capacity to be incongruous with the regime's adherence to Shi'i Islam. Several of these identity groups possess irredentist agendas, thus posing challenges to the territorial integrity of the state. The response of the state has been to restrict the political, cultural and religious space of most identity groups; however, attempts to resolve the internal security dilemma have often resulted in the manifestation of violence.

The response to internal security dilemmas has fed into wider levels of identity incongruence across the Gulf and also manifested themselves in an external security dilemma between Saudi Arabia and Iran.

In undertaking analysis of the impact of this, it is necessary to firstly examine each of the spheres of competition within the rivalry, considering the impact of identity incongruence upon each sphere, before turning to the nature of the rivalry as a whole.

The first sphere, of ideological competition, has evolved, on the back of increasing sectarian competition post 1979. The events of 1979 brought sectarian issues to the forefront of Middle Eastern politics, immediately fostering competition between the two dominant Islamic states. Indeed, this sectarian competition comprises both symbolic moves and exchanges in an effort to demonstrate Islamic legitimacy and power. This ideological competition has the obvious capacity to feed into geopolitical competition, which demonstrates the importance of ideology.

The second sphere, geopolitical competition, has also evolved, because of the proliferation of ideological competition into the geopolitical sphere, in conjunction with the increasing involvement of Iran in what have previously been seen as Arab portfolios, along with Tehran's apparent quest for nuclear weapons. Indeed, geopolitical relations have been inflamed by the increase in sectarian tensions. Furthermore, the geopolitical sphere has evolved around the notion that both Saudi Arabia and Iran are competing for regional dominance, more so given the decline of Iraq post 2003.

Given these two spheres, one can see the impact of identity incongruence and an internal-external security dilemma upon the rivalry. While the levels of incongruence differ depending upon structural factors, the notion that identity incongruence can impact upon, and to some extent determine, the nature of the rivalry is undeniable. Having discussed the varying notions of change within ideological and geopolitical spheres, it is possible to differentiate between the levels of change between spheres. It is undeniable that change has occurred within ideological competition and that this has fed in to the evolution of the geopolitical sphere. However, a greater level of change has occurred within the geopolitical sphere, albeit partially stemming from the resulting evolution of the ideological sphere.

CONCLUSIONS

The claim that Middle Eastern security throughout the twentieth and twenty-first centuries has been driven by identity and ideology is undeniable. Pan-Arabism, Pan-Islamism and sectarian conflict have all shaped the regional security environment and continue to do so. National, religious and ethno-tribal identities have guided the behaviour of actors, both internationally and domestically, challenging states, and contesting their sovereignty. In particular, the rise of Pan-Arabism and Pan-Islamism across the region throughout the 1950s and 1960s demonstrates the power of trans-state ideologies. However, in addition to the existence of these ideologies and identities, state sovereignty within the Middle East is also challenged by the existence of powerful identities operating within states. The interplay of these identities and ideologies can best be seen within the Gulf; indeed, post 1979, the Gulf became a contested security environment, which transcended pure hard power competition, becoming a region embroiled in soft power competition.

The events of 1979 in both Saudi Arabia and Iran demonstrate the importance of ideology, seen with the emergence of the Islamic Republic in Iran and the rise of Islamic opposition in Saudi Arabia. The importance of Islam within the Kingdom, coupled with the emergence of a belligerent neighbour claimng legitimacy within the Islamic world, posed a serious challenge to the Al Saud. Yet, in addition to this religious competition, the two states also became increasingly involved in geopolitical competition, both in the Gulf and MENA regions.

In understanding the nature of both ideological and geopolitical competition, it is imperative to consider the internal dynamics of each state. This book has demonstrated how identity incongruence has formed internal security dilemmas in Saudi Arabia and Iran, the response to which has added a soft power dimension to the external security dilemma between the two states. In achieving this, the argument has unpacked the notion of identity incongruence, examining the multifarious identities located within each state. The argument discussed the nature of the threat posed by each identity group, suggesting that identity groups within Saudi Arabia and Iran challenge both the ideological and territorial integrity of each state, stemming from ideological incompatibility with the regime, and/or irredentist or secessionist desires. The state then faces the two dilemmas at the heart of the security dilemma, notably the dilemma of interpretation and the dilemma of response. In responding to these threats, each state becomes embroiled in an external soft power security dilemma as a consequence of a shared normative environment.

By referring to nationalistic and Islamic rhetoric in an effort to unite disparate groups and secure internal legitimacy, coupled with the importance of Islam for the other, any reference to Islamic legitimacy necessitates a response from the other, resulting in a spiral of ideological competition. This is supplemented by reference to an external other, again in an attempt to foster internal unity. Further, by responding in often violent ways to identity groups with irredentist agendas, the trans-state nature of many identities within the region means that neighbouring states often offer support for these identity groups.

Given the competing doctrinal strands within Saudi Arabia and Iran, within both Riyadh and Tehran is a perception that the other is seeking to manipulate the internal security dilemma. The action of both states across the Middle East adds to this perception, particularly when considering action in Iraq, Lebanon, Bahrain and Syria. Thus, one can see the influence of ideology in shaping the nature of the geopolitical environment. However, while this can be viewed in zero-sum terms, perhaps it would be more appropriate to suggest that Saudi Arabia and Iran are seeking to block the other's growth, in the Persian Gulf, Middle East and Central Asia.

While both states seek to increase their legitimacy internally and externally, action in the aftermath of the "Arab Spring" may well undermine this quest for legitimacy. Indeed, the hypocrisy of both Riyadh and Tehran can be seen in the provision of support both for regimes and opposition groups, despite the apparently contradictory nature of this position. This hypocrisy may well go some way to eroding the legitimacy of each state, particularly in light of the changing nature of the Middle East.

In improving the nature of Saudi-Iranian relations there are five areas that must be addressed.

1. The Resolution of Domestic Problems within Saudi Arabia and Iran

If each state resolved internal security dilemmas, then internal stability would be increased, along with reducing the perception that groups are manipulated by external powers. However, while not addressed in this book, both states are facing growing calls for moves towards democracy, which threaten regimes in both Saudi Arabia and Iran. The response to this challenge has the capacity to both unite and divide populations. While the end of Ahmadinejad's second term in office approaches in 2013, it is likely that the conservatives will win the next presidential election and will retain power. Although the death of Crown Prince Nayef has prevented an incredibly hard-line member of the Al Saud, with close ties to the *ulama*, from becoming king, an opportunity was lost to move succession from the sons of Ibn Saud to a different generation of the Al Saud family, more open to reform.

2. A Wider Acceptance and Tolerance of Doctrinal Differences within Islam

A more tolerant position of other facets of Islam by both states will achieve a two-fold result. Firstly, increasing tolereance will reduce the severity of internal security dilemmas driven by religious differences. Secondly, this would remove an important degree of competition from the rivalry, which has often been seen as a zero-sum area of competition.

3. Restrained Behaviour within the Middle East

The action of both states across the region has sought to increase legitimacy, spread ideology and counter the gains of the other, a strategy that is increasing tensions between the two. This can particularly be seen when offering support for groups across the region, particularly within Iraq, Bahrain and Syria. In behaving in a more restrained manner, this would reduce the number of proxy conflicts. Furthermore, both states must remove hypocrisy from their regional strategies, which has been inherent since the outbreak of the "Arab Spring". This would increase the legitimacy of Saudi Arabia and Iran, both internally and externally and improve the stability of the region.

4. Reconsidering the Role of the United States in the Persian Gulf

While regional security has long been a source of contentious discussion between the two states, the role of the United States both in the Persian Gulf and Middle East has been an area of antagonism. The United States maintains a strong visibile presence within the Persian Gulf and Middle East, which challenges Iran's desire for regional security, to be engendered solely by regional actors. Given the strategic importance of the Middle East for the United States, a reconsidered role would have to come from Washington, meaning that a key aspect of the rivalry remains beyond the control of Saudi Arabia or Iran. However, concerns about the nature of regional security have led to point four.

5. A Resolution of the Iranian Nuclear Problem

This resolution must prevent the proliferation of nuclear weapons across the Middle East while maintaining Iranian integrity. The Iranian nuclear programme has fostered much concern within Saudi Arabia and recent new stories have suggested that were Iran to gain the bomb,

Saudi Arabia would follow suit. This would then trigger a spate of proliferation across the Persian Gulf and Middle East. However, the nuclear programme is a source of prestige for many in Iran and as, such, the situation needs to be handled delicately.

While acknowledging the difficulty in resolving any of these problems, steps towards resolution would create scope for *rapprochement.* Unfortunately, unlike prior to the revolution of 1979 when Saudis and Iranians were suspicious of each other but had learned to live together, it appears that, post revolution, to invert the words of Fred Halliday, Saudis and Iranians are currently struggling to live together.

NOTES

Preface to the Paperback Edition

1. See: Richard Spencer, 'Revealed: Saudi Arabia's 'Great Wall' to keep out Isil', (The Telegraph, 14 January 2015) Available from: http://www.telegraph.co.uk/news/worldnews/middleeast/saudiarabia/11344116/Revealed-Saudi-Arabias-Great-Wall-to-keep-out-Isil.html [Accessed 19 June 2015].

Introduction

1. Charlie Savage and Scott Shane, 'Iranians Accused of a Plot to Kill Saudis' US Envoy' (*The New York Times*, 11 October 2011). Available from: http://www.nytimes.com/2011/10/12/us/us-accuses-iranians-of-plotting-to-kill-saudi-envoy.html?_r=1&ref=middl eeast [Accessed 11 October 2011].
2. Taieb Mahjoub and Wissam Keyrouz, *GCC leaders host Ahmadinejad at summit* (Middle East Online, 3 December 2007). Available from: http://www.middle-east-online.com/english/?id=23340 [Accessed 20 January 2009].
3. Fred Halliday, *Nation and Religion in the Middle East* (London: Saqi Books, 2000), p118.
4. *Ibid.*
5. Fred Halliday, *Iran: Dictatorship and Development* (Harmondsworth: Penguin, 1979), p248.
6. *Ibid.*, p249.
7. Madawi Al-Rasheed, *A History of Saudi Arabia* (Cambridge: Cambridge University Press 2002), pp117–118.
8. *Ibid.*, pp118–119.
9. *Ibid.*

10. Formally occurring in 1971, although this was a longer-than-envisaged process.
11. Al-Rasheed, Op. Cit., p118.
12. F. Gregory Gause, *The International Relations of the Persian Gulf* (Cambridge: Cambridge University Press, 2010), p19.
13. *Ibid.*, pp21–2.
14. Halliday, 2000, Op. Cit., p119.
15. Post 1979, this reliance on external powers for security provides one of the main areas of contention within the rivalry.
16. Many Wahhabis would prefer to be called Salafis or Unitarians, reflecting the belief in the one God, receiving Islamic guidance directly from the Qur'an and Sunna, rather than following the teachings of Muhammad ibn Abd al-Wahhab. Despite this, given the body of work exploring Wahhabism, many of which use the term, this work refers to Wahhabism and those who adhere to its teachings as Wahhabis. This does not, however, assume the existence of coherence within Wahhabism.
17. A point illustrated by first the postponement, then cancellation, of the Islamic Solidarity Games, due to be held in Iran in April 2010. Arab nations took issue with Iranian organisers using the name "Persian Gulf" on the logo and medals. See BBC, 'Islamic Solidarity Games cancelled over Gulf dispute' (18 January 2010). Available from: http://news.bbc.co.uk/1/hi/world/middle_east/8465235.stm [Accessed 18 January 2010].
18. Although one should note the legacy of interference within Iran since this time, which appears to somewhat challenge the notion of a natural state, free from external influence. See chapter three for more information.
19. In particular, see Shahram Chubin and Charles Tripp, *Iran-Saudi Arabia Relations and Regional Order* (London: Oxford University Press for IISS, 1996); and Henner Furtig, *Iran's Rivalry with Saudi Arabia between the Gulf Wars* (Reading: Ithaca Press, 2002).
20. John R. Bradley, 'Iran's Ethnic Tinderbox', *The Washington Quarterly,* Vol. 30, No. 1 (2006–7), p181.

1 The Middle East in International Relations

1. Fred Halliday, *The Middle East in International Relations: Power, Politics and Ideology* (Cambridge: Cambridge University Press 2005), p6.
2. Raymond Hinnebusch, *The International Politics of the Middle East* (Manchester University Press: Manchester 2003), pp 54–72.
3. Barry Buzan, *People, States and Fear* (Harlow: Pearson Education Limited 1991); and Barry Buzan, Ole Wæver, Jaap de Wilde, *Security: A New Fra mework for Analysis* (London: Lynne Rienner Publishers, 1998). While this

book does not specifically apply Buzan's work, it seeks to broaden concepts of security, thus sharing a similar agenda to Buzan.

4. Michael N. Barnett, *Dialogues in Arab Politics* (New York: Columbia University Press 1998).
5. See p28.
6. See: Barnett, Op. Cit., Louise Fawcett, *International Relations of the Middle East* (Oxford: Oxford University Press 2005); Gause, 2010 Op. Cit., Halliday, Op. Cit.; Hinnebusch, Op. Cit.; Raymond Hinnebusch, and Anoushiravan Ehteshami (eds.), *The Foreign Policies of Middle East States* (London: Lynne Reiner Publishers 2002); and Gerd Nonneman (ed.), *Analyzing Middle East Foreign Policies and the Relationship with Europe* (Oxon: Routledge 2005).
7. Edward H. Carr, *The Twenty Years' Crisis, 1919–1939: An Introduction to the Study of International Relations* (London: Macmillan, 1946).
8. Hans J. Morgenthau, *Politics Among Nations: The Struggle for Power and Peace* (New York: Knopf, 1967).
9. Although as J. Samuel Barkin correctly points out, "this premise was more a matter of observation than of deduction [...] States were the organisations in international politics with power". Barkin continues, highlighting how Carr suggests that the state may not remain the dominant actor. See J. Samuel Barkin, 'Realist Constructivism', *International Studies Review*, Vol. 5, No. 3 (2003), pp325–342, p328.
10. Morgenthau, Op. Cit., p5.
11. Carr, Op. Cit., p14. Carr's work responded to Liberal Internationalism, which failed to account for power in its explanation of the international system, and as such, failed to explain Japanese and Italian actions towards Manchuria and Abyssinia, respectively.
12. Morgenthau, Op. Cit., p3. This demonstrates the difference between Realism and Liberal Internationalism. Further, while Carr's Realism was predominantly concerned with the notion of scarcity, Morgenthau's Realism was driven by interpretations of human nature. Supporting this claim, Morgenthau set out six principles that he defines as the fundamental principles of Realism, through which he demonstrates politics is governed by objective laws, rooted in human nature.
13. *Ibid.*, p4.
14. Kenneth Waltz, *A Theory of International Politics* (New York: Random House 1979). See also John J. Mearshimer, *The Tragedy of Great Power Politics* (New York: Norton, 2001).
15. A further integral part of Neo-Realism is the Security Dilemma, discussed later in the chapter.

16. Outlined below are several criticisms that this book seeks to address. There are, of course, many criticisms from Constructivists, Marxists, Post-Modernists, amongst others, that this book does not possess scope to cover.
17. Although it is important to note that Waltz is more concerned with structure than actors.
18. Barnett, Op. Cit., pp153–159.
19. Barnett's argument will be discussed in greater detail later in the chapter.
20. Barak Ravid, 'WikiLeaks blows cover off Israel's covert Gulf states ties', (*Haaretz*, 29 November 2010). Available from: http://www.haaretz.com/news/diplomacy-defense/WikiLeaks-blows-cover-off-israel-s-covert-gulf-states-ties-1.327758 [Accessed 6 June 2011].
21. Thucydides c.460 BC-c.395 BC: Greek historian and author of *History of the Peloponnesian War* (London: Heinemann, 1919–1930).
22. Gideon Rose, 'Neo-Classical Realism and Theories of Foreign Policy', *World Politics*, Vol. 51, No. 1, (1998), pp144–172.
23. *Ibid.*, p146.
24. Barkin, Op. Cit., p326.
25. Nicholas Onuf, *World of Our Making* (Columbia: University of South Carolina Press).
26. Alexander Wendt, 'Anarchy is what states make of it: the social construction of power politics', *International Organisation*, Vol. 46, No. 2, (1992), pp391–425.
27. This demonstrates the ontologically opposed positions held by the Constructivist and Realist, respectively.
28. In contrast to other Constructivist thinkers such as Onuf. While I acknowledge the attraction of such approaches, given the prominence of the state in the Middle East, this work shall focus predominantly on Wendt's approach, rather than using a broader Constructivism.
29. *Ibid.* As such, one can see the evolution relationships through the transformation of identities and interests.
30. Maja Zehfuss, *Constructivism in International Relations* (Cambridge: Cambridge University Press 2002), p93.
31. For greater discussion of this problem, see chapters three and four.
32. This idea can be further elaborated if one considers an authoritarian regime maintaining control of civil society through the use of force. Few would argue that the identity imposed by an authoritarian regime is a true reflection of the state's natural identity.
33. The emergence of irredentism suggests an "outgrowth of the complexities inherent in the nation state" and is understood as "any political effort to unite ethnically, historically, or geographically related segments of a

population in adjacent countries within a common political framework". Naomi Chazan, ed. *Irredentism and International Politics* (Boulder: Lynne Reinner, 1991), p1.

34. Fred Halliday, 'For an International Sociology', in: Steven Hobden and John M. Hobson (eds.), *Historical Sociology of International Relations* (Cambridge: Cambridge University Press 2002), pp244–264.
35. Halliday, 2005, Op. Cit.
36. *Ibid.*, p39.
37. Immanuel Wallerstein, 'World-systems analysis', in George Modelski, (ed.), *World System History* (Oxford: Eolss Publishers, 2004).
38. See: Jack Levy, 'The Diversionary Theory of War: A Critique', in Manus I. Midlarsky (ed.), *Handbook of War Studies* (New York and Boston: Unwin Hyman, 1989).
39. Graeme Davies, 'Inside out or outside in: The impact of domestic politics and the great powers on Iranian-US relations 1990–2004', *Foreign Policy Analysis*, Vol. 4, No. 3 (2008), pp209–225, p214.
40. *Ibid.*
41. Hinnebusch and Ehteshami, Op. Cit.
42. Further discussion of Hinnebusch's position occurs in the following works: Hinnebusch, 2003; Op. Cit., Fawcett, Op. Cit.; and Nonneman, Op. Cit.
43. Johan Galtung, 'A structural theory of imperialism', *Journal of Peace Research*, Vol. 8, No. 2 (1971), pp81–117. Galtung argues that imperialism fragmented the region into a multitude of weak and artificial states, forming a classical form of dependence, wherein states are reliant upon external powers, notably for security.
44. Hinnebusch and Ehteshami, Op. Cit. p7.
45. *Ibid.*, p20.
46. Barnett, Op. Cit.
47. *Ibid.*, p25.
48. *Ibid.*, p34.
49. *Ibid.*, p27.
50. Erving Goffman, *The Presentation of Self in Everyday Life* (London: Allen Lane 1969).
51. Barnett, Op. Cit., p33.
52. *Ibid.*, p39.
53. *Ibid.*, p39.
54. *Ibid.*, p40. However, Barnett's position is subject to strong criticisms on ontological grounds, notably the idea that events can and do have objective meaning.
55. *Ibid.*, p49.
56. *Ibid.*, p49

57. See in particular: Barkin, Op. Cit.; Jeffrey Checkel, 'The Constructivist turn in International Relations theory', *World Politics*, Vol. 50, No. 2 (1998), pp324–348; Patrick T. Jackson, Daniel H. Nexon, Jennifer Sterling-Folker, *et al.*, 'Bridging the gap: Toward a Realist-Constructivist dialogue', *International Studies Review*, 6 February 2004, pp337–352.
58. Barkin, Op. Cit., p329.
59. *Ibid.*, p326.
60. *Ibid.*, p332.
61. Although one must stress that these are modified positions, and that a serious criticism levied at Realists is that they generally fail to acknowledge the importance of identity.
62. A term originally coined by John Herz who, along with Herbert Butterfield was responsible for the initial development of the security dilemma. This early work on the security dilemma predominantly focussed upon uncertainty. See John H. Herz, *Political Realism and Political Idealism: A Study in Theories and Realities* (Chicago: University of Chicago Press 1951); and Herbert Butterfield, *History and Human Relations* (London: Collins 1951).
63. Ken Booth and Nicholas J. Wheeler, *The Security Dilemma: Fear, Cooperation and Trust in World Politics* (Basingstoke: Palgrave Macmillan 2008), p1.
64. *Ibid.*, p4.
65. Joseph Nye, *Bound to Lead: The Changing Nature of American Power* (New York: Basic Books, 1990).
66. Joseph Nye, *Soft Power* (New York: Public Affairs, 2004).
67. *Ibid.*, p5.
68. *Ibid.*, p6.
69. Barry R. Posen, 'The security dilemma and ethnic conflict', *Survival*, Vol. 35, No. 1 (1993), p29. Although it is important to note that Posen suggests this occurs when central authority has collapsed. This argument suggests that internal security dilemmas occur with the existence of a belligerent form of identity incongruence that challenges sovereignty, either territorially or ideologically.
70. Clive A. Jones, 'Saudi Arabia after the Gulf War: The internal-external security dilemma', *International Relations*, Vol. 12, No. 6 (1995), pp31–51.
71. Hinnebusch and Ehteshami, Op. Cit., p20.
72. However, it is important to note that while the external security dilemma as posed above shares many characteristics of standard security dilemmas, the debate between Kenneth Waltz and John Mearshimer over defensive and offensive Realism is not applicable, given the focus upon soft power rather than hard power. See John J. Mearsheimer, *The Tragedy of Great Power Politics* (New York: Norton, c2001); and Waltz, Op. Cit.

73. There is, however, a need to focus upon the regional security environment and the international system within which identity groups operate.
74. Halliday, 2000, Op. Cit., p110. However, one should not underestimate the importance of Islam or history in this conflict.
75. Where nation-states represent a congruence between a nationality and a state whereas state-nations do not represent such congruence.
76. Mostafa Rejai, and Cynthia H Enloe, 'Nation-states and state-nations', *International Studies Quarterly*, Vol. 13, No. 2 (1969), pp140–158.
77. We must then define what is understood by the term *interaction.* There are several types of interaction that must be considered, notably legitimate and illegitimate interaction. Moreover, there are two levels of interaction that must be considered: between those identity groups comprising identity incongruence, and between an identity group and the state, or state-society relations. The nature of interaction is contingent upon notions of political space.
78. This is a Sociological/Philosophical definition of Realism, rather than an IR definition of Realism, accepting the existence of identities.
79. Linda Martin Alcoff, Michael Hames-Garcia, Satya P. Mohanty, and Paula M.L. Moya (eds.), *Identity Politics Reconsidered* (New York: Palgrave MacMillan, 2006), p6.
80. Hinnebusch and Ehteshami, Op. Cit., p7.
81. The distinction between ideas of positive and negative freedoms was explicitly articulated by Isaiah Berlin, who speaks of how negative liberty permits individuals to have the political freedoms, or *space*, to act free from government interference. Isaiah Berlin, *Four Essays on Liberty* (Oxford: Oxford University Press, 1969).
82. M.M. Mohammed M. Hafez, *Why Muslims Rebel: Repression and Resistance in the Islamic World* (Colorado: Lynne Reiner Publications, 2003), p28.
83. *Ibid.*
84. Augustus R. Norton, (ed.) *Civil Society in the Middle East: Volume One* (Leiden: E.J.Brill, 2005), p7.
85. *Ibid.*, p11.
86. *Ibid.*
87. Hafez, Op. Cit., p27.
88. For the purposes of this chapter, illegitimate interaction will be defined as the engagement of groups with one another, or with the regime, that transcends legal frameworks within a respective state.
89. Taken to be the disintegration of a state. Posen, Op. Cit.
90. Brian L. Job, 'The Insecurity Dilemma: National, regime and state securities in the Third World', in Brian L. Job (ed.), *The Insecurity Dilemma: National Security of Third World State* (Boulder, CO: Lynne Rienner), p12.

91. Buzan, Op. Cit.
92. When considering the nature of the bi-lateral relationship, an additional layer of interaction is considered: that of state-state interaction.
93. Barnett, Op. Cit., p39.
94. Francesco Cavatorta, 'The convergence of governance: Upgrading authoritarianism in the Arab World and downgrading democracy elsewhere?', *Middle East Critique*, Vol. 19, No. 3 (2010), pp217–232.
95. *Ibid.*, p224.
96. It is pertinent to note that legitimacy may be sought from both internal and external sources.
97. Assuming the space and capacity to act.

2 Arabian Gulf vs Persian Gulf

1. Anoushiravan Ehteshami, 'Iran and its immediate neighbourhood', in Anoushiravan Ehteshami and Mahjoob Zweiri (eds.), *Iran's Foreign Policy from Khatami to Ahmadinejad* (Reading: Ithaca Press, 2008), pp129-130.
2. Halliday, 2000, Op. Cit.
3. *Ibid.*, p110.
4. Chubin and Tripp, Op. Cit., p3.
5. *Ibid.*, p53.
6. For more information, see: Sam Knight, 'Briefing: the 444-day US embassy siege, Tehran 1979' (*The Times*, 30 June 2005). Available from: http://www.timesonline.co.uk/tol/news/world/article538994.ece [Accessed 6 November 2009].
7. Mahmoud Ahmadinejad took office on 3 August 2005 after winning the election with 60 per cent of the vote. Cornwell, Rupert, 'Iran's new leader accused of role in US embassy siege' (1 July 2005). Available from: http://www.independent.co.uk/news/world/americas/irans-new-leader-accused-of-role-in-us-embassy-siege-497146.html [Accessed 6 November 2009].
8. Michael Axworthy, *Iran, Empire of the Mind: A History from Zoroaster to the present day* (London: Penguin, 2008), p12.
9. *Ibid.*, p76.
10. *Ibid.*, p77.
11. *Ibid.*, p78.
12. See: Nazi N.M. Ayubi, *Political Islam: Religion and Politics in the Arab World* (London: Routledge, 1991); Fazlur Rahman, *Islam* (Chicago: Chicago University Press, 1979), amongst others.
13. Figures from 2009. *Mapping The Global Muslim Population: A Report on the Size and Distribution of the Muslim Population* (The Pew Forum, 7 October 2009). Available from: http://pewforum.org/Mapping-the-Global-Muslim-Population.aspx [Accessed 28 September 2010].

14. *Ibid.*
15. A recent report mapping the Muslim population of the world posited a statistic of 10-13 per cent of Muslims adhering to Shi'i doctrine, with the the remaining 87-90 per cent of Muslims following Sunni doctrine. *Ibid.*, p8.
16. Rahman, Op. Cit., p11.
17. *Ibid.*, p13.
18. *Ibid.*, p14.
19. Literal translation, tradition.
20. Rahman, Op. Cit., p14.
21. *Ibid.*, p20.
22. *Ibid.*, p25.
23. Axworthy, Op. Cit., p126.
24. *Ibid.*
25. *Ibid.*
26. Axworthy, Op. Cit., p128. Throughout the duration of this work, unless otherwise stated, "Shi'a" is taken to be Twelver Shi'ism.
27. The first of the four *madhahib,* the Hanifa *madhahib*, emerged 200 years after the death of the Prophet, in the eighth century, while the last, the Hanbali *madhahib*, emerged in the ninth century; the four *madhahib* remain to this day.
28. For a more detailed discussion of Wahhabism, see chapter four.
29. A motif that features on the modern day flag of Saudi Arabia.
30. David Commins, *The Wahhabi Mission and Saudi Arabia* (London: I.B.Tauris, 2006), p158.
31. For Sunni Muslims the Five Pillars are: *Shahada*: monotheism; *Salah*: to pray five times per day; *Sawm*: fasting during the month of Ramadan; *Zakat*: the giving of alms to the poor; and the *Hajj*: pilgrimage to Mecca. The Five Pillars of Shi'ism presuppose those of Sunni Muslims, with a more introspective, abstract outlook.
32. Rahman, Op. Cit., pp68-9.
33. Muhammad Al-'Ashmawi, '*Shari'a*: The codification of Islamic law', in Charles Kurzman (ed.), *Liberal Islam: A Sourcebook* (Oxford: Oxford University Press, 1998), p51.
34. Rahman, Op. Cit., p55.
35. *Ibid.*, p57.
36. *Ibid.*, pp53-4.
37. *Ibid.*, p43
38. The role of *Ijtihad* is important within Shi'i thought. Indeed, it is "the most elevated state of learning in Shi'ism whereby one is thought to be learned and trained sufficiently to interpret religion, allowing the jurisprudent to wield much power in the way of providing or withdrawing legitimacy". See: Farid

Mirbaghari, 'Shi'ism and Iran's foreign policy', *The Muslim World*, Vol. 94 (2004), pp555-563, p557.

39. Anoushiravan Ehteshami, 'The foreign policy of Iran', in Raymond Hinnebusch and Anoushiravan Ehteshami (eds.), *The Middle East in the International System* (London: Lynne Reiner Publishers, 2002), p284.
40. Chubin and Tripp, Op. Cit., p9.
41. See chapter three for the implementation and discussion of *velayat-e faqih*.
42. Ruhollah Khomeini, *Islam and Revolution: Writing and Declarations of Imam Khomeini*, translated and annotated by Hamid Algar (Berkely: Mizan Press, 1981), p61.
43. See pp.139-142.
44. See: Shaul Bakhash, *The Reign of the Ayatollahs* (London: I.B.Tauris, 1985).
45. Fred Halliday, 'Iranian foreign policy since 1979: Internationalism and nationalism in the Islamic Revolution', in Juan R.I. Cole and Nikki R. Keddie (eds.), *Shi'ism and Social Protest* (New Haven: Yale University Press 1986), pp106-7.
46. Chubin and Tripp, Op. Cit., p15.
47. *Organisation of the Islamic Conference*. Available from: http://www.oic-oci.org/page_detail.asp?p_id=52 [Accessed May 2011]
48. Peter Mandaville, *Global Political Islam* (Oxon: Routledge, 2007), p287.
49. *Ibid.*, p287.
50. Martin Kramer, 'Muslim congresses', in John L. Esperito (ed.), *The Oxford Encyclopedia of the Modern Islamic World* (Oxford: Oxford University Press, 1995), p309.
51. *Ibid.*, p310.
52. *Ibid.*
53. Furtig, Op. Cit., p226.
54. The fifth pillar of Islam: a pilgrimage to Mecca that must be carried out at least once in their life time by all able-bodied Muslims who can afford to do so.
55. Jacob Goldberg, 'The Saudi Arabian Kingdom', in Itovar Rabinovich, and Haim Shaked (eds.) *Middle East Contemporary Survey Volume XI: 1987* (Boulder: Westview Press, 1987), p590. The allegations stem from the "confessions" of Iranian pilgrims arrested after the attacks.
56. *Ibid.*, p602.
57. Frederick Wehrey, Theodore W. Karasik, Alireza Nader, Jeremy J. Ghez, Lydia Hansell, Robert A. Guffey, *Saudi-Iranian Relations Since the Fall of Saddam: Rivalry, Cooperation, and Implications for U.S. Policy* (Santa Monica, CA: RAND Corporation, 2009), p42.
58. Chubin and Tripp, Op. Cit., p18.

59. *Ibid.*, p17.
60. *Ibid.*
61. Paul Wood, 'Life and legacy of King Fahd' (BBC, 1 August 2005). Available from: http://news.bbc.co.uk/1/hi/world/middle_east/4734505.stm [Accessed 12 November 2009].
62. For instance, Osama Bin Laden. For greater analysis, see chapter six.
63. Al-Rasheed, 2002, Op. Cit., pp146–7.
64. *Ibid.*, p148.
65. Robin Wright and Peter Baker, 'Iraq, Jordan see threat to election from Iran: Leaders warn against forming religious state' (*The Washington Post*, 8 December 2004), Available from: http://www.washingtonpost.com/wp-dyn/articles/A43980-2004Dec7.html [Accessed 1 May 2010].
66. For greater analysis, see Chubin and Tripp, Op. Cit., p16.
67. Conversation between King Fahd and the German foreign minister, 1 November 1993 in FBIS-NES-93-210, 2 November 1993, in Chubin and Tripp, Op. Cit., p16.
68. Furtig, Op. Cit., p143. It is pertinent to note that Iran has threatened to close the Strait of Hormutz in response to what it perceives to be Western/Israeli aggression.
69. For greater discussion of this issue, see chapter six.
70. Frederick Wehrey, Theodore W. Karasik, Alireza Nader, *et al.*, Op. Cit., pxiii.
71. Kevin M. Woods, Williamson Murray, Elizabeth A. Nathan, Laila Sabara, Ana M. Venegas, *Saddam's Generals, Perspectives of the Iran-Iraq War* (Virginia: Institute for Defence Analysis, 2010), p8.
72. *Ibid.*, p9.
73. Global Security, *Iran-Iraq War (1980-1988).* Available from: http://www.globalsecurity.org/military/world/war/iran-iraq.htm [Accessed 10 October 2009].
74. Halliday suggests this support was given reluctantly, due to a suspicion and fear of Iraq, 2000, Op. Cit., pp122-123.
75. *Ibid.*, p123.
76. *Ibid.*
77. See: Ann Wroe, *Lives, Lies and the Iran-Contra Affair* (London: I.B.Tauris, 1991).
78. Chubin and Tripp, Op. Cit., p10.
79. *Ibid.*, p11.
80. *Ibid.*, p11.
81. *Ibid.*, p12.
82. Rachel Bronson, 'Understanding US-Saudi Relations', in Paul Aarts and Gerd Nonneman (eds.) *Saudi Arabia in the Balance: Political Economy, Society, Foreign Affairs* (London: C.Hurst & Co., 2005), p385.

83. *Ibid.*
84. Chubin and Tripp, Op. Cit., p20.
85. *Ibid.*
86. Bronson, Op. Cit. p386.
87. *Ibid.*
88. CNN, 'Bush State of the Union Address' (29 January 2002). Available from: http://edition.cnn.com/2002/ALLPOLITICS/01/29/bush.speech.txt/ [Accessed 13 January 2009].
89. Frederick Wehrey, *et al.*, Op. Cit., p60.
90. John E., Peterson, *Saudi Arabia and the Illusion of Security* (Oxford: Oxford University Press for the International Institute for Strategic Studies, 2002), p14.
91. *Ibid.*, p7.
92. Chubin and Tripp, Op. Cit., p8.
93. Ehteshami, 2002, Op. Cit., p285.
94. Bronson, Op. Cit., p387.
95. Ehteshami, A., 2002 Op. Cit., p286.
96. *Ibid.*, p285.
97. Notably desires to export revolutionary goals and to create any form of Shi'i bloc throughout the region.
98. The NPT sought to end the nuclear arms race of the Cold War, limiting the number of states in possession of nuclear weapons to five, each of whom has an obligation to take steps towards disarmament. The treaty prohibits those states without nuclear weapons from attempting to purchase or develop such weapons, in return permitting the use of nuclear energy for use in civilian reactors.
99. UN Security Council, 'SC/9792 Security Council demands Iran suspend uranium enrichment of face possible economic, diplomatic sanctions.' Available from: http://www.un.org/News/Press/docs//2006/sc8792.doc.htm [Accessed: 24 August 2009].
100. BBC, 'Q&A: Iran and the nuclear issue' (10 January 2011). Available from: http://news.bbc.co.uk/1/hi/world/middle_east/4031603.stm [Accessed 24 August 2009].
101. Richard L. Russell, *Weapons Proliferation and War in the Greater Middle East* (New York: Routledge, 2005), p78.
102. *Ibid.*
103. *Ibid.*, p62.
104. It is important to note that the text of this *fatwa* has never been released. Gawdat Bahghat, 'Nuclear proliferation: The Islamic Republic of Iran', *International Studies Perspectives*, Vol. 7, No. 2 (2006), p124-136.
105. Frederick Wehrey, *et al.*, Op. Cit., pxv.

106. Chemi Shalev, 'Dennis Ross: Saudi king vowed to obtain bomb after Iran' (*Ha'aretz*, 30 May 2012). Available from: http://www.haaretz.com/news/diplomacy-defense/dennis-ross-saudi-king-vowed-to-obtain-nuclear-bomb-after-iran-1.433294 [Accessed 30 May 2012].
107. *Ibid.*, p63.
108. *The Guardian*, 'US embassy cables: Saudi king urges US strike on Iran' (28 November 2010). Available from: http://www.guardian.co.uk/world/us-embassy-cables-documents/150519 [Accessed 29 November 2010].
109. Frederick Wehrey, *et al.*, Op. Cit., p67.
110. 'Taghier negrash nesbat beh barbame atomi Iran [A change in the level of anxiety among Arabs regarding Iran's nuclear program]', *Tabnak.ir*, 15 April 2008. In Frederick Wehrey, *et al.*, Op. Cit., p71.
111. Notably by the IAEA, and UN alongside numerous states, predominantly the United States, UK and Israel.
112. This idea builds upon the work of William Thomas, and his Thomas' Theorem, which states, "If men define situations as real, they are real in their consequences". See William I. Thomas, and Dorothy S. Thomas, *The Child in America: Behavior Problems and Programs* (New York: Knopf, 1928), pp571-2.
113. As seen with regard to North Korea strengthening its position during the Six Party Talks on the back of a nuclear test.
114. Although Pakistan possesses a nuclear arsenal, the argument is concerned by the existence of an Islamic state at the heart of the Middle East gaining a nuclear weapon.
115. Notably Israel and the United States, with many Israelis portraying a nuclear Iran as an "existential threat".
116. Indeed, many Sunni states remain concerned by the threat posed by Iran.
117. Michael Eisenstadt, Michael Knights, Ahmed Ali, *Iran's Influence in Iraq: Countering Tehran's Whole-of-Government Approach* (Washington: Washington Institute for Near East Policy, 2011).
118. In particular see the increasing level of financial support for Hamas. See: Wehrey, F., Karasik, T. W., *et al.*, *Saudi-Iranian Relations Since the Fall of Saddam: Rivalry, Cooperation, and Implications for U.S. Policy* (Santa Monica, CA: RAND Corporation, 2009), p23.
119. 08RIYADH649, *Saudi King Abdullah and Senior Princes on Saudi Policy towards Iraq* (Wikileaks 20 April 2008) Available from: http://WikiLeaks.as50620.net/cable/2008/04/08RIYADH649.html [Accessed: 7 December 2010].

120. Paul Aarts and Joris van Duijne, 'Saudi Arabia and Iran: Less antagonism, more pragmatism', in Viewpoints Special Edition, *The Kingdom of Saudi Arabia, 1979-2009: Evolution of a Pivotal State* (Middle East Institute), p71.
121. A term referring to general public opinion within Arab states. See: Aarts and van Duijne, Op. Cit., p70. See also: Frederick Wehrey, *et al.*, Op. Cit., pp21-24.
122. *Ibid.*, p4.
123. *Ibid.*, p22.
124. Aarts and van Duijne, Op. Cit., p70.
125. *Ibid.*
126. Al-Rasheed, 2002, Op. Cit., p130.
127. Shaul Shai, *The Axis of Evil: Iran, Hizballah, and the Palestinian Terror* (Piscataway, NJ: Transaction Books, 2005), p149. In Frederick Wehrey, *et al.*, Op. Cit., p23.
128. RAND interviews in Riyadh, March 2007, in Frederick Wehrey, *et al.*, Op. Cit., p24.
129. Aarts and van Duijne, Op. Cit., p70.
130. Frederick Wehrey, *et al.*, Op. Cit., p24.
131. *Ibid.*
132. Aarts and van Duijne, Op. Cit., p70.
133. Baghat Korany and Moataz A Fattah, 'Irreconcilable role-partners? Saudi foreign policy between the Ulama and the U.S.', in Baghat Korany and Ali E Hillal Dessouki (eds.), *The Foreign Policies of Arab States: The Challenge of Globalization* (Cairo: Cairo Press, 2009), p374.
134. Aarts and van Duijne, Op. Cit., p70.
135. Roni Bart, 'The second Lebanon war: The plus column', *Strategic Assessment* Vol. 9, No. 3, (2006). Available from: http://www.inss.org.il/publications.php?cat=25&incat=0&read=85 [Accessed 12 May 2009].
136. Jeffrey White, *If War Comes: Israel vs Hizballah and its Allies* (Washington: Washington Institute for Near East Policy, 2010).
137. Reuters, 'Israel Warns Hizbullah War Would Invite Destruction' (*Reuters*, 10 March 2008). Available from: http://www.ynetnews.com/articles/0,7340,L-3604893,00.html [Accessed 3 June 2009].
138. Frederick Wehrey, *et al.*, Op. Cit., p78.
139. *Ibid.*, p86.
140. The Israeli incursion in Gaza resulted in over 1000 deaths and approximately $2 billion's worth of damage to Gazan assets. The international community condemned the military action, with the United Nations Office for the Coordination of Humanitarian Affairs proclaiming a significant

humanitarian crisis. A UN Report led by Justice Richard Goldstone offered damning criticism of Israeli actions, further concluding that the Israeli Defence Force and Palestinian armed groups committed actions amounting to war crimes.

141. Frederick Wehrey, *et al.*, Op. Cit., p78.
142. International Crisis Group, *Lebanon's Politics: The Sunni Community and Hariri's Future Current.* Available from: http://www.crisisgroup.org/~/media/Files/Middle%20East%20North%20Africa/Iraq%20Syria%20Lebanon/Lebanon/96%20Lebanons%20Politics%20-%20The%20Sunni%20Community%20and%20Hariris%20Future%20Current.pdf [Accessed 13 February 2012], p2. Hariri was assassinated on 14 February 2005, with "converging evidence pointing at both Lebanese and Syrian involvement in this terrorist act". United Nations, *Report of the International Independent Investigation Commission Established Pursuant to Security Council Resolution 1595* (2005). Available from: http://www.un.org/News/dh/docs/mehlisreport/ [Acccessed 13 Febraury 2012], p53.
143. Frederick Wehrey, *et al.*, Op. Cit., p79.
144. *Ibid.*, pp81-2.
145. Yakin Ertuk, *Turmoil in Syria: failed "Arab Spring" or sectarian nightmare?* (Open Democracy, 8 May 2012). Available from: http://www.opendemocracy.net/5050/yakin-erturk/turmoil-in-syria-failed-%E2%80%9Carab-spring%E2%80%9D-or-sectarian-nightmare [Accessed 12 May 2012].
146. International Crisis Group, *Syria's Phase of Radicalisation.* Available from: http://www.crisisgroup.org/~/media/Files/Middle%20East%20North%20Africa/Iraq%20Syria%20Lebanon/Syria/b033-syrias-phase-of-radicalisation [Accessed 12 April 2012], p3.
147. *Ibid.*, p2.
148. Madawi Al-Rasheed, 'The Saudi response to the "Arab Spring": containment and co-option' (*Open Democracy*, 10 January 2012). Available from: http://www.opendemocracy.net/5050/madawi-al-rasheed/saudi-response-to-%E2%80%98arab-spring%E2%80%99-containment-and-co-option [Accessed 15 January 2012].
149. International Crisis Group, *Syria's Phase of Radicalisation*, Op. Cit., p8.
150. Al Arabiya, 'Saudi Arabia has never given "one single arm" to Syrian opposition: source' (*Al Arabiya*, 10 April 2012). Available from: http://english.alarabiya.net/articles/2012/04/10/206761.html [Accessed: 12 April 2012].
151. The Qods (Jerusalem) force is a unit within the IRGC that is tasked with extra-territorial action and exporting revolutionary goals. It is alleged that members of the Qods force were involved in the failed assassination attempt on the Saudi ambassador to the US in October 2011. For greater analysis of the IRGC, see pp146-8.

152. Saeed Kamali Dehghan, 'Syrian army being aided by Iranian forces', (*The Guardian*, 28 May 2012). Available from: http://www.guardian.co.uk/world/2012/may/28/syria-army-iran-forces [Accessed: 28 May 2012].
153. International Crisis Group interview in April 2008, in International Crisis Group, *Iraq After The Surge 1: The New Sunni Landscape.* Available from: http://www.crisisgroup.org/~/media/Files/Middle%20East%20North%20Africa/Iraq%20Syria%20Lebanon/Iraq/74_iraq_after_the_surge_i_the_new_sunni_landscape.pdf Accessed 12 February 2012], p15.
154. International Crisis Group, *Iraq's Transition: On a Knife Edge.* Available from: http://www.crisisgroup.org/~/media/Files/Middle%20East%20North%20Africa/Iraq%20Syria%20Lebanon/Iraq/Iraqs%20Transition%20On%20a%20Knife%20Edge.pdf [Accessed 12 February 2012], p6.
155. Crisis Group interview, senior Sadrist official, November 2007, in International Crisis Group, *Iraq's Civil War, The Sadrists and the Surge.* Available from: http://www.crisisgroup.org/~/media/Files/Middle%20East%20North%20Africa/Iraq%20Syria%20Lebanon/Iraq/72_iraq_s_civil_war_the_sadrists_and_the_surge.pdf [Accessed 12 February 2012].
156. Frederick Wehrey, *et al.*, Op. Cit., p62.
157. *Ibid.*, p62.
158. Notably in the Yemeni civil war and the Dhofar Rebellion in Oman.
159. Nawaf Obaid, 'Stepping into Iraq: Saudi Arabia Will Protect Sunnis If the U.S. Leaves' (*The Washington Post*, 26 Novemeber 2006). Available from: http://www.washingtonpost.com/wp-dyn/content/article/2006/11/28/AR2006112801277.html [Accessed 30 November 2008].
160. Frederick Wehrey, *et al.*, Op. Cit., p63.
161. *Ibid.*, pp64-7.
162. For more indepth analysis, see: Simon Mabon, 'The Battle for Bahrain, Iranian-Saudi rivalry in the aftermath of the Arab Spring', *Middle East Policy*, Vol. 19, No. 2 (2012), which draws upon analysis within this chapter.
163. *Ibid.*, p53.
164. Laura Guazzone, 'Gulf co-operation council: The security policies', *Survival: Global Politics and Strategy*, Vol. 30, No. 2 (1988), pp134-48. However, the International Crisis Group suggests that this is only 70 per cent. International Crisis Group, *Bahrain's Sectarian Challenge.* Available from: http://www.crisisgroup.org/~/media/Files/Middle%20East%20North%20Africa/Iran%20Gulf/Bahrain/Bahrains%20Sectarian%20Challenge.pdf [Accessed 28 January 2012], p1.
165. *2010 Census.* Available from: www.cio.gov.bh/CIO_ARA/English/Publications/census/General%20%20%202011%2002%2006%20-%203.pdf [Accessed: 9 February 2012].

166. Husain Al-Baharna, 'The fact-finding mission of the United Nations Secretary-General and the settlement of the Bahrain-Iran Dispute, May 1970', *International and Comparative Law Quarterly*, Vol. 22, No. 3 (1973), pp541-52.
167. *Ibid.*
168. Frederick Wehrey, *et al.*, Op. Cit., p54.
169. *Ibid.*, p54.
170. Although this remains an important factor driving Saudi policy towards Bahrain.
171. In addition to providing military support, Saudi Arabian support for the Al Khalifa includes bankrolling items on Bahrain's national budget, while also paying for King Hamad's Boeing 747-400. See: Simon Henderson, *Iran's Shadow over Reform in Bahrain* (Washington Institute for Near East Policy, 11 April 2011). Available from: http://www.washingtoninstitute.org/templateC05.php?CID=3347 [Accessed 12 April 2011].
172. Simon Henderson, *Saudi Arabia's Fears for Bahrain* (Washington Institute for Near East Policy, 17 February 2011). Available from: http://www.washingtoninstitute.org/templateC05.php?CID=3309[Accessed 12 October 2011]. The charge of ties with Iran is also levied at the Shi'a of Saudi Arabia's Eastern Province.
173. Dalia Dassa Kaye and Frederic M. Wehrey, 'A nuclear Iran: The reactions of neighbours', *Survival: Global Politics and Strategy*, Vol. 49, No. 2 (2007), pp111-28, p116.
174. Hamad Al Khalifa changed the title of the state from "State of Bahrain" to "Kingdom of Bahrain" in 2002, also changing the title of the ruler from Emir to King, although it is possible to trace political dissatisfaction much earlier than that.
175. For greater discussion of this see: International Crisis Group, *Popular Protests in North Africa and the Middle East (III): The Bahrain Revolt*. Available from: http://www.crisisgroup.org/~/media/files/middle%20east%20north%20africa/iran%20gulf/bahrain/105-%20popular%20protests%20in%20north%20africa%20and%20the%20middle%20east%20-iii-the%20bahrain%20revolt.pdf [Accessed 12 April 2011], pp2-4.
176. Michelle Dunne, *The Deep Roots of Bahrain's Unrest* (Washington D.C.: Carnegie Endowment for International Peace, 2011).
177. International Crisis Group, *Popular Protests in North Africa and the Middle East*, Op. Cit., p6.
178. *Ibid.*, pi.
179. Martin Chulov, 'Saudi Arabian troops enter Bahrain as regime asks for help to quell uprising' (*The Guardian*, 14 March 2011). Available from: http://www.

guardian.co.uk/world/2011/mar/14/saudi-arabian-troops-enter-bahrain [Accessed 14 March 2011]; and William Butler, 'Saudi Arabian intervention in Bahrain driven by visceral Sunni fear of Shias' (*The Observer*, 20 March 2011) Available from: http://www.guardian.co.uk/world/2011/mar/20/bahrain-saudi-arabia-rebellion [Accessed 20 March 2011].

180. Jean Francois Seznec, 'Saudi Arabia strikes back' (*Foreign Policy*, 14 March 2011). Available from: http://www.foreignpolicy.com/articles/2011/03/14/saudi_arabia_strikes_back [Accessed: 15 March 2011].
181. Henderson, Op. Cit.
182. Hasan T. Alhasan, 'The Role of Iran in the failed coup of 1981: The IFLB in Bahrain', *Middle East Journal*, Vol. 65, No. 4 (2011), pp603-617, p603.
183. Hinnebusch, 2003, Op. Cit., p194.
184. Alhasan, Op. Cit., p604.
185. Mehdi Khalaji, *Iran's Policy Confusion about Bahrain* (Washington Institute for Near East Policy, 27 June 2011). Available from: http://www.washingtoninstitute.org/templateC05.php?CID=3376 [Accessed 1 August 2011].
186. Such as Ayatollah Ali Al Sistani.
187. Michael Slackman, 'The proxy battle in Bahrain' (*The New York Times*, 19 March 2011). Available from: http://www.nytimes.com/2011/03/20/weekinreview/20proxy.html?pagewanted=all [Accessed 27 January 2012].
188. F. Gregory Gause, 'Is Saudi Arabia really counter-revolutionary?' in Pomeps Briefings, *Arab Uprisings: The Saudi Counter Revolution*, 9 August 2011. Available from: http://www.pomeps.org/wp-content/uploads/2011/08/POMEPS_BriefBooklet5_SaudiArabia_web.pdf [Accessed 10 August 2011].
189. Khalaji, 27 June 2011, Op. Cit.
190. Khomeini, Op. Cit., p50.
191. Organisation of the Petroleum Exporting Countries, *Annual Statistical Bulletin 2008*. Available from: http://www.opec.org/opec_web/static_files_project/media/downloads/publications/ASB2009.pdf [Accessed 27 June 2009], p6.
192. Chubin and Tripp, Op. Cit., p68.
193. *Ibid.*
194. Keith Kohl, *A Civil War inside OPEC* (Energy & Capital, 2 February 2007). Available from: http://www.energyandcapital.com/articles/opec-oil-cuts/354 [Accessed 11 January 2011].
195. *Ibid.*
196. John Vidal, 'WikiLeaks cables: Saudi Arabia cannot pump enough oil to keep a lid on prices' (*The Guardian*, 8 February 2011). Available from: http://www.guardian.co.uk/business/2011/feb/08/saudi-oil-reserves-overstated-wikileaks [Accessed 8 February 2011].

197. *Ibid.*
198. *Ibid.*
199. Chubin and Tripp, Op. Cit., p69.
200. *Ibid.*, pp67-70.
201. Gerd Nonneman, 'Determinants and patterns of Saudi foreign policy: "Omnibalancing" and "Relative Autonomy" in multiple environments', in Paul Aarts and Gerd Nonneman (eds.), *Saudi Arabia in the balance: Political Economy, Society, Foreign Affairs* (London: C.Hurst & Co., 2005), p321.
202. *Ibid.*, p332.
203. Frederick Wehrey, *et al.*, Op. Cit.,px.
204. Kohl, Op. Cit.
205. Nonneman, Op. Cit., p332.
206. For greater discussion of this, see chapter six.
207. Aarts and van Duijne, Op. Cit., p63.
208. *Ibid.*
209. Frederick Wehrey, *et al.*, Op. Cit., pxiii.
210. Interview with King Abdullah, in *al-Siyasa* (Kuwait), 27 January 2008, quoted in Frederick Wehrey, *et al.*, Op. Cit., p7.
211. *Ibid.*
212. For more information see: Knight, Op. Cit.

3 History, Politics and Narratives of State-Building

1. Halliday, 2000, Op. Cit., p110.
2. Second largest if taking the wider definition of Middle East, to include North Africa, then Sudan is bigger.
3. Central Intelligence Agency, *The World Factbook: Saudi Arabia.* Available from: https://www.cia.gov/library/publications/the-world-factbook/geos/sa.html [Accessed: 1 July 2009].
4. *Ibid.*
5. *Ibid.*
6. Joseph Nevo, 'Religion and national identity in Saudi Arabia', *Middle Eastern Studies*, Vol. 34, No. 3 (1998), p34.
7. Within which there was a war of "every man against every man". See Thomas Hobbes, *Leviathan* (London: Dent, 1973).
8. Al-Rasheed, 2002, Op.Cit., pp191–2.
9. Darryl Champion, *The Paradoxical Kingdom: Saudi Arabia and the Momentum of Reform* (London: C. Hurst & Co., 2003), p28.
10. *Ibid.*

11. However, one must not overplay the role of the British,
12. For more discussion of the role played by the *ikhwan,* see chapter five.
13. Al-Rasheed, 2002, Op. Cit., p3.
14. *Ibid.*
15. Champion, Op. Cit., p68. It is also believed that Ibn Saud had 45 legitimate sons. The number of daughters was not counted.
16. Al-Rasheed, 2002, Op. Cit., p196.
17. Royal Embassy of Saudi Arabia, *Government.* Available from: http://www.mofa.gov.sa/Detail.asp?InSectionID=1545&InNewsItemID=24409 [Accessed: 8 July 2009].
18. Royal Embassy of Saudi Arabia, *The Basic Law of Governance.* Available from: http://www.saudiembassy.net/about/country-information/laws/The_Basic_Law_Of_Governance.aspx [Accessed: 8 July 2009].
19. The Allegiance Council contains one of the purest forms of democracy within Saudi Arabia, with one prince, one vote.
20. Simon Henderson, *After King Abdullah, Succession in Saudi Arabia* (Washington: Washington Institute for Near East Policy, August 2009), p6.
21. Royal Embassy of Saudi Arabia, *Council of Ministers System.* Available from: http://www.saudiembassy.net/about/country-information/government/council_of_ministers_system.aspx [Accessed: 8 July 2009].
22. *Ibid.*
23. None of whom are currently women, although women have served in the *Majlis.* See: Inter-Parliamentary Union, *General Information.* Available from: http://www.ipu.org/parline-e/reports/2373_A.htm [Accessed: 9 July 2009].
24. Inter-Parliamentary Union, *Electoral System.* Available from: http://www.ipu.org/parline-e/reports/2373_B.htm [Accessed: 9 July 2009].
25. Martin Chulov, 'Saudi women to be given right to vote and stand for election in four years' (*The Guardian*, 25 September 2011). Available from: http://www.guardian.co.uk/world/2011/sep/25/saudi-women-right-to-vote [accessed 25 September 2011].
26. Daniel Howden, 'Saudis jail academics who petitioned for reforms' (*The Independent*, 18 May 2005). Available from: http://www.independent.co.uk/news/world/middle-east/saudis-jail-academics-who-petitioned-for-reforms-491111.html [Accessed: 15 July 2009].
27. F. Gregory Gause, *Oil Monarchies: Domestic and Security Challenges in the Arab Gulf States* (New York: Council on Foreign Relations Press, 1994), p78.
28. Peterson, Op. Cit., p53.
29. Organisation of the Petroleum Exporting Countries, Op. Cit., p9.

30. Chubin and Tripp, Op. Cit., p66.
31. Jack Shenker, 'Saudi Arabia king accused of misjudgement bribery in attempt to avoid unrest' (*The Guardian*, 24 February 2011). Available from: http://www.guardian.co.uk/world/2011/feb/24/saudi-arabia-king-accused-bribery [Accessed 24 February 2011].
32. F. Gregory Gause, *Saudi Arabia in the New Middle East* (New York: Council on Foreign Relations, 2011), p6.
33. Lyon, A., Op. Cit.
34. Peterson, Op. Cit., p44.
35. *Ibid.*, p46.
36. *Ibid.*
37. *Ibid.*, p47.
38. *Ibid.*, p55.
39. 'Saudi Arabia: The royal house is rattled too' (*The Economist,* 3 May 2011). Available from: http://www.economist.com/node/18291511 [Accessed 4 May 2011].
40. Mordechai Abir, *Saudi Arabia: Government, Society, and the Gulf Crisis* (London, 1993), pp66–99. In: Commins, Op. Cit., p158.
41. Commins, Op. Cit., p159.
42. Nevo, Op. Cit., p35.
43. Ibn Taymiyya, 1263–1328.
44. Hamid Algar, *Wahhabism: A Critical Essay* (Islamic Publications International: New York, 2002), p8.
45. Commins, Op. Cit., p19.
46. *Ibid.*
47. *Ibid.*, p72.
48. *Ibid.*, p77.
49. Nevo, Op. Cit., p40.
50. Joseph Kostiner, 'State, Islam and Opposition in Saudi Arabia, The Post Desert Storm Phase', *Middle East Review of International Affairs*, Vol. 1, No. 2 (1997), [Online]. Available from: http://meria.idc.ac.il/JOURNAL/1997/issue2/jv1n2a8.html.
51. See: Nevo, Op. Cit., p50; and Al-Rasheed, 2002, Op. Cit., p144.
52. Kostiner, Op. Cit., p7.
53. Peterson, Op. Cit., p48.
54. Anthony H. Cordesman, *Saudi Arabia: Guarding the Desert Kingdom* (Oxford: Westview Press, 1997), p26.
55. *Ibid.*, p27.
56. *Ibid.*, p26.

57. John Bradley, *Saudi Arabia Exposed: Inside a Kingdom in Crisis* (New York: Palgrave Macmillan, 2005), pp90–1.
58. Peterson, Op. Cit., p80.
59. Bradley, Op. Cit., p221.
60. Al-Rasheed, Op. Cit., p146.
61. Fouad N. Abrahim, *The Shi'is of Saudi Arabia* (London: Saqi, 2006), p117.
62. *Ibid.*, pp106–17.
63. F. Gregory Gause III, 'The Foreign Policy of Saudi Arabia', in Raymond Hinnebusch and Anoushiravan Ehteshami (eds.), *The Middle East in the International System* (London: Lynne Reiner Publishers, 2002), p193.
64. Frederick Wehrey, *et al.*, Op. Cit., p61.
65. International Crisis Group, *Popular Protests in North Africa and the Middle East*, Op. Cit., pi.
66. Khalaji, 27 June 2011, Op. Cit.
67. Central Intelligence Agency, *The World Factbook-Iran.* Available from: https://www.cia.gov/library/publications/the-world-factbook/geos/ir.html [Accessed: 1 July 2009].
68. *Ibid.*
69. Shirin Hakimzadeh, *Iran: A Vast Diaspora Abroad and Millions of Refugees at Home* (Migration Information Source, September 2006). Available from: http://www.migrationinformation.org/Profiles/display.cfm?ID=424 [Accessed 12 July 2009].
70. Bradley, 2006–7, Op. Cit., pp181–190.
71. *Ibid.*, p181.
72. *Ibid.*, pp.181–90.
73. Schaeffer, Brenda., 'Iran's volatile ethnic mix' *(International Herald Tribune)*. Available from: http://www.nytimes.com/2006/06/02/opinion/02iht-edshaffer.1874687.html?_r=1 [Accessed 7 July 2009].
74. Central Intelligence Agency, *Iran*, Op. Cit.
75. See chapter four for greater analysis of religious identities within Iran.
76. Farideh Farhi, 'Creating a national identity amidst contentious politics in contemporary Iran', in Homa Katouzian and Hossein Shahidi (eds.), *Iran in the 21st Century, Politics, Economics and Conflict* (Oxon: Routledge, 2008), p13.
77. Axworthy, Op. Cit., p5.
78. *Ibid.*, pxv.
79. *Ibid.*, p12.
80. Farhi, Op. Cit., p13.
81. Axworthy, Op. Cit., p131.

82. Homa Omid, *Islam and the Post-Revolutionary State in Iran* (Basingstoke: Macmillan, 1994), p43.
83. Ervand Abrahamian, *A History of Modern Iran* (Cambridge: Cambridge University Press, 2008), p36.
84. Homa Katouzian, 'Nationalist Trends in Iran 1921–1926', *International Journal of Middle East Studies*, Vol. 10, No. 4 (1979), p533.
85. Percy Sykes, 'South Persia and the Great War', *The Geographical Journal*, Vol. 58, No. 2 (1921), p102.
86. Katouzian, Op. Cit., p534.
87. James L. Gelvin, *The Modern Middle East: A History* (Oxford: Oxford University Press, 2005), p278.
88. Ali Ansari, *Confronting Iran* (New York: Basic Books, 2006), p20.
89. Katouzian, Op,. Cit., p538.
90. *Ibid.* For more information on the political environment within Iran during this time, see also Axworthy, Op. Cit., pp189–224; and Stephanie Cronin, 'Riza Shah and the Disintegration of Bakhtiyari Power in Iran, 1921–1934', *Iranian Studies,* Vol. 33, No. 3/4 (2000), pp349–76.
91. The Anglo-Iranian Agreement of 1919 contained six clauses, beginning with a reiteration of Persian independence and including the offer of assistance necessary for the restructuring of the Persian government. Katouzian suggests that all Iranians, regardless of political persuasion, are in agreement that the Anglo-Iranian Agreement was designed "by the British government to turn Iran into a British protectorate". This suspicion ultimately caused the agreement to be revoked. See: Homa Katouzian, 'The campaign against the Anglo-Iranian Agreement of 1919', *British Journal of Middle Eastern Studies*, Vol. 25, No. 1 (1998), p5.
92. Ali Ansari, *Modern Iran: The Pahlavis and After* (Harlow: Pearson Education Limited, 2007), p32.
93. *Ibid.*
94. *Ibid.*
95. Axworthy, Op. Cit., p223.
96. *Ibid.*, p231.
97. A politician renowned for his vehement opposition to foreign involvement within Iran, who was removed from power in the aftermath of Operation Ajax, the CIA code name for the operation to restore the Shah in 1953.
98. Ansari, 2006, Op. Cit., p25.
99. *Ibid.*, p26.
100. Mokhtari, Op. Cit., p470.
101. Fariborz Mokhtari, 'Iran's 1953 Coup Revisited: Internal Dynamics versus External Intrigue', *Middle East Journal,* Vol. 62, No. 3 (2008), p467.

102. General Razmara was assassinated on 7 March 1951, while Hossein Ala resigned within two weeks, unable to withstand the pressure to nationalise AIOC. See Mokhtari, Op. Cit., p469.
103. Axworthy, Op. Cit., p240.
104. Geoffrey Jones, *Banking and Empire in Iran* (Cambridge: Cambridge University Press, 1986), p318.
105. Mokhtari, Op. Cit., p470.
106. Although as Stephen Kinzer articulates, the United States was initially against the idea of overthrowing a nationalist movement. Indeed, it was only with the election to president of Dwight Eisenhower that this position changed. Further, rather than framing events in Iranian in the context of nationalist groups seizing British property, the Iranian threat was located within a Cold War context. See: Stephen Kinzer, *All The Shah's Men: An American Coup and the Roots of Middle East Terror* (Hoboken: John Wiley & Sons Ltd, 2003), pp3–4.
107. *Ibid.*, pp173–6.
108. *Ibid.*, p176.
109. Axworthy, Op. Cit., p242.
110. Robert Fisk, *The Great War for Civilization* (London: Harper Perennial, 2006), p121.
111. See section on Iran and Islam.
112. Axworthy, Op. Cit., pp261–3.
113. Day of mourning for the martyrdom of Hosein. The parallels between Hosein and the protesters are important to note here.
114. Alireza Asgharzadeh, *Iran and the Challenge of Diversity* (New York: Palgrave MacMillan, 2007), p107.
115. Axworthy, Op. Cit., p269.
116. Furthermore, it is suggested that there were at least 8 grand ayatollahs and 200 ayatollahs who were more senior than Khameini in the religious hierarchy at this time. See: Masoud Kazemzadeh, 'Intra-Elite factionalism and the 2004 Majles elections in Iran', *Middle Eastern Studies*, Vol. 44, No. 2 (2008), p192.
117. It is important to note that while Islam is the dominant religion within Iran, there exist several other religious denominations, the discussion of which shall occur within chapter four.
118. Wilfried Buchta, *Who Rules Iran? The Structure of Power in the Islamic Republic* (Washington DC: The Washington Institute for Near East policy, 2000), p2.
119. BBC, *Iran, Who Holds the Power?* Available from: http://news.bbc.co.uk/1/shared/spl/hi/middle_east/03/iran_power/html/ [Accessed 12 October 2008].

120. Anoushiravan Ehteshami, *After Khomeini: The Iranian Second Republic* (London: Routledge, 1995), p48.
121. *Ibid.*
122. Ayatikkah Montazeri speaking in support of the Guards, *Kayhan*, 27 April 1982, in Omid, Op. Cit., p106.
123. Frederic Whehrey, Jerrold D. Green, Brian Nichiporuk, *et al.*, *The Rise of the Pasdaran: Assessing the Domestic Roles of Iran's Islamic Revolutionary Guards Corps* (Santa Monica: Rand Corporation, 2009), pxi.
124. *Ibid.*
125. Barbara Slavin, *The Iran Stalemate and the Need for Strategic Patience* (Atlantic Council: Iran Task Force, 2010), p4.
126. *Ibid.*, p5.
127. Ali Alfoneh, *The Basij Resistance Force* (USIP The Iran Primer). Available from: http://iranprimer.usip.org/sites/iranprimer.usip.org/files/The%20Basij%20Resistance%20Force.pdf [Accessed 10 December 2011].
128. Butcha, Op. Cit., p66.
129. *Ibid.*
130. Ehteshami, 1995, Op. Cit., p48.
131. As seen in the 2011–12 power struggle between Ahmadinejad and Khamenei, in which Khamenei undoubtably emerged victorious. See: Mehdi, Khalaji, *Iran's Continuing Power Struggles* (Washington Institute for Near East Policy, 20 April 2011). Available from: http://www.washingtoninstitute.org/policy-analysis/view/irans-continuing-power-struggles [Accessed: 14 April 2011].
132. Butcha, Op. Cit., p23.
133. Slavin, Op. Cit., pp3–4.
134. Butcha, Op. Cit., p2. For greater analysis of informal power structures in Iran, see pp6–73.
135. Khalaji, 27 June 2011, Op. Cit.
136. Lamine Ghanmi, 'Morocco cuts ties with Iran over Bahrain' (*Reuters*, 7 March 2009). Available from: http://af.reuters.com/article/topNews/idAFJOE52601D20090307 [Accessed 12 January 2011].
137. Khalaji, 27 June 2011, Op. Cit.
138. Michael Eisenstadt, Michael Knights, Ahmed Ali, Op. Cit., ppix-x.
139. Frederick Wehrey, Theodore W. Karasik, *et al.*, Op. Cit., p62.
140. Vali Nasr, 'Regional implications of Shi'a revival in Iraq', *The Washington Quarterly*, Vol. 27, No. 3 (2004), p18.
141. Michael Eisenstadt, Michael Knights, Ahmed Ali, Op. Cit., p12.

142. Abbas William Samii, 'A stable structure on shifting sands: Assessing the Hizballah-Iran-Syria relationship', *Middle East Journal*, Vol. 62, No. 1, (2008), pp32–53.
143. Iranian Constitution, Article 3.16. Available from: www.alaviandassociates.com/documents/constitution.pdf [Accessed 24 October 2010].
144. Augustus R. Norton, *Hezbollah* (Princeton: Princeton University Press, 2007), p29.
145. *Ibid.*, p33.
146. *Ibid.*, p34.
147. Judith Palmer Harik, *Hezbollah: The Changing Face of Terrorism* (London: I.B.Tauris, 2004), p40.
148. It was believed by many that Hizballah could have won the election, which was instead won by the March 14 coalition. See: *BBC*, 'Lebanon Confirms Hariri Election Win' (8 June 2009). Available from: http://news.bbc.co.uk/1/hi/world/middle_east/8089285.stm [Accessed 13 September 2010].
149. Frederick Wehrey, Theodore W. Karasik, *et al.*, Op. Cit., p24.
150. See Magnus Norell, *A Victory for Islamism: The Second Lebanon War and Its Repercussions* (Washington: Washington Institute for Near East Policy, 2009), p5. And Frederick Wehrey, Theodore W. Karasik, *et al.*, Op. Cit., p25.
151. See: Ambassador Henry Crumpton, cited by Caroline Drees, 'Syria, Iran Lack Full Hizbullah Control: US Official', *Reuters*, 25 July 2006, in Samii, Op. Cit., p50.
152. Norell, Op. Cit., pp11–12.
153. Amos Harel, and Avi Issacharoff, *34 Days Israel, Hezbollah, and the War in Lebanon* (New York: Palgrave Macmillan, 2008), p257.
154. El-Husseini, Op. Cit., p810.
155. *Al-Siyassa*, 14 December 2006, in Norell, Op. Cit., p12.
156. El-Husseini, Rola., 'Hezbollah and the Axis of Refusal: Hamas, Iran and Syria', *Third World Quarterly*, Vol. 31, No. 5 (2010), pp808–9.
157. *Al Jazeera*, 'Ahmadinejad: Holocaust a myth' (14 December 2005). Available from: http://english.aljazeera.net/archive/2005/12/200849154418141136.html [Accessed 12 May 2009]. See also: *BBC*, 'Holocaust comments spark outrage', (14 December 2005). Available from: http://news.bbc.co.uk/1/hi/world/middle_east/4529198.stm [Accessed 12 December 2009].
158. See: Patrick Clawson and Michael Eisenstadt, *The Last Resort: Consequences of Preventative Military Action against Iran* (Washington: Washington Institute for Near East Policy, 2008).

4 Religious Incongruence

1. Hinnebusch, 2003, Op. Cit., p55.
2. *Ibid.*, p55.
3. *Ibid.*, p62.
4. Martin Kramer, *Ivory Towers on Sand: The Failure of Middle Eastern Studies in America* (Washington: Washington Institute for Near East Policy, 2001), p61.
5. Hinnebusch, 2003, Op. Cit., p93.
6. Ervin Staub and Daniel Bar-Tal, 'Genocide, mass killing, and intractable conflict, roots, evolution, prevention, and reconciliation', in David O. Sears, Leonie Huddy, and Robert Jervis (eds.), *Oxford Handbook of Political Psychology* (Oxford: Oxford University Press, 2003), p711.
7. *Ibid.*
8. *Ibid.*, referencing Ervin Staub, *The Roots of Evil: The Origins of Genocide and Other Group Violence* (New York: Cambridge University Press, 1989).
9. Daniel Bar-Tal, 'Introduction: Conflicts and social psychology', in Daniel Bar-Tal (ed.), *Intergroup Conflicts and Their Resolution: Social Psychological Perspective* (New York: Psychology Press, 2011), p4.
10. Yona Teichman and Daniel Bar-Tal, 'Acquisition and development of a shared psychological intergroup repertoire in a context of an intractable conflict', in Stephen M. Quintana and Clark McKown (eds.), *Handbook of Race, Racism, and the Developing Child* (New Jersey: John Wiley & Sons, 2008), p453.
11. Bar-Tal, Op. Cit., p12.
12. Staub and Bar-Tal, Op. Cit., p716.
13. *Ibid.*, p714.
14. Bar-Tal, Op. Cit., p4.
15. Staub and Bar-Tal, Op. Cit., p715.
16. *Ibid.*, p718.
17. *Ibid.*, p720.
18. Bar-Tal, Op. Cit., p15.
19. Staub and Bar-Tal, Op. Cit., p721.
20. *Ibid.*
21. Schwartz, Op. Cit., p261.
22. *Ibid.*
23. Algar, Op. Cit., p10.
24. Commins, Op. Cit., p11.
25. *Ibid.*, p12.
26. Algar, 2002, Op. Cit., p6.

27. Commins, Op. Cit., p10.
28. *Ibid.*
29. Commins, Op. Cit., p12.
30. *Ibid.*, p14.
31. Albert Hourani, *A History of the Arab Peoples* (London: Faber and Faber Limited, 1991), p258.
32. Commins, Op. Cit., pvii.
33. Derek Hopwood, 'The ideological basis: Ibn Abd Al-Wahhab's Muslim revivalism', in Tim Niblock (ed.), *State, Society and Economy in Saudi Arabia*, (Croom Helm Ltd: Breckenham, 1982), p32.
34. Commins, Op. Cit., pvii.
35. *Ibid.*
36. *Ibid.*, p92.
37. Gwenn Okrunhlik, 'State power, religions privilege, and myths about political reform', in Mohammad Ayoob and Hasan Kosebalaban (eds.), *Religion and Politics in Saudi Arabia* (Colorado: Lynne Rienner, 2009), pp92–3.
38. *Ibid.*, p94.
39. Al-Rasheed, Op. Cit., p144. This demonstrated a belief in millenarianism, a convinction in the return of the rightly guided one, typically found in Shi'i thought rather than Sunni. See: Commins, Op. Cit., p163–8.
40. Al-Rasheed, Op. Cit., p144.
41. This was achieved by employing French paratroopers to carry out the military action.
42. Al-Rasheed, Op. Cit., pp145–6.
43. Sherifa Zuhur, *Saudi Arabia: Islamic Threat, Political Reform, and the Global War on Terror* (Strategic Studies Institute U.S. Army War College, 2005), p23.
44. Commins, Op. Cit., p72.
45. *Ibid.*, p77.
46. Mohammad Ayoob and Hasan Kosebalaban, 'Introduction: Unraveling the myths', in: Mohammad Ayoob and Hasan Kosebalaban (eds.), *Religion and Politics in Saudi Arabia* (Colorado: Lynne Rienner, 2009), p3.
47. Commins, Op. Cit., p78.
48. *Ibid.*, p95.
49. *Ibid.*, p97.
50. *Ibid.*, p105.
51. John S. Habib, 'Wahhabi origins of the contemporary Saudi state', in Mohammad Ayoob and Hasan Kosebalaban (eds.), *Religion and Politics in Saudi Arabia* (Colorado: Lynne Rienner, 2009), p63.
52. Commins, Op. Cit., p4.

53. *Ibid.*, p5.
54. Schwartz, Op. Cit., p181.
55. Commins, Op. Cit., p129.
56. *Ibid.*, pp113–4.
57. *Ibid.*, p120.
58. Jones, C., Op. Cit., p32.
59. Commins, Op. Cit., p156.
60. Ayoob and Kosebalaban, Op. Cit., p3.
61. Jones, C., Op. Cit., p32.
62. *9/11 Commission Report.* Available from: www.911commission.gov/report/911Report.pdf [Accessed 4 November 2010], p156.
63. *Ibid.*
64. *Ibid.*
65. *Ibid.*
66. Schwartz, Op. Cit., p265.
67. Lionel Beehner, *Shi'a Muslims in the Middle East* (Council on Foreign Relations, 16 June 2006). Available from: http://www.cfr.org/publication/10903/shia_muslims_in_the_mideast.html [Accessed 7 November 2010].
68. Joseph Teitelbaum, *The Shiites of Saudi Arabia* (Centre on Islam, Democracy and the Future of the Muslim World, 2010). Available from: http://www.currenttrends.org/research/detail/the-shiites-of-saudi-arabia [Accessed 25 Augsut 2010], p1.
69. Al-Rasheed, 2002, Op.Cit., p146.
70. Teitelbaum, Op. Cit., p2.
71. Toby Jones, 'Rebellion on the Saudi periphery: Modernity, marginalisation and the Shi'a uprising of 1979', *International Journal of Middle East Studies*, Vol. 38, No. 2 (2006), p215.
72. *Ibid.*, p213.
73. Al-Rasheed, 2002, Op.Cit., p147.
74. Schwartz, Op. Cit., p266.
75. *Ibid.*, p275.
76. Teitelbaum, Op. Cit., p2.
77. Toby Matthieson, 'The Shi'a of Saudi Arabia at a Crossroads', *Middle East Report Online* (6 May 2009). Available from: http://www.merip.org/mero050609.html [Accessed 7 November 2010].
78. *9/11 Commission Report*, Op. Cit., p60.
79. Global Security, *Saudi Hezbollah.* Available from: http://www.globalsecurity.org/military/world/para/saudi-hezbollah.htm [Accessed: 7 November 2010]. See also *9/11 Commission Report*, Op. Cit., p60.

80. Roger Hardy, 'Hezballah capture marks new escalation', *(BBC*, 12 July 2006). Available from: http://news.bbc.co.uk/1/hi/world/middle_east/5172760.stm [Accessed 12 November 2010].
81. Teitelbaum, Op. Cit., p1.
82. *Ibid.*, p7.
83. *Ibid.*, p5.
84. *Ibid.*, p7.
85. Stephen Blank, Lawrence E. Grinter, Jerome W. Klingaman, *et al.*, *Low Intensity Conflict in the Third World* (Air University Press, 1988), p8.
86. Simon Henderson, *Riot Report Will Force Bahrain to Choose a Direction*, (Washington Institute for Near East Policy, 21 November 2011). Available from: http://www.washingtoninstitute.org/templateC05.php?CID=3424 [Accessed 22 November 2011].
87. Teitelbaum, Op. Cit., p5.
88. *Ibid.*, p4. The Committee for the Defence of Legitimate Rights (CDLR) is a group of prominent Saudi academics, supported by the Najdi *ulama* who are in opposition to the rule of the Al Saud, on grounds of non-compliance with the Shari'a, and on human rights violations. For more information on the CDLR, see chapter six.
89. *Ibid.*, although it is not stated as to which Shi'i strand was accepted.
90. *Ibid.*, p6.
91. Thomas Hegghammer, 'Islamist violence and regime stability in Saudi Arabia', *International Affairs*, Vol. 84, No. 4 (2008), pp701–15.
92. It is imperative to note that Hegghammer makes no distinction between Sunni and Shi'i violence within the Kingdom. Furthermore, Hegghammer outlines the need to make a distinction between socio-revolutionary action, and Pan-Islamism, given the idea that if the regime supports the latter, then it can prevent the development of the former, giving an added layer of security to the state. Moreover, one should note the distinction between classical jihad, which is located within specific theatres of action and global jihad, which seeks to operate in all theatres, using any means possible.
93. *Ibid.*, p702.
94. *Ibid.*
95. This argument is not concerned with attempting to explain the rise of Islamist movements and attempts to differentiate between them. For more information, see: Hegghammer, 2008, Op. Cit.
96. Jason Burke, *Al Qaeda: The True Story of Radical Islam* (London: Penguin, 2007), p3.
97. *Ibid.*

98. Although it is possible that they were chosen as a consequence of their nationality, and due to the ease of attaining US visas for Saudi citizens in comparison with citizens of other Arab states.
99. John Bradley, 'Al Qaeda and the House of Saud: Eternal enemies or secret bedfellows?', *The Washington Quarterly*, Vol. 28, No. 4 (2005), pp139–52. See also, Hegghammer, 2008, Op. Cit., p707.
100. Bradley, 2005, Op. Cit., p139.
101. Bruce Ridel and Bilal Y. Saab, 'Al Qaeda's third front: Saudi Arabia', *The Washington Quarterly*, Vol. 31, No. 2 (2008), p33.
102. See Hegghammer, 2008, Op. Cit., p708, footnote 31.
103. George Tenet, *At the Center of the Storm: My Years at the CIA* (New York: Harper Collins, 2007), p248.
104. Hegghammer, 2008, Op. Cit., p708.
105. Bradley, 2005, Op. Cit., p141. Quoting: Nick Fielding, 'Saudis paid Bin Laden 200 million pounds' (*The Sunday Times,* 25 August 2002) Available from: http://www.timesonline.co.uk/article/0,,2089–393584,00.html [Accessed: 21 July 2009].
106. Hegghammer, 2008, Op. Cit., p709.
107. Ridel and Saab, Op. Cit., p36.
108. For more information see: Ridel and Saab, Op. Cit., p36; and Bradley, 2005, Op. Cit., p142.
109. For more information on the development of Al Qa'ida in the Arabian Peninsula and their capacity to operate within Saudi Arabia, see: Hegghammer, 2008, Op. Cit., pp710–12.
110. Anthony H. Cordesman and Nawaf Obaid, *Al Qaeda in Saudi Arabia: Asymmetric Threats and Islamic Extremists* (Centre for Strategic and International Studies, 26 January 2005). Available from: http://csis.org/files/media/csis/pubs/050106_al-qaedainsaudi.pdf [Accessed 11 April 2010], p4.
111. Thomas Hegghammer, 'Terrorist recruitment in Saudi Arabia', *Middle East Policy*, Vol. 13, No. 4 (2006), p41.
112. *Ibid.*
113. See: Hegghammer, 2006, Op. Cit., p41; and Cordesman and Obaid, Op. Cit., p5.
114. *BBC*, '"Smoke and screams" on board plane', (26 December 2009). Available from: http://news.bbc.co.uk/1/hi/world/americas/8430664.stm [Accessed 26 December 2009].
115. CNN Wire Staff, Yemen-based al Qaeda group claims responsibility for parcel bomb plot (6 November 2010). Available from; http://edition.cnn.com/2010/WORLD/meast/11/05/yemen.security.concern/?hpt=T2 [Accessed: 7 November 2010].

116. Al Qa'ida in the Arabian Peninsula, *Inspire*. Available from: http://publicintelligence.net/complete-inspire-al-qaeda-in-the-arabian-peninsula-aqap-magazine/ [Accessed 1 August 2010], p4.
117. *Ibid.*, p13.
118. *Ibid.*, p14.
119. Toby Matthiesen, 'Hizballah al-Hijaz: A history of the most radical Saudi Shi'a opposition group', *Middle East Journal*, Vol. 64, No. 2 (2010), p194.
120. *Ibid.*, p179.
121. *Ibid.*, p185.
122. Interview with an unnamed cleric of Hizballah al-Hijaz in *Risalat al-Haramayn,* No.0 (1989), in Matthiesen, 2010, Op. Cit., p189.
123. *Ibid.*, p196.
124. Press communique by Hizballah al-Hijaz refuting statements made by al-Safar to Al Arabiya TV Channel, 9 March 2005. Available from: http://www.alhraman. Translated by: Matthiesen, 2010, Op. Cit., p197.
125. Commission on Human Rights, *E/CN.4/Sub.2/AC.5/2003/WP.10 Ethnic and Religious Groups in the Islamic Republic of Iran.* Available from: http://ap.ohchr.org/documents/E/SUBCOM/other/E-CN_4-SUB_2-AC_5-2003-WG_10.pdf [Accessed 7 April 2010], p11.
126. CIA World Fact Book, *Iran.* Available from: https://www.cia.gov/library/publications/the-world-factbook/geos/ir.html [Accessed 2 November 2010].
127. Kazem Alamdari, 'The power structure of the Islamic Republic of Iran: Transition from populism to clientelism, and militarization of the government', *Third World Quarterly*, Vol. 26, No. 8 (2005), p1287.
128. Mirbaghari, Op. Cit., p556.
129. *Ibid.*, p556.
130. As opposed to *akhbariyoon*, which denotes the importance of adhering to the Qur'an and Sunna.
131. *Ibid.*, p557.
132. *Ibid.*
133. Masoud Kamali, *Revolutionary Iran: Civil Society and State in the Modernization Process* (Aldershot: Algate Publishing Ltd, 1998), p156.
134. *Ibid.*, p157.
135. Khomeini, Op. Cit., p41.
136. Kamali, Op. Cit., p157.
137. *Ibid.*, p157.
138. *Surat-e Mashruh-ye Mozakerat-e Majles Baresi-ye Nahai'e-ye Qanun-e Asai-ye Jomhuri-ye Eslami-ye Iran* (The Detailed Deliberations of the Proceedings of the Council on the Final Review of the Constitution of the Islamic Republic

of Iran, *Majles-e* Elamiye Iran), (Tehran), 1986, p73. In: Milani, Mohsen, 'Shi'ism and the State in the Constitution of the Islamic Republic of Iran', in Samih K. Farsoun and Mehrdad Mashayekhi, (eds.), *Iran: Political Culture in the Islamic Republic* (London: Routledge, 1992), p143.

139. Khomeini, Op. Cit., p56.
140. Milani, Op. Cit., p138.
141. Hossein Aryan, 'Blaming Outsiders Won't Solve Iran's Baluchistan Problem'. Available from: http://www.rferl.org/content/Blaming_Outsiders_Wont_Solve_Irans_Baluchistan_Problem/2104613.html [Accessed: 10 August 2010].
142. CIA World Fact Book, *Iran.* Available from: https://www.cia.gov/library/publications/the-world-factbook/geos/ir.html [Accessed 2 November 2010]. The Human Rights Watch Report posits the Sunni population as closer to 20 per cent. Human Rights Watch, *Iran, Religious and Ethnic Minorities: Discrimination in Law and Practice.* Available from: http://www.hrw.org/legacy/reports/1997/iran/ [Accessed 11 August 2010], p21.
143. For more information on ethnic groupings, see chapter five.
144. *Iran Press Service*, 'Iranians told about atrocities against religious minorities' (London: 11 February 1997), In Human Rights Watch, Op. Cit.,p21.
145. Eliz Sanasarian, *Religious Minorities in Iran* (Cambridge: Cambridge University Press, 2000), p43.
146. Human Rights Watch, Op. Cit., p14.
147. *Ibid.*, p15.
148. *Ibid.*
149. *Ibid.*, p17.
150. *Ibid.*; and Commission on Human Rights, Op. Cit., p17.
151. Human Rights Watch, Op. Cit., p19.
152. Sanasarian, Op. Cit., p45.
153. Zoroastrianism is based upon the teachings of the prophet Zoraster/Zarathustra, and is predicated upon a belief that there is one universal and transcendental God.
154. Sanasarian, Op. Cit, p48.
155. Human Rights Watch, Op. Cit., p19.
156. Sanasarian, Op. Cit., p50.
157. *Ibid.*
158. Sanasarian, Op. Cit., p52.
159. Whilst the Baha'i faith was born in Iran, the Baha'i faith is now based in Haifa, after the leaders of the faith were forced to leave Iran.
160. Human Rights Watch, Op. Cit., p10.
161. *Ibid.*
162. *Ibid.*, p11.
163. *Ibid.*, p13.

164. Commission on Human Rights, Op. Cit., p14.
165. *Ibid.*, p14.
166. Human Rights Watch, Op. Cit., p10.
167. *Ibid.*, p14.
168. Commission on Human Rights, Op. Cit., p19.
169. See discourse on Zoroastrians. Human Rights Watch, Op. Cit., p19.

5 Ethno-Tribal Incongruence

1. Peterson, Op. Cit., p297.
2. Nevo, Op. Cit., p34.
3. *Ibid.*
4. Madawi Al-Rasheed and Loulouwa Al-Rasheed, 'The politics of encapsulation: Saudi policy towards tribal and religious opposition', *Middle Eastern Studies,* Vol. 32, No. 1 (Jan., 1996), p106.
5. Joseph Kostiner, *The Making of Saudi Arabia 1916–1936* (Oxford University Press: Oxford, 1993), p3.
6. Champion, Op. Cit., pp66–7.
7. Eleanor A. Doumato, 'Tribalism', in Phillip Mattar, *Encyclopaedia of the Modern Middle East and North Africa* Vol. 4 (Detroit, MI: Macmillan Reference USA, 2004), p2209.
8. Al-Rasheed and Al-Rasheed, Op. Cit., p99.
9. *Ibid.*
10. Doumato, Op. Cit., p2209.
11. Donald P Cole, 'Where have the Bedouin gone?', *Anthropological Quarterly*, Vol. 76, No. 2 (2003), p236.
12. *Ibid.*, p237.
13. *Ibid.*, p251.
14. Ugo Fabietti, 'Sedentarisation as a means of detribalisation: Some policies of the Saudi Arabian government towards the nomads', in Tim Niblock (ed.), *State, Society and Economy in Saudi Arabia* (Croom Helm Ltd: Breckenham, 1982), p187.
15. *Ibid.*, p252.
16. *Ibid.*
17. Al-Rasheed and Al-Rasheed, Op. Cit., p102.
18. Doumato, Op. Cit., p2214
19. Al-Rasheed and Al-Rasheed, Op. Cit., p102.
20. Madawi Al-Rasheed, 'Durable and non-durable dynasties, the Rashidis and Saudis in Central Arabia', *British Journal of Middle Eastern Studies*, Vol. 19, No. 2 (1992), p144.
21. *Ibid.*

22. Joseph Kostiner, 'Transforming dualities: Tribe and state formation in Saudi Arabia', in Phillip S., Khoury and Joseph Kostiner (eds.) *Tribe and State Formation in the Middle East* (Berkeley: University of California Press, 1990), p237.
23. *Ibid.*, p244.
24. *Ibid.*, pp244–5.
25. Tim Niblock, *Social Structure and the Development of the Saudi Arabian Political System* (Beckenham: Croom Helm Ltd, 1982), p90.
26. Champion, Op. Cit., p64.
27. Ibn Khaldun, *The Muqaddimah, Book 1, An Introduction to History,* translated by Franz Rosenthal (Pantheon Books Inc: New York, 1958), p263.
28. *Ibid.*
29. *Ibid.*, p264.
30. *Ibid.*, p314.
31. *Ibid.*, p319.
32. Kostiner, 1990, Op. Cit., p237.
33. *Ibid.*
34. Champion, Op. Cit., p69.
35. Nevo, Op. Cit., p45.
36. Champion, Op. Cit., p66.
37. Kostiner, 1990, Op. Cit., p226.
38. *Ibid.*
39. *Ibid.*, p230. Quoting Harry St. J. Philby, *The Heart of Arabia* (London: Constable and Company, 1922).
40. Champion alleges Ibn Saud married into 30 tribal families to engender support. *Ibid.*, p68.
41. Kostiner, 1990, Op. Cit., p231.
42. Al-Rasheed, Madawi, 1992, Op. Cit., pp150–51.
43. John S. Habib, *Ibn Saud's Warriors of Islam* (Leiden: Brill, 1978), p16, Quoted in Al-Rasheed, 1992, Op. Cit., p150.
44. Joseph Kostiner, 'On Instruments and their desingers: The *Ikhwan* of Najd and the emergence of the Saudi state', *Middle East Studies*, Vol. 21, No. 3 (1985), p298.
45. Kostiner, 1993, Op. Cit., p74
46. *Ibid.*
47. For more information on the *ikhwan* rebellion, see: Daniel Silverfarb, 'Great Britain, Iraq, and Saudi Arabia: The revolt of the *Ikhwan*, 1927–1930', *International History Review*, Vol. 4, No. 2 (1982), pp222; and Champion, Op. Cit., pp48–51.
48. Al-Rasheed and Al-Rasheed, Op. Cit., p99.

49. Kostiner, 1993, Op. Cit., p3.
50. Al-Rasheed and Al-Rasheed, Op. Cit., p108.
51. *Ibid.*
52. *Ibid.*, p115.
53. Fabietti, Op. Cit., pp189–90.
54. *Ibid.*, p195.
55. Niblock, 1982, Op. Cit., p96.
56. *Ibid.*, p93.
57. Al-Rasheed, 1992, Op. Cit., p156.
58. Gause, 1994, Op. Cit., p18.
59. *Ibid.*, p20.
60. *Ibid.*, p23.
61. Al-Rasheed and Al-Rasheed, Op. Cit., p101.
62. Al-Rasheed, 1992, Op. Cit., p150.
63. Al-Rasheed and Al-Rasheed, Op. Cit., p104.
64. Al-Rasheed, 1992, Op. Cit., p104.
65. Al Rashed and Al-Rasheed, Op. Cit., p105.
66. Gause, 1994, Op. Cit., p24.
67. Al-Rasheed and Al-Rasheed, Op. Cit., p105.
68. *Ibid.*, p116.
69. Gause, 1994, Op. Cit., p26.
70. *Ibid.*, p27.
71. *Ibid.*, p26.
72. Hassan Al-Husseini, *The Expatriate Population in Saudi Arabia.* Available from: http://americanbedu.com/2009/06/06/the-expatriate-population-in-saudi-arabia/ [Accessed 8 September 2010].
73. *Ibid.*
74. AMEinfo, *Saudi Arabia – Demographic Trends to Watch For* (AMEinfo, 18 June 2007). Available from: www.ameinfo.com/123859.html [Accessed 8 September 2010].
75. Al-Husseini, Op. Cit.
76. Mohammed Bosbait and Rodney Wilson, 'Education, school to work transitions and unemployment in Saudi Arabia', *Middle Eastern Studies*, Vol. 41, No. 4 (2005), p534.
77. *Ibid.*, p536.
78. David Pollock, *Saudi Arabia by the Numbers* (ForeignPolicy.com, 12 February 2010). Available from: http://www.washingtoninstitute.org/templateC06.php?CID=1414 [Accessed 19 May 2011].
79. Caryle Murphy, 'Saudi Arabia's King Abdullah promises $36 billion in benefits' *(Christian Science Monitor*, 23 February 2011). Available from: http://

www.csmonitor.com/World/Middle-East/2011/0223/Saudi-Arabia-s-King-Abdullah-promises-36-billion-in-benefits [Accessed 28 February 2011].

80. Madawi Al-Rasheed, 'Yes, It Could Happen Here: Why Saudi Arabia is ripe for revolution' *(Foreign Policy*, 28 February 2011). Available from: http://www.foreignpolicy.com/articles/2011/02/28/yes_it_could_happen_here?page=0,0 [Accessed 28 Febraury 2011].
81. *Ninth Five-Year Plan Includes $385 Billion in New Spending.* Available from: http://www.us-sabc.org/custom/news/details.cfm?id=775 [Accessed 18 May 2011].
82. Staff, 'Saudi five-year plan sees stronger private sector' *(Emirates 24/7 News*, 18 October 2010). Available from: http://www.emirates247.com/news/region/saudi-five-year-plan-sees-stronger-private-sector-2010–10–18–1.305509 [Accessed 18 May 2011].
83. It is often believed that religion and language are two of the defining characteristics of ethnic minorities within Iran.
84. These include Armenians, Lors and Turkmen.
85. Max Weber, *Economy and Society: An Outline of Interpretive Sociology*, Guenther Roth, and Claus Wittich (eds.); translated by Ephraim Fischoff, *et al.*, (New York: Bedminster Press, 1968), p389.
86. Perhaps due to the failure to export revolutionary goals beyond the boundaries of the state. It is interesting to consider how a trans-national religious movement has been utilised in an attempt to define a national project. See Farhi, Op. Cit., for further consideration of this.
87. Farhi, Op. Cit., p15.
88. Although this is challenged by irredentist and separatist agendas.
89. *Ibid.*, p17.
90. *Ibid.*, p19.
91. As previously noted, demographic information cannot be taken as wholly accurate. Bradley, 2006–07, Op. Cit., p181.
92. Farhi, Op. Cit., p13.
93. See chapter three for discussion of Persian history.
94. *The Constitution of the Islamic Republic of Iran.* Available from: http://www.iranchamber.com/government/laws/constitution.php [Accessed 12 March 2010].
95. Hussein D. Hassan, *Iran: Ethnic and Religious Minorities* (CRS Report for Congress, 25 November 2008). Available from: http://www.fas.org/sgp/crs/mideast/RL34021.pdf [Accessed 7 April 2010].
96. Human Rights Watch, Op. Cit., p27. While Azeris comprise approximately 40 per cent of the Iranian population, there are some who suggest that Iran is home to 75 per cent of Azeris worldwide. Moreover, the size of the Republic of Azerbaijan is estimated to be a third the size of the combined

areas of a united Azerbaijan. See Nasib Nassibli, *The Azerbaijan Question in Iran: A Crucial Issue For Iran's Future*, Available from: http://www.zerbaijan.com/azeri/nasibzade2.html [Accessed 12 March 2010].

97. See Cameron S. Brown, 'Wanting to have their cake and their neighbour's Too: Azerbaijani attitudes towards Karabakh and Iranian Azerbaijan', *Middle East Journal*, Vol. 58, No. 4 (Autumn 2004).
98. Mahan Abedin, 'Iran at sea over Azerbaijan' (*Asia Times*, 28 September 2009). Available from: http://www.atimes.com/atimes/Middle_East/FI28Ak01.html [Accessed 12 October 2004].
99. Ali M. Koknar, *Iranian Azeris: A Giant Minority* (Washington: Washington Institute for Near East Policy, 6 June 2006).
100. *Ibid.*
101. Human Rights Watch, Op. Cit., p28.
102. Nassibli, Op. Cit.
103. On 12 May 2006, the state-run newspaper *Iran* published a caricature depicting a Persian boy attempting to communicate with a cockroach, which responded in the Azeri tongue. This caricature demonstrates an underlying stereotype within Iran, one that is defamatory towards Azeris. See: Iason Athanasiadis, 'Foreign plots and cockroaches in Iran' (*Asia Times*, 8 June 2006). Available from: http://www.atimes.com/atimes/Middle_East/HF08Ak02.html [Accessed 15 July 2010].
104. Human Rights Watch, Op. Cit., p29.
105. Brown, Op. Cit., p577.
106. *Ibid.*, p578.
107. Human Rights Watch, Op. Cit., p28.
108. Brown, Op. Cit., p594.
109. James Ciment, *The Kurds: State and Minority in Turkey, Iraq and Iran* (New York: Facts on File, 1996), p1.
110. Human Rights Watch, Op. Cit., p24.
111. Evidence of such a military heritage can be seen with regard to arguably the most famous of Kurds, Saladin, the military leader responsible for reclaiming the Holy Land from the Christian Crusaders of Richard Lionheart. See Ciment, Op. Cit., p37.
112. Edgar O'Ballance, *The Kurdish Struggle* (London: Macmillan, 1996), p1.
113. Ciment, Op. Cit., p37.
114. Jawad Mella, *Kurdistan and the Kurds: A Divided Homeland and a Nation Without a State* (London: Western Kurdistan Association), p27.
115. Gerald Chaliand, *The Kurdish Tragedy* (London: Zed Books, 1994), pp19–20.
116. O'Ballance, Op. Cit., p5.

117. *Ibid.*, p4; and Chaliand, Op. Cit., pp19–20.
118. Ciment, Op. Cit., p7.
119. For more information on the Mahabad Republic, see Arichabald B. Roosevelt, Jr., 'The Kurdish Republic of Mahabad', *Middle East Journal*, Vol. 1, No. 3 (1947); or O'Ballance, Op. Cit., pp21–35.
120. O'Ballance, Op. Cit., p43.
121. *Ibid.*, p120.
122. For anecdotal observations of Khalkhadi's tenure as an Islamic judge, see Fisk, Op. Cit., pp158–164.
123. Human Rights Watch, Op. Cit., p26.
124. David McDowall, *The Kurds* (London: Minority Rights Group International, December, 1996), p22.
125. One should observe however, that Human Rights Watch, responsible for reporting this allegation, were unable to confirm this independently. See Human Rights Watch, Op. Cit., p26.
126. Human Rights Watch, Op. Cit., p26.
127. *Ibid.*
128. Zalmay Khalilzad, 'The politics of ethnicity in Southwest Asia: Political development or political decay?', *Political Science Quarterly*, Vol. 99, No. 4 (1984–5), p677.
129. It is worth noting that while the majority of Baluchis are Sunni, there are small numbers who subscribe to Shi'ism and to the Zikriyya sect.
130. Hassan places this number at 1.4 million, while Aryan suggests the figure is 2.5 million. See: Hassan, Op. Cit.; and Aryan, Op. Cit.
131. Alireza Nader and Laha Joya, *Iran's Balancing Act in Afghanistan* (Santa Monica, CA: RAND Corporation, 2011), p11.
132. Aryan, Op. Cit.
133. Human Rights Watch, Op. Cit., p29.
134. *Ibid.*, p30.
135. Aryan, Op. Cit.
136. Human Rights Watch, Op. Cit., p31.
137. *Ibid.*
138. *Ibid.*
139. Aryan, Op. Cit.
140. *Gozinesh* is literally translated as an ideological screening, enshrined within Iranian law in 1988, which determines guidelines for employment and education.
141. *Taqiyah* is the principle of lying when faced with imminent danger, predominantly practiced by Shi'i Muslims. The majority of Sunni Muslims do not believe in the principle.

142. Massoud Ansari, 'We will cut them until Iran asks for mercy' (*The Telegraph*, 15 January 2006). Available from: http://www.telegraph.co.uk/news/worldnews/middleeast/iran/1507890/We-will-cut-them-until-Iran-asks-for-mercy.html [Accessed 13 April 2010].
143. Robert F. Worth, 'Iran says capture of rebel is blow to U.S.' (*The New York Times*, 23 February 2010). Available from: http://www.nytimes.com/2010/02/24/world/middleeast/24insurgent.html [Accessed 13 April 2010].
144. Human Rights Watch, Op. Cit., p30.
145. Bradley, 2006–7, Op. Cit., p183.
146. *Ibid.*
147. Alam B. Saleh, *Identity and Societal Security in Iran* (Unpublished PhD diss., University of Leeds, 2010), pp145–149.
148. *Ibid.*, p146.
149. Ali Ansari, *Modern Iran Since 1921* (London: Pearson Education, 2003), p231.
150. Bradley, 2006–7, Op. Cit., p184. It is important to note that coverage of these riots by Al Jazeera led to the station's ban within Iran. See *BBC*, 'Iran bans Al Jazeera after riots' (19 April 2005). Available from; http://news.bbc.co.uk/1/hi/world/middle_east/4459033.stm [Accessed 22 May 2010].
151. Rasmus C. Elling, 'State of mind, state of order: Reactions to ethnic unrest in the Islamic Republic of Iran', *Studies in Ethnicity and Nationalism*, Vol. 8, No. 3 (2008), p486.
152. UNPO, *Iran Parliamentary Think Tank Warns of Ethnic Unrest.* Available from: http://www.unpo.org/article/3460 [Accessed 17 June 2009].
153. *Ibid.*
154. *Ibid.*
155. Sanasarian, Op. Cit., p12.
156. Muhammad Tahir, *Turkmen Identity on the Wane in Iran* (Institute for War and Peace Reporting: 27 March 2006). Available from: http://www.iwpr.net/report-news/turkmen-identity-wane-iran [Accessed 13 April 2010].
157. *Ibid.*
158. *Ibid.*
159. Saleh, Op. Cit., p154.
160. *Press TV*, 'Iran-Turkmenistan ties unbreakable' (17 April 2010). Available from: http://www.presstv.ir/detail.aspx?id=123531§ionid=351020101 [Accessed 18 May 2010].
161. *BBC*, 'Turkmenistan opens new Iran gas pipeline' (6 January 2010). Available from: http://news.bbc.co.uk/1/hi/8443787.stm [Accessed 8 January 2010].

162. *Press TV*, 'Iran, Turkmenistan launch new gas pipeline' *(Press TV*, 29 December 2009). Available from: http://www.presstv.ir/detail.aspx?id=114878§ionid=351020103 [Accessed 8 January 2010].
163. Firoozeh Kashani-Sabet, *Frontier Fictions, Shaping the Iranian Nation, 1804–1946* (New Jersey: Princeton University Press, 1999), p211.
164. Farhi, Op. Cit., p17.
165. Bradley, 2006–7, Op. Cit., p182.
166. Nayereh Tohidi, *Iran: Regionalism, Ethnicity and Democracy* (Open Democracy, 29 June 2006). Available from: http://www.opendemocracy.net/content/articles/PDF/3695.pdf [Accessed 14 April 2010].
167. *Ibid.*
168. Bradley, 2006–7, Op. Cit., p184.
169. *Ibid.*
170. Elling, Op. Cit., p486.
171. Bradley, 2006–07, Op. Cit., p185.
172. *Ibid.*
173. Bradley, 2006–07, Op. Cit., p186.
174. Worth, Op. Cit.
175. Mark Tran and Saeed K. Dehghan, 'Iran mosque bombing kills dozens' (*The Guardian*, 15 December 2010). Available from: http://www.guardian.co.uk/world/2010/dec/15/iran-chahbahar-suicide-bombing-mosque [Accessed 15 December 2010].
176. Ian Black, 'Iran bombing: Profile of Sunni group Jundallah' (*The Guardian*, 15 December 2010). Available from: http://www.guardian.co.uk/world/2010/dec/15/iran-suicide-bombing-jundallah-profile [Accessed: 15 December 2010].
177. Elling, Op. Cit., p486.
178. Ahmadzadeh Hasham and Gareth Stansfield, 'The political, cultural, and military re-awakening of the Kurdish Nationalist Movement in Iran', *Middle East Journal*, Vol. 64, No. 1 (2010), p22.
179. The Kurdish Democratic Party, the Kurdish Workers' Party, and the Free Life Party of Kurdistan.
180. Hasham, Op. Cit., p26.
181. *BBC*, 'Iranian forces clash with Kurdish separatist group' (27 January 2010). Available from: http://news.bbc.co.uk/1/hi/8482802.stm [Accessed 11 February 2010].
182. Bradley, 2006–07, Op. Cit., pp181–2.
183. *Ibid.*, and Amir Taheri, 'Why some parts of Iran are beyond Ahmadinejad's reach' (*Gulf News*, 31 May 2006). Available from: http://gulfnews.com/opinions/columnists/why-some-parts-of-iran-are-beyond-ahmadinejad-s-reach-1.238982 [Accessed: 7 March 2010].

184. Bradley draws attention to the possibility of a Jundallah attack on Ahmadinejad, referencing an earlier attack on a presidential convoy. Bradley, 2006–07, Op. Cit., p187.
185. Tahir, Op. Cit.

6 The Response of the State

1. These ideas of de-politicisation are all internal to a state. Thus, while an organisation may be de-politicised from one state, through being exported, that does not necessarily mean their political agenda has been eradicated.
2. Hooshang Amirahmadi and Nader Entessar (eds.), *Iran and the Arab World* (Basingstoke: Macmillan, 1993), p3.
3. Con Coughlin, *Khomeini's Ghost* (London: Macmillan, 2009), p274.
4. '*Excerpts from Khomeini's Speeches*', (*The New York Times*, 4 August 1987). Available from: http://www.nytimes.com/1987/08/04/world/excerpts-from-khomeini-speeches.html?pagewanted=all&src=pm [Accessed 10 June 2009].
5. *The New York Times*, 4 August 1987, Op. Cit.
6. Goldberg, Op. Cit., p589.
7. *The New York Times*, 4 August 1987, Op. Cit.
8. Furtig, Op. Cit., p219.
9. Goldberg, Op. Cit., p589.
10. *Ibid.*
11. *Ibid.*, p602.
12. *Ibid.*
13. Baqer Moin, *Khomeini: Life of the Ayatollah* (London: I.B.Tauris, 1999), p305.
14. *Ibid.*
15. Vali Nasr, *The Shia Revival: How Conflicst within Islam Will Shape the Future* (New York: W.W. Norton, 2007), p236.
16. Frederick Wehrey, Theodore W. Karasik, *et al.*, Op. Cit., p38.
17. *Ibid.*, p39.
18. *The Guardian*, 'US embassy cables: Saudi youths "frolic under princely protection"', (7 December 2010). Available from: http://www.guardian.co.uk/world/us-embassy-cables-documents/235420 [Accessed: 7 December 2010].
19. Said K. Aburish, *The Rise, Corruption and Coming Fall of The House of Saud* (London: Bloomsbury, 1994), p304.
20. *Ibid.*, p303.
21. *Ibid.*, p78. For Aburish, the two evils were "booze and violence".

22. The creation of this film provoked a diplomatic crisis between Saudi Arabia and the UK. See Aburish, Op. Cit., pp80–1.
23. Hegghammer, 2008, Op. Cit., p704.
24. *Ibid.*
25. *Ibid.* This figure demonstrates the symbolic nature of the Palestinian cause, in contrast to the level of support given to Muslims in the Balkans.
26. Schwartz, Op. Cit., p154.
27. *Ibid.*, p155.
28. Haroon Siddique and agencies, 'BBC's Panorama claims Islamic schools teach anti-Semitism and homophobia' (*The Guardian*, 22 November 2010). Available from: http://www.guardian.co.uk/media/2010/nov/22/bbc-panorama-islamic-schools-antisemitism [Accessed: 22 Novemeber 10].
29. *Ibid.*
30. A third strategy concerns the nature of tribal opposition. As articulated in chapter five, the Al Saud has faced opposition in the form of rival tribes, notably the Al-Rasheed. The Al Saud sought to marginalise the Al-Rasheed, in order to prevent the rise of an opposition group possessing a perceived greater legitimacy than the House of Saud.
31. C. Jones, Op. Cit., p35.
32. Joseph A. Kechichian, *Succession in Saudi Arabia* (New York: Palgrave Macmillan, 2001), p109.
33. C. Jones, Op. Cit., p35.
34. *Ibid.*, p36.
35. Commins, Op. Cit., p168. Commins articulates how those charged, were found guilty of seven crimes, notably violating the Haram's sanctity, killing fellow Muslims, and disobeying legitimate authorities.
36. Fouad N. Ibrahim, *The Shi'is of Saudi Arabia* (London: Saqi, 2006), p120.
37. Ridel and Saab, Op. Cit., p37.
38. *Ibid.*
39. *Ibid.*
40. Matthiesen, 2010, Op. Cit., p186.
41. *Ibid.*, p191.
42. This was not explicitly the phrase used.
43. Frederick Wehrey, Theodore W. Karasik, *et al.*, Op. Cit., p34.
44. *Ibid.*, p35.
45. Ascertained through conversations with an Iranian Arab and an Iraqi Kurd.
46. Frederick Wehrey, Theodore W. Karasik, *et al.*, Op. Cit., p35.

47. See: Bradley, 2005, Op. Cit., pp145–6; and Ridel and Saab, Op. Cit., pp33–46.
48. Declan Walsh, 'WikiLeaks cables portray Saudi Arabia as a cash machine for terrorists' (*The Guardian*, 5 December 2010). Available from: http://www.guardian.co.uk/world/2010/dec/05/wikileaks-cables-saudi-terrorist-funding [Accessed 6 December 2010].
49. Hegghammer, 2008, Op. Cit., p714.
50. Although this does not appear to be the case when considering Saudi policy towards Hizballah.
51. 08RIYADH768, *Lebanon: SAG FM says UN Peace Keeping Force Needed* (Wikileaks, 14 May 2008). Available from: http://WikiLeaks.ch/cable/2008/05/08RIYADH768.html#parl [Accessed 15 December 2010]. See also: Ewan MacAskill, 'WikiLeaks cables: Saudis proposed Arab force to invade Lebanon' (*The Guardian*, 7 December 2010). Available from: http://www.guardian.co.uk/world/2010/dec/07/wikileaks-saudi-arab-invasion-Lebanon [Accessed: 8 December 2010].
52. Elling, Op. Cit., p482.
53. Bradley, 2006–07, Op. Cit., p181.
54. Elling, Op. Cit., p487.
55. In particular, the invasions of Arab/Mongol armies; the Soviet invasion during World War II; the 1953 CIA sponsored coup; perceived Western imperialist agendas across the Middle East.
56. Iraj Pezeshkzad, *My Uncle Napoleon* (Washington DC: Mage Publishers, 2006).
57. Elling, Op. Cit., pp490–1.
58. *Ibid.*, p491.
59. *Ibid.*, p488, quoting from *Kayhan* (daily) 2005a. 'Name-ye ja'li be daftar-e riyasat-e jomhuri, dar ahvaz moshkel-saz shod', 16 April: *kayhannews.ir.*
60. Elling, Op. Cit., p488.
61. However, some may argue that this continued "involvement" of foreign powers in Iranian affairs demonstrates the failings of *velayat-e faqih*.
62. *Ibid.*, p493.
63. Human Rights Watch, Op. Cit., p28.
64. Elling, Op. Cit., p497.
65. *Ibid.*, p496.
66. *Ibid.*, p487.
67. Saleh, Op. Cit., p286.
68. See: *The New York Times*, 'Text of Mahmoud Ahmadeinejad's speech' (*The New York Times*, 30 October 2005). Available from: http://www.nytimes.com/2005/10/30/weekinreview/30iran.html?pagewanted=1&_r=1&ei=507

0&en=26f07fc5b7543417&ex=1161230400 [Accessed: 24 February 2010]. Also: The Middle East Media Research Institute, *The Holocaust and Its Denial* (30 January 2009). Available from: http://www.memri.org/report/en/0/0/0/0/0/0/3060.htm [Accessed 24 February 2010].

69. *The Jerusalem Post*, 'Iran hosts the World Without Zionism' (*The Jerusalem Post*, 26 October 2005). Available from: http://www.jpost.com/servlet/Satellite?pagename=JPost%2FJPArticle%2FShowFull&cid=1129540603434 [Accessed: 24 July 2007].
70. United Nations Economic and Social Council, *E/CN.4/2006/NGO/*. Available from: http://domino.un.org/unispal.nsf/3822b5e39951876a85256b6e0058a478/258eda552cbb854a852571310058a594?OpenDocument [Accessed: 22 August 2007].
71. Juan Cole, *Ahmadinejad: We Are Not a Threat to Any Country, Including Israel* (27 August 2006), Available from: http://www.juancole.com/2006/08/ahmadinejad-we-are-not-threat-to-any.html [Accessed: 26 July 2007].
72. *BBC*, 'Iran leader's comments attacked', (27 October 2005). Available from: http://news.bbc.co.uk/1/hi/world/middle_east/4378948.stm [Accessed: 26 July 2007].
73. *CNN*, 'Iranian leader: Holocaust a "myth"' (14 December 2005). Available from: http://www.cnn.com/2005/WORLD/meast/12/14/iran.israel/index.html [Accessed: 24 September 2009].
74. *BBC,* 'Holocaust comments spark outrage', (14 December 2005), Available from: http://news.bbc.co.uk/1/hi/world/middle_east/4529198.stm [Accessed 12 May 2009].
75. For more information see: Ed Pilkington, 'Ahmadinejad accuses US of "orchestrating" 9/11 attacks to aid Israel' (*The Guardian*, 23 September 2010). Available from: http://www.guardian.co.uk/world/2010/sep/23/iran-united-nations [Accessed 24 September 2010].
76. Barry Buzan, 'Societal security, state security and internationalisation', in Ole Waever, Barry Buzan, Morten Kelstrup, Pierre Lemaitre (eds.), *Identity, Migration and the New Security Agenda in Europe* (London: Pinter Publishers Ltd, 1993), p43.
77. Elling, Op. Cit., p493.
78. *Ibid.*, p487.
79. *Ibid.*, p490.
80. *Ibid.*, p488.
81. Salman Rushdie, *The Satanic Verses* (London: Viking, 1988).
82. Gary Sick, 'Iran: Confronting terrorism', *The Washington Quarterly*, Vol. 26, No. 4, (2003), p84.
83. *Ibid.*, p86.

84. *Ibid.*, p84.
85. *CNN*, 'Transcript of interview with Iranian president Mohammad Khatami', *(CNN*, 7 January 1998). Available from: www.cnn.com/WORLD/9801/07/iran/interview.html [Accessed: 01 December 2010].
86. Sick, Op. Cit., p89.
87. Samii, Op. Cit. See also: Eitan Azani, *Hezbollah: The Story of the Party of God* (New York: Palgrave Macmillan, 2009), p62.
88. Also known as the Khobar Towers bombing.
89. Sick, Op. Cit., p88.
90. *Ibid.*, p92.
91. See chapter two.
92. Ali Rahigh-Aghsan and Peter V. Jakobsen, 'The rise of Iran: How durable, how dangerous?', *Middle East Journal*, Vol. 64, No. 4 (2010), pp560–1.
93. *Ibid.*, p563.
94. *Ibid.*, p564.
95. *Ahlul Bayt News Agency*, 'Akhtari: Arab spring inspired by Iran 1979 revolution' (10 September 2011). Available from: http://www.abna.ir/data.asp?lang=3&Id=264658 [Accessed: 12 Septemeber 2011].
96. *Deutsche Welle*, 'Iran's supreme leader: Using nuclear weapons is Un-Islamic', (4 June 2006). Available from: http://www.dw-world.de/dw/article/0,,2043328,00.html [Accessed: 7 December 2010].

7 Internal-External Security Dilemmas

1. *The Guardian*, 'US embassy cables: Saudi king urges US strike on Iran' (28 November 2010). Available from: http://www.guardian.co.uk/world/us-embassy-cables-documents/150519 [Accessed: 29 November 2010].
2. Chubin and Tripp, Op. Cit., p9.
3. *Ibid.*
4. Ali Ansari, 'Iran under Ahmadinejad: populism and its malcontents', in *International Affairs*, Vol. 84, No. 4 (2008), p16.
5. Shahram Chubin, *Iran's Nuclear Ambitions* (Washington DC: Carnegie Endowment for International Peace, 2006), p33.
6. Chubin and Tripp, Op. Cit., p17.
7. See Matthieson, 2010, Op. Cit.
8. Chubin and Tripp, Op. Cit., p17.
9. Mabon, Op. Cit., p90.
10. Chubin and Tripp, Op. Cit., p15.
11. *Ibid.*, p9.
12. See the Thomas Theorum in chapter two.

13. However, it is important to note that ties between Hamas and Saudi Arabia are not always harmonious, despite shared ideological traits. This suggests an overarching geopolitical importance. See: *BBC*, 'Hamas claims strong Saudi Support' (11 March 2006). Available from: http://news.bbc.co.uk/1/hi/world/middle_east/4795574.stm [Accessed: 12 May 2010]; Ashraf Khalil, 'Saudi Arabia offers $1 billion to rebuild Gaza as fragile cease-fires hold' (*Los Angeles Times*, 20 January 2009). Available from: http://articles.latimes.com/2009/jan/20/world/fg-gaza20 [Accessed: 12 May 2010]; Ian Black, 'Saudis blame Hamas amid calls for talks with Fatah' (*The Guardian*, 1 January 2009). Available from: http://www.guardian.co.uk/world/2009/jan/01/saudi-arabia-hamas-gaza [Accessed: 12 May 2010].
14. See: Al Jazeera, 'Leaked cable: Gulf Sates "funded extremism"' *(Al Jazeera*, 22 May 2011). Available from: http://www.aljazeera.com/news/middleeast/2011/05/2011522154717683995.html [Accessed: 22 May 2011]. and *PBS*, 'Frontline: Saudi Time Bomb'. Available from: http://www.pbs.org/wgbh/pages/frontline/shows/saudi/interviews/nasr.html [Accessed: 18 May 2011].
15. Mabon, Op. Cit.
16. Shahram Chubin, 'Iran and regional security in the Persian Gulf', *Survival: Global Politics and Strategy*, Vol. 34, No. 3 (1992), pp62–80, p73.
17. International Crisis Group, *Popular Protests in North Africa and the Middle East*, Op. Cit., 2011, pii.
18. Simon Henderson, *A Testing Weekend in Bahrain* (Washington Institute for Near East Policy, 6 January 2012). Available from: http://www.washingtoninstitute.org/templateC06.php?CID=1790 [Accessed: 27 January 2012].
19. Shahram Chubin, 'Iran's Power in Context', *Survival: Global Politics and Strategy*, Vol. 51, No. 1 (2009), pp165–190, p167.
20. Henderson, 6 January 2012, Op. Cit.

BIBLIOGRAPHY

Books

Abir, Mordechai. *Saudi Arabia: Government, Society, and the Gulf Crisis* (London, 1993).

Abrahamian, Ervand. *A History of Modern Iran* (Cambridge: Cambridge University Press, 2008).

Abrahim, Fouad N. *The Shi'is of Saudi Arabia* (London: Saqi, 2006).

Aburish, Said K. *The Rise, Corruption and Coming Fall of The House of Saud* (London: Bloomsbury, 1994).

Alcoff, Linda M., Hames-Garcia, Michael. Mohanty, Satya P., Moya, Paula M. L., (eds.), *Identity Politics Reconsidered* (New York: Palgrave MacMillan, 2006).

Algar, Hamid. *Wahhabism: A Critical Essay* (Islamic Publications International: New York, 2002).

Amirahmadi, Hooshan, Entessar, Nader. (eds.) *Iran and the Arab World* (Basingstoke: Macmillan, 1993).

Ansari, Ali. *Confronting Iran* (New York: Basic Books, 2006).

Ansari, Ali. *Modern Iran: The Pahlavis and After* (Harlow: Pearson Education Limited, 2007).

Archer, Margaret S. *Realist Social Theory: The Morphogenetic Approach* (Cambridge: Cambridge University Press, 1995).

Asgharzadeh, Alireza., *Iran and the Challenge of Diversity* (New York: Palgrave MacMillan, 2007).

Axworthy, Michael. *Iran, Empire of the Mind: A History from Zoroaster to the Present Day* (London: Penguin, 2008).

Ayoub, Mahmoud. *Islam: Faith and History* (Oxford: Oneworld Publications, 2004).

Ayubi, Nazi N. M. *Political Islam: Religion and Politics in the Arab World* (London: Routledge, 1991).

Azani, Eitan. *Hezbollah: The Story of the Party of God* (New York: Palgrave Macmillan, 2009).

Bakhash, Shaul. *The Reign of the Ayatollahs* (London: I.B.Tauris, 1985).

Barnett, Michael N. *Dialogues in Arab Politics* (New York: Columbia University Press, 1998).

Bell, Richard. *The Qur'an: Translated, with a Critical Re-arrangement of the Surahs* (Edinburgh: T. & T. Clark, 1937–9).

Berlin, Isaiah. *Four Essays on Liberty* (Oxford: Oxford University Press, 1969).

Blank, Stephen, Grinter, Lawrence E., Klingaman, Jerome W., *et al.*, *Low Intensity Conflict in the Third World* (Air University Press, 1988).

Bradley, John R. *Saudi Arabia Exposed: Inside a Kingdom in Crisis* (New York: Palgrave Macmillan, 2005).

Booth, Ken, Wheeler, Nicholas J. *The Security Dilemma: Fear, Cooperation and Trust in World Politics* (Basingstoke: Palgrave Macmillan, 2008).

Buchta, Wilfried. *Who Rules Iran? The Structure of Power in the Islamic Republic* (Washington, DC: The Washington Institute for Near East Policy, 2000).

Burke, Jason. *Al Qaeda: The True Story of Radical Islam* (London: Penguin, 2007).

Butterfield, Herbert. *History and Human Relations* (London: Collins, 1951).

Buzan, Barry. *People, States and Fear* (Harlow: Pearson Education Limited, 1991).

Buzan, Barry, Wæver, Ole, de Wilde, Jaap. *Security: A New Framework for Analysis* (London: Lynne Rienner Publishers, 1998).

Carr, Edward H. *The Twenty Years' Crisis, 1919–1939: An Introduction to the Study of International Relations* (London: Macmillan, 1946).

Chaliand, Gerald. *The Kurdish Tragedy* (London: Zed Books, 1994).

Champion, Darryl. *The Paradoxical Kingdom: Saudi Arabia and the Momentum of Reform* (London: C. Hurst & Co., 2003).

Chazan, Naomi, (ed.) *Irredentism and International Politics,* (Boulder: Lynne Reinner, 1991).

Chubin, Shahram. *Iran's Nuclear Ambitions* (Washington, DC: Carnegie Endowment for International Peace, 2006).

Chubin, Shahram, and Tripp, Charles. *Iran-Saudi Arabia Relations and Regional Order* (London: Oxford University Press for IISS, 1996).

Ciment, James. *The Kurds: State and Minority in Turkey, Iraq and Iran* (New York: Facts on File, 1996).

Clawson, Patrick., and Eisenstadt, Michael., The Last Resort: Consequences of Preventative Military Action against Iran, (Washington: Washington Institute for Near East Policy, 2008).

Commins, David D. *The Wahhabi Mission and Saudi Arabia* (London: I.B.Tauris, 2006).

Cordesman, Anthony H. *Saudi Arabia: Guarding the Desert Kingdom* (Oxford: Westview Press, 1997).

Coughlin, Con. *Khomeini's Ghost* (London: Macmillan, 2009).

Davis, Paul K., and Cragin, Kim. *Social Science for Terrorism: Putting the Pieces Together* (Santa Monica, CA: RAND Corporation, 2009).

Ehteshami, Anoushiravan. *After Khomeini: The Iranian Second Republic* (London: Routledge, 1995).

Ehteshami, Anoushiravan. *Globalization and Geopolitics in the Middle East: Old Games, New Rules* (Oxon: Routledge, 2007).

Eisenstadt, Michael., Knights, Michael., Ali, Ahmed., *Iran's Influence in Iraq: Countering Tehran's Whole-of-Government Approach*, (Washington: Washington Institute for Near East Policy, 2011)

Fawcett, Louise. *International Relations of the Middle East* (Oxford: Oxford University Press, 2005).

Fisk, Robert. *The Great War for Civilization* (London: Harper Perennial, 2006).

Furtig, Henner. *Iran's Rivalry with Saudi Arabia between the Gulf Wars* (Reading: Ithaca Press, 2002).

Gause, F. Gregory. *Oil Monarchies: Domestic and Security Challenges in the Arab Gulf States* (New York: Council on Foreign Relations Press, 1994).

Gause, F. Gregory. *The International Relations of the Persian Gulf* (Cambridge: Cambridge University Press, 2010).

Gelvin, James L. *The Modern Middle East. A History* (Oxford: Oxford University Press, 2005).

Goffman, Erving. *The Presentation of Self in Everyday Life* (London: Allen Lane, 1969).

Hafez, Mohammed M. *Why Muslims Rebel: Repression and Resistance in the Islamic World* (Colorado: Lynne Reiner Publications, 2003).

Halliday, Fred. *Iran: Dictatorship and Development* (Harmondsworth: Penguin, 1979).

Halliday, Fred. *Nation and Religion in the Middle East* (London: Saqi, 2000).

Halliday, Fred. *The Middle East in International Relations: Power, Politics and Ideology* (Cambridge: Cambridge University Press, 2005).

Harel, Amos. and Issacharoff, Avi. *34 Days Israel, Hezbollah, and the War in* Lebanon (New York: Palgrave Macmillan, 2008).

Herz, John H. *Political Realism and Political Idealism: A Study in Theories and Realities* (Chicago: University of Chicago Press, 1951).

Hinnebusch, Raymond, and Ehteshami, Anoushiravan (eds) *The Foreign Policies of Middle East States* (London: Lynne Reiner Publishers, 2002).

Hinnebusch, Raymond. *The International Politics of the Middle East* (Manchester University Press: Manchester, 2003).

Hobbes, Thomas. *Leviathan* (London: Dent, 1973).

Hourani, Albert. *A History of the Arab Peoples* (London: Faber and Faber Limited, 1991).

Ibrahim, Fouad N. *The Shi'is of Saudi Arabia* (London: Saqi, 2006).

Jones, Geoffrey. *Banking and Empire in Iran* (Cambridge: Cambridge University Press, 1986).

Kamali, Masoud. *Revolutionary Iran: Civil Society and State in the Modernization Process* (Aldershot: Algate Publishing Ltd, 1998).

Kashani-Sabet, Firoozeh. *Frontier Fictions, Shaping the Iranian Nation, 1804–1946* (New Jersey: Princeton University Press, 1999).

Katouzian, Homa, and Shahidi, Hossein (eds.). *Iran in the 21st Century, Politics, Economics and Conflict* (Oxon: Routledge, 2008).

Kechichian, Joseph A. *Succession in Saudi Arabia* (New York: Palgrave Macmillan, 2001).

Khaldun, Ibn. *The Muqaddimah, Book 1, An Introduction to History,* translated by Franz Rosenthal. (Pantheon Books Inc: New York, 1958).

Khomeini, R. *Islam and Revolution.* Writing and Declarations of Imam Khomeini, ranslated and annotated by Hamid Algar (Berkely: Mizan Press, 1981).

Kinzer, Stephen. *All The Shah's Men: An American Coup and the Roots of Middle East Terror* (Hoboken: John Wiley & Sons Ltd, 2003).

Koknar, Ali M. *Iranian Azeris: A Giant Minority*, (Washington: Washington Institute for Near East Policy, 6 June 2006).

Kostiner, Joseph. *The Making of Saudi Arabia 1916–1936* (Oxford: Oxford University Press, 1993).

Kramer, Martin. *Ivory Towers on Sand: The Failure of Middle Eastern Studies in America* (Washington: Washington Institute for Near East Policy, 2001).

Mandaville, Peter. *Global Political Islam* (Oxon: Routledge, 2007).

McDowall, David. *The Kurds* (London: Minority Rights Group International, December 1996).

Mearsheimer, John J. *The Tragedy of Great Power Politics* (New York: Norton, c2001).

Mella, Jawad. *Kurdistan and the Kurds: A Divided Homeland and a Nation without State* (London: Western Kurdistan Association, 2005).

Moin, Baqer. *Khomeini: Life of the Ayatollah* (London: I.B.Tauris, 1999).

Morgenthau, Hans J. *Politics Among Nations: The Struggle for Power and Peace* (New York: Knopf, 1967).

Nader, Alireza, and Joya, Laha., *Iran's Balancing Act in Afghanistan* (Santa Monica, CA: RAND Corporation, 2011).

Nasr, Vali. *The Shia Revival: How Conflicst within Islam Will Shape the Future* (New York: W.W. Norton, 2007).

Nonneman, Gerd. (ed.). *Analyzing Middle East Foreign Policies and the Relationship with Europe* (Oxon: Routledge, 2005).

Norell, Magnus. *A Victory for Islamism: The Second Lebanon War and Its Repercussions*, (Washington: Washington Institute for Near East Policy, 2009).

Norton, Augstus R. (ed.). *Civil Society in the Middle East: Volume One* (Leiden: E.J.Brill, 1995–6).

Norton, Augustus R. *Hezbollah* (Princeton: Princeton University Press, 2007).

Nye, Joseph S. *Bound to Lead: The Changing Nature of American Power* (New York: Basic Books, 1990).

Nye, Joseph S. *Soft Power: The Means to Success in World Politics* (New York: Public Affairs, 2004).

O'Ballance, Edgar. *The Kurdish Struggle* (London: Macmillan, 1996).

Omid, Homa. *Islam and the Post-Revolutionary State in Iran* (Basingstoke: Macmillan, 1994).

Onuf, Nicholas. *World of Our Making* (Columbia: University of South Carolina Press, 1989).

Palmer Harik, Judith. *Hezbollah: The Changing Face of Terrorism* (London: I.B.Tauris, 2004).

Peterson, John E. *Saudi Arabia and the Illusion of Security* (Oxford: Oxford University Press for the International Institute for Strategic Studies, 2002).

Pezeshkzad, Iraj. *My Uncle Napoleon* (Washington, DC: Mage Publishers, 2006).

Philby, Harry St. J. *The Heart of Arabia* (London: Constable and Company, 1922).

Rahman, Fazlur. *Islam* (Chicago: Chicago University Press, 1979).

Al-Rasheed, Madawi., *A History of Saudi Arabia* (Cambridge: Cambridge University Press 2002).

Rushdie, Salman. *The Satanic Verses* (London: Viking, 1988).

Russell, Richard L. *Weapons Proliferation and War in the Greater Middle East* (New York: Routledge, 2005).

Sanasarian, Eliz. *Religious Minorities in Iran* (Cambridge: Cambridge University Press, 2000).

Schwartz, Stephen. *The Two Faces of Islam: The House of Sa'ud from Tradition to Terror* (Random House: New York, 2002).

Shay, Shaul. *The Axis of Evil: Iran, Hizballah, and the Palestinian Terror* (Piscataway, NJ: Transaction Books, 2005).

Staub, Ervin. *The Roots of Evil: The Origins of Genocide and Other Group Violence* (New York: Cambridge University Press, 1989).

Telhami, Shibley, and Barnett, Michael (eds.). *Identity and Foreign Policy in the Middle East* (New York: Cornell University Press, 2002).

Tenet, George. *At the Center of the Storm: My Years at the CIA* (New York: Harper Collins, 2007).

Thucydides. *History of the Peloponnesian War* (London: Heinemann, 1919–1930).

Thomas, William I., and Thomas, Dorothy S. *The Child in America: Behavior Problems and Programs* (New York: Knopf, 1928).

Waltz, Kenneth. *A Theory of International Politics* (New York: Random House, 1979).

Weber, Max. *Economy and Society: An Outline of Interpretive Sociology.* Edited by Guenther Roth and Claus Wittich translated by Ephraim Fischoff, *et al.*, (New York: Bedminster Press, 1968).

Wehrey, Frederick, Karasik, Theodore W., Nader, Alireza, Ghez, Jeremy J., Hansell, Lydia, and Guffey, Robert A. *Saudi-Iranian Relations Since the Fall of Saddam: Rivalry, Cooperation, and Implications for U.S. Policy* (Santa Monica, CA: RAND Corporation, 2009).

Wehrey, F., Green, Jerrold D., Nichiporuk, B., Nader, Alireza, Hansell, Lydia, and Nafisi, Rasool. *The Rise of the Pasdaran: Assessing the Domestic Roles of Iran's Islamic Revolutionary Guards Corps* (Santa Monica: Rand Corporation, 2009).

Woods, Kevin M., Murray, Williamson, Nathan, Elizabeth A., Sabara, Laila and Venegas, Ana M. *Saddam's Generals, Perspectives of the Iran-Iraq War* (Virginia: Institute for Defence Analysis, 2010).

Wroe, Ann. *Lives, Lies and the Iran-Contra Affair* (London: I.B.Tauris, 1991).

Zehfuss, Maja. *Constructivism in International Relations* (Cambridge: Cambridge University Press, 2002).

Zuhur, Sherifa. *Saudi Arabia: Islamic Threat, Political Reform, and the Global War on Terror* (Strategic Studies Institute U. S. Army War College, 2005).

Chapters in Edited Books

Al-'Ashmawi, Muhammad. '*Shari'a*: The codification of Islamic law', in Kurzman, Charles, (ed.). *Liberal Islam: A Sourcebook* (Oxford: Oxford University Press, 1998).

Ayoob, Mohammad, and Kosebalaban, Hasan. 'Introduction: Unraveling the myths', in Ayoob, Mohammad, and Kosebalaban, Hasan, (eds.). *Religion and Politics in Saudi Arabia* (Colorado: Lynne Rienner, 2009).

Bar-Tal, Daniel, 'Introduction: Conflicts and social psychology', in Bar-Tal, Daniel, (ed.). *Intergroup Conflicts and Their Resolution: Social Psychological Perspective* (New York: Psychology Press, 2011).

Bronson, Rachel. 'Understanding US-Saudi relations', in Aarts, Paul, and Nonneman, Gerd, (eds.). *Saudi Arabia in the Balance: Political Economy, Society, Foreign Affairs* (London: C.Hurst & Co., 2005).

Buzan, B. 'Societal security, state security and internationalisation', in Waever, Ole, Buzan, Barry, Kelstrup, Morten, and Lemaitre, Pierre, (eds.). *Identity, Migration and the New Security Agenda in Europe* (London: Pinter Publishers Ltd, 1993).

Cole, Donald P., 'The household, marriage and family life among the Al Murrah nomads of Saudi Arabia', in Hopkins, Nicholas S., and Ibrahim, Saad E. (eds.). *Arab Society: Social Science Perspectives* (American University in Cairo Press: Cairo, 1985).

Davis, Paul K., and Cragin, Kim. 'Introduction', in Davis, Paul K., and Cragin, Kim., (eds.). *Social Science for Terrorism: Putting the Pieces Together* (Santa Monica, CA: RAND Corporation, 2009).

Davis, Paul K., and Cragin, Kim. 'Summary', in Davis, Paul K., and Cragin, Kim., (eds.). *Social Science for Terrorism: Putting the Pieces Together* (Santa Monica, CA: RAND Corporation, 2009).

Doumato, Eleanor A., 'Tribalism', in Mattar, Phillip, (ed.). *Encyclopaedia of the Modern Middle East and North Africa,* Vol. 4 (Detroit, MI: Macmillan Reference USA, 2004).

Ehteshami, Anoushiravan. 'Iran and its immediate neighbourhood', in Ehteshami, Anoushiravan, and Zweiri, Mahjoob, (eds.). *Iran's Foreign Policy from Khatami to Ahmadinejad* (Reading: Ithaca Press, 2008).

Ehteshami, Anoushiravan, 'The foreign policy of Iran', in Hinnebusch, Raymond, Ehteshami, Anoushiravan, (eds.). *The Middle East in the International System* (London: Lynne Reiner Publishers, 2002).

Fabietti, Ugo, 'Sedentarisation as a means of detribalisation: Some policies of the Saudi Arabian government towards the nomads', in Niblock, Tim, (ed.). *State, Society and Economy in Saudi Arabia* (Breckenham: Croom Helm Ltd, 1982).

Farhi, Farideh, 'Creating a national identity amidst contentious politics in contemporary Iran', in Katouzian, Homa, and Shahidi, Hossein, (eds.). *Iran in the 21st Century, Politics, Economics and Conflict* (Oxon: Routledge, 2008).

Gause, F. Gregory. 'The foreign policy of Saudi Arabia', in Hinnebusch, Raymond, and Ehteshami, Anoushiravan, (eds.). *The Middle East in the International System* (London: Lynne Reiner Publishers, 2002).

Goldberg, Jacob, 'The Saudi Arabian Kingdom', in Rabinovich, Itovar, and Shaked, Haim, (eds.). *Middle East Contemporary Survey Volume XI: 1987* (Boulder: Westview Press, 1987).

Habib, John S. 'Wahhabi origins of the contemporary Saudi state', in Ayoob, Mohammad, and Kosebalaban, Hasan, (eds.). *Religion and Politics in Saudi Arabia* (Colorado: Lynne Rienner, 2009).

Halliday, Fred. 'For an international sociology', in Hobden, Stephen, and Hobson, John M. (eds.). *Historical Sociology of International Relations* (Cambridge: Cambridge University Press 2002).

Halliday, Fred. 'Iranian Foreign Policy Since 1979: Internationalism and Nationalism in the Islamic Revolution', in Cole, Juan R.I., and Keddie, Nikki R., (eds.). *Shi'ism and Social Protest* (New Haven: Yale University Press, 1986).

Hopwood, Derek. 'The ideological basis: Ibn Abd Al-Wahhab's Muslim revivalism', in Niblock, Tim, (ed.). *State, Society and Economy in Saudi Arabia* (Breckenham: Croom Helm Ltd, 1982).

Job, Brian L. 'The insecurity dilemma: National, regime and state securities in the third world', in Job, Brian L., (ed.). *The Insecurity Dilemma: National Security of Third World States* (Boulder, CO: Lynne Rienner, 1992).

Korany, Baghat, and Fattah, Moataz A. 'Irreconcilable role-partners? Saudi foreign policy between the Ulema and the U.S.', in Korany, Baghat, and Hillal Dessouki, Ali E., (eds.). *The Foreign Policies of Arab States: The Challenge of Globalization* (Cairo: Cairo Press, 2009).

Kostiner, Joseph. 'Transforming dualities: Tribe and state formation in Saudi Arabia', in Khoury, Phillip S., and Kostiner, Joseph, (eds.). *Tribe and State Formation in the Middle East* (Berkeley: University of California Press, 1990).

Kramer, Martin. 'Muslim congresses', in Esposito, John L., (ed.). *The Oxford Encyclopedia of the Modern Islamic World* (Oxford: Oxford University Press, 1995).

Levy, Jack. 'The diversionary theory of war: A critique', in Midlarsky, Manus I., (ed.). *Handbook of War Studies* (New York and Boston: Unwin Hyman, 1989).

Lockwood, David. 'Social integration and system integration', in Zollschan, George K., and Hirsch, Walter, (eds.). *Explorations in Social Change* (Boston: Houghton Mifflin, 1964).

Milani, Mohsen. 'Shi'ism and the state in the constitution of the Islamic Republic of Iran', in Farsoun, Samih K., and Mashayekhi, Mehrdad, (eds.). *Iran: Political Culture in the Islamic Republic* (London: Routledge, 1992).

Niblock, Tim. 'Social structure and the development of the Saudi Arabian political system', in Niblock, Tim, (ed.). *State, Society and Economy in Saudi Arabia* (Breckenham: Croom Helm, 1982).

Nonneman, Gerd. 'Determinants and patterns of Saudi foreign policy: "Omnibalancing" and "relative autonomy" in multiple environments', in Aarts, Paul, and Nonneman, Gerd, (eds.). *Saudi Arabia in the Balance: Political Economy, Society, Foreign Affairs* (London: C.Hurst & Co., 2005).

Noricks, Darcy. 'The root causes of terrorism', in Davis, Paul K., and Cragin, Kim, (eds.). *Social Science for Terrorism: Putting the Pieces Together* (Santa Monica, CA: RAND Corporation, 2009).

Okrunhlik, Gwenn. 'State power, religious privilege, and myths about political reform', in Ayoob, Mohammad, and Kosebalaban, Hasan, (eds.). *Religion and Politics in Saudi Arabia* (Colorado: Lynne Rienner, 2009).

Staub, Ervin, and Bar-Tal, Daniel. 'Genocide, mass killing, and intractable conflict, roots, evolution, prevention, and reconciliation', in Sears, David O., Huddy, Leonie, and Jervis, Robert, (eds.). *Oxford Handbook of Political Psychology* (Oxford: Oxford University Press, 2003).

Teichman, Yona, and Bar-Tal, Daniel. 'Acquisition and development of a shared psychological intergroup repertoire in a context of an intractable conflict', in Quintana, Stephen M., and McKown, Clark, (eds.). *Handbook of Race, Racism, and the Developing Child* (New Jersey: John Wiley & Sons, 2008).

Wallerstein, Immanuel. 'World-systems analysis', in Modelski, George, (ed.). *World System History* (Oxford: Eolss Publishers).

Zweiri, Mahjoob., 'Arab-Iranian relations: New realities?', in Ehteshami, Anoushiravan, and Zweiri, Mahjoob, (eds.). *Iran's Foreign Policy from Khatami to Ahmadinejad* (Reading: Ithaca Press, 2008).

Articles

Aarts, Paul, and van Duijne, Joris. 'Saudi Arabia and Iran: Less antagonism, more pragmatism', Viewpoints Special Edition, *The Kingdom of Saudi Arabia, 1979–2009: Evolution of a Pivotal State*, Middle East Institute, pp62–4.

Alamdari, Kazem. 'The power structure of the Islamic Republic of Iran: Transition from populism to clientelism, and militarization of the government', *Third World Quarterly*, Vol. 26, No. 8 (2005), pp1285–1301.

Alhasan, Hasan T. 'The role of Iran in the failed coup of 1981: The IFLB in Bahrain', *Middle East Journal*, Vol. 65, No. 4 (2011), pp603–17.

Ansari, Ali. 'Iran under Ahmadinejad: populism and its malcontents', *International Affairs*, Vol. 84, No. 4 (2008), pp683–700.

Archer, Margaret S. 'The trajectory of the morphogenetic approach: An account in the first person', *Sociologia, Problems E Práticas,* Vol. 54, No. 3 (2007), pp35–47.

Al-Baharna, Husain. 'The fact-finding mission of the United Nations secretary-general and the settlement of the Bahrain-Iran dispute, May 1970', *International and Comparative Law Quarterly*, Vol. 22, No. 3 (1973), pp541–52.

Bahghat, Gawdat. 'Nuclear proliferation: The Islamic Republic of Iran', *International Studies Perspectives*, Vol. 7, No. 2 (2006), pp124–36.

Barkin, J. Samuel. 'Realist constructivism', *International Studies Review,* Vol. 5, No. 3 (2003), pp325–42.

Bart, R. 'The Second Lebanon War: The plus column', *Strategic Assessment* Vol. 9, No. 3 (2006). Available from: http://www.inss.org.il/publications.php?cat=25&incat=0&read=85 [Accessed 12 May 2009].

Bosbait, Mohammed, and Wilson, Rodney. 'Education, school to work transitions and unemployment in Saudi Arabia', *Middle Eastern Studies*, Vol. 41, No. 4 (2005), pp533–46.

Bradley, John R. 'Al Qaeda and the House of Saud: Eternal enemies or secret bedfellows?', *The Washington Quarterly*, Vol. 28, No. 4 (2005), pp139–52.

Bradley, John R. 'Iran's ethnic tinderbox', *The Washington Quarterly,* Vol. 30, No. 1 (2006–07), pp181–90.

Brown, Cameron S. 'Wanting to have their cake and their neighbour's too: Azerbaijani attitudes towards Karabakh and Iranian Azerbaijan', *Middle East Journal,* Vol. 58, No. 4 (Autumn, 2004), pp576–96.

Cavatorta, Francesco. 'The convergence of governance: Upgrading authoritarianism in the Arab World and downgrading democracy elsewhere?', *Middle East Critique*, Vol. 19, No. 3 (2010), pp217–32.

Checkel, Jeffrey. 'The Constructivist Turn in International Relations Theory', *World Politics,* Vol. 50, No. 2 (1998), pp324–48.

Chubin, Shahram. 'Iran and regional security in the Persian Gulf', *Survival: Global Politics and Strategy*, Vol. 34, No. 3 (1992), pp62–80.

Chubin, Shahram. 'Iran's power in context', *Survival: Global Politics and Strategy*, Vol. 51, No. 1 (2009), pp165–90.

Cole, Donald P. 'Where have the Bedouin gone?', *Anthropological Quarterly,* Vol. 76, No. 2 (2003), pp235–67.

Cronin, Stephanie. 'Riza Shah and the disintegration of Bakhtiyari power in Iran, 1921–1934', *Iranian Studies*, Vol. 33, No. 3/4 (2000), pp349–76.

Davies, Graeme. 'Inside out or outside in: The impact of domestic politics and the great powers on Iranian-US relations 1990–2004', *Foreign Policy Analysis,* Vol. 4, No. 3 (2008), pp209–25.

Elling, Rasmus C. 'State of mind, state of order: Reactions to ethnic unrest in the Islamic Republic of Iran', *Studies in Ethnicity and Nationalism,* Vol. 8, No.3 (2008), pp481–501.

Galtung, Johan. 'A structural theory of imperialism', *Journal of Peace Research*, Vol. 8, No. 2 (1971), pp81–117.

Guazzone, Laura. 'Gulf co-operation council: The security policies', *Survival: Global Politics and Strategy*, Vol. 30, No. 2 (1988), pp134–48.

Hasham, Ahmadzadeh, and Stansfield, Gareth. 'The political, cultural, and military re-awakening of the Kurdish Nationalist Movement in Iran', *Middle East Journal*, Vol. 64, No. 1 (2010), pp11–27.

Hegghammer, Thomas. 'Terrorist recruitment in Saudi Arabia', *Middle East Policy*, Vol. 13, No. 4 (2006), pp39–60.

Hegghammer, Thomas. 'Islamist violence and regime stability in Saudi Arabia', *International Affairs*, Vol. 84, No.4 (2008), pp701–15.

El-Husseini, Rola. 'Hezbollah and the axis of refusal: Hamas, Iran and Syria', *Third World Quarterly*, Vol. 31, No. 5 (2010), pp803–15.

Jackson, Patrick T., Nexon, Daniel H., Sterling-Folker, Jennifer, Mattern, Janice B., Lebow, Richard N., and Barkin, J. Samuel. 'Bridging the gap: Toward a Realist-Constructivist dialogue', *International Studies Review* (February 2004), pp337–52.

Jones, Clive A. 'Saudi Arabia after the Gulf War: The internal-external security dilemma', *International Relations,* Vol. 12, No. 6 (1995), pp31–51.

Jones, Toby. 'Rebellion on the Saudi periphery: Modernity, marginalisation and the Shi'a uprising of 1979', *International Journal of Middle East Studies,* Vol. 38, No. 2 (2006), pp213–33.

Katouzian, Homa. 'Nationalist trends in Iran 1921–1926', *International Journal of Middle East Studies*, Vol. 10, No. 4 (1979), pp533–51.

Katouzian, Homa. 'The campaign against the Anglo-Iranian Agreement of 1919', *British Journal of Middle Eastern Studies*, Vol. 25, No. 1 (1998), pp5–46.

Kaye, Dalia Dassa, and Wehrey, Frederic M. 'A nuclear Iran: The reactions of neighbours', *Survival: Global Politics and Strategy*, Vol. 49 No. 2 (2007), pp111–28.

Kazemzadeh, Masoud. 'Intra-elite factionalism and the 2004 Majles elections in Iran', *Middle Eastern Studies*, Vol. 44, No. 2 (2008), pp189–214.

Khalilzad, Zalmay. 'The politics of ethnicity in Southwest Asia: Political development or political decay?', *Political Science Quarterly*, Vol. 99, No. 4 (1984–85), pp657–79.

Kostiner, Joseph. 'On instruments and their designers: The Ikhwan of Najd and the emergence of the Saudi state', *Middle East Studies,* Vol. 21, No. 3 (1985), pp298–323.

Kostiner, Joseph. 'State, Islam and opposition in Saudi Arabia, The post-Desert Storm phase', *Middle East Review of International Affairs,* Vol. 1, No. 2 (1997).

Mabon, Simon. 'The battle for Bahrain', *Middle East Policy,* Vol. 19, No. 2 (2012), pp84–97.

Matthiesen, Toby. 'Hizballah al-Hijaz: A history of the most radical Saudi Shi'a opposition group', *Middle East Journal*, Vol. 64, No. 2 (2010), pp179–97.

Mirbaghari, Farid. 'Shi'ism and Iran's foreign policy', *The Muslim World,* Vol. 94 (2004), pp555–63.

Mokhtari, Fariborz. 'Iran's 1953 coup revisited: Internal dynamics versus external intrigue', *Middle East Journal,* Vol. 62, No. 3 (2008), pp457–88.

Nasr, Vali. 'Regional implications of Shi'a revival in Iraq', *The Washington Quarterly*, Vol. 27, No. 3 (2004), pp7–24.

Nevo, Joseph. 'Religion and national identity in Saudi Arabia', *Middle Eastern Studies*, Vol. 34, No. 3 (1998), pp34–53.

Peterson, J.E. 'Tribes and politics in Eastern Arabia', *Middle East Journal*, Vol. 31, No. 3 (1997), pp297–312.

Posen, Barry R. 'The security dilemma and ethnic conflict', *Survival*, Vol. 35, No. 1 (1993), pp27–47.

Rahigh-Aghsan, Ali, and Jakobsen, Peter V. 'The rise of Iran: How durable, how dangerous?', *Middle East Journal*, Vol. 64, No. 4 (2010), pp559–73.

Al-Rasheed, Madawi. 'Durable and non-durable dynasties: The Rashidis and Saudis in Central Arabia', *British Journal of Middle Eastern Studies*, Vol. 19, No. 2 (1992), pp144–58.

Al-Rasheed, Madawi, and Al-Rasheed, Loulouwa. 'The politics of encapsulation: Saudi policy towards tribal and religious opposition', *Middle Eastern Studies,* Vol. 32, No. 1 (Jan. 1996), pp96–119.

Rejai, Mostafa, and Enloe, Cynthia H. 'Nation-states and state-nations', *International Studies Quarterly*, Vol. 13, No. 2 (1969), pp140–58.

Ridel, Bruce, and Saab, Bilal Y. 'Al Qaeda's third front: Saudi Arabia', *The Washington Quarterly*, Vol. 31, No. 2 (2008), pp33–46.

Roosevelt, Jr., Arichabald B. 'The Kurdish Republic of Mahabad', *Middle East Journal,* Vol. 1, No. 3 (1947), pp247–69.

Rose, Gideon. 'Neo-Classical realism and theories of foreign policy', *World Politics*, Vol. 51, No. 1 (1998), pp144–72.

Samii, Abbas William. 'A stable structure on shifting sands: Assessing the Hizballah-Iran-Syria relationship', *Middle East Journal*, Vol. 62, No. 1 (2008), pp32–53.

Sick, Gary. 'Iran: confronting terrorism', *The Washington Quarterly*, Vol. 26, No. 4 (2003), pp83–98.

Silverfarb, Daniel. 'Great Britain, Iraq, and Saudi Arabia: The revolt of the *Ikhwan*, 1927–1930', *International History Review,* Vol. 4, No. 2 (1982), pp222–48.

Sykes, Percy. 'South Persia and the Great War', *The Geographical Journal*, Vol. 58, No. 2 (1921), pp101–16.

Wallerstein, Immanuel. 'The rise and future demise of the world-capitalist system: Concepts for comparative analysis', *Comparative Studies in Society and History*, Vol. 16, No. 4 (1974), pp387–415.

Waltz, Kenneth. 'Neo-Realism: Confusion and criticisms', *Journal of Politics and Society* Vol. 15, No. 1 (2004), pp2–6.

Wendt, Alexander. 'Anarchy is what states make of it: the social construction of power *International Organisation*, Vol. 46, No. 2 (1992), pp391–425.

White, Jeffrey. *If War Comes: Israel vs Hizballah and Its Allies* (Washington: Washington Institute for Near East Policy, 2010).

Reports

9/11 Commission Report. Available from: www.911commission.gov/report/911Report.pdf. [Accessed: 4 November 2010].

Beehner, Lionel. *Shi'a Muslims in the Middle East* (Council on Foreign Relations, 16 June 2006). Available from: http://www.cfr.org/publication/10903/shia_muslims_in_the_mideast.html [Accessed: 7 November 2010].

Commission on Human Rights. *E/CN.4/Sub.2/AC.5/2003/WP.10 Ethnic and Religious Groups in the Islamic Republic of Iran*. Available from: http://ap.ohchr.org/documents/E/SUBCOM/other/E-CN_4-SUB_2-AC_5–2003-WG_10.pdf [Accessed: 7 April 2010].

Cordesman, Anthony H., and Obaid, Nawaf. *Al Qaeda in Saudi Arabia: Asymmetric threats and Islamic Extremists* (Centre for Strategic and International Studies, 26 January 2005). Available from: http://csis.org/files/media/csis/pubs/050106_al-qaedainsaudi.pdf [Accessed 11 April 2010].

Dunne, Michelle. *The Deep Roots of Bahrain's Unrest* (Washington, DC: Carnegie Endowment for International Peace, 2011).

Gause, F. Gregory. *Saudi Arabia in the New Middle East* (New York: Council on Foreign Relations, 2011).

Hassan, Hussein D. *Iran: Ethnic and Religious Minorities* (CRS Report for Congress, 25 November 2008). Available from: http://www.fas.org/sgp/crs/mideast/RL34021.pdf [Accessed: 7 April 2010].

Henderson, Simon. *After King Abdullah, Succession in Saudi Arabia* (Washington: Washington Institute for Near East Policy, August 2009).

Human Rights Watch. *Iran, Religious and Ethnic Minorities: Discrimination in Law and Practice,* Available from: http://www.hrw.org/legacy/reports/1997/iran/ [Accessed: 11 August 2010].

International Crisis Group. *Bahrain's Sectarian Challenge*. Available from: http://www.crisisgroup.org/~/media/Files/Middle%20East%20North%20Africa/Iran%20Gulf/Bahrain/Bahrains%20Sectarian%20Challenge.pdf [Accessed: 28 January 2012].

International Crisis Group. *Iraq after the Surge 1: The New Sunni Landscape*. Available from: http://www.crisisgroup.org/~/media/Files/Middle%20East%20North%20Africa/Iraq%20Syria%20Lebanon/Iraq/74_iraq_after_the_surge_i_the_new_sunni_landscape.pdf [Accessed: 12 February 2012].

International Crisis Group. *Iraq's Civil War, The Sadrists and the Surge*. Available from: http://www.crisisgroup.org/~/media/Files/Middle%20East%20North%20Africa/Iraq%20Syria%20Lebanon/Iraq/72_iraq_s_civil_war_the_sadrists_and_the_surge.pdf [Accessed: 12 February 2012].

International Crisis Group. *Lebanon's Politics: The Sunni Community and Hariri's Future Current.* Available from: http://www.crisisgroup.org/~/media/Files/Middle%20East%20North%20Africa/Iraq%20Syria%20Lebanon/Lebanon/96%20Lebanons%20Politics%20-%20The%20Sunni%20Community%20and%20Hariris%20Future%20Current.pdf [Accessed: 13 February 2012].

International Crisis Group. *Popular Protests in North Africa and the Middle East (III): The Bahrain Revolt.* Available from: http://www.crisisgroup.org/~/media/files/middle%20east%20north%20africa/iran%20gulf/bahrain/105-%20popular%20protests%20in%20north%20africa%20and%20the%20middle%20east%20-iii-the%20bahrain%20revolt.pdf [Accessed: 12 April 2011].

International Crisis Group. *Syria's Phase of Radicalisation* Available from: http://www.crisisgroup.org/~/media/Files/Middle%20East%20North%20Africa/Iraq%20Syria%20Lebanon/Syria/b033-syrias-phase-of-radicalisation [Accessed: 12 April 2012].

Mapping The Global Muslim Population: A Report on the Size and Distribution of the Muslim Population (The Pew Forum, 7 October 2009). Available from: http://pewforum.org/Mapping-the-Global-Muslim-Population.aspx [Accessed: 28 September 2010].

Matthieson, Toby. 'The Shi'a of Saudi Arabia at a crossroads', *Middle East Report Online* (6 May 2009). Available from: http://www.merip.org/mero050609.html [Accessed: 10 May 2010].

Nassibli, Nasib. *The Azeri Question in Iran: The Crucial Issue for Iran's Future.* Available from: http://www.zerbaijan.com/azeri/nasibzade2.html [Accessed: 12 August 2010].

Slavin, Barbara. *The Iran Stalemate and the Need for Strategic Patience* (Atlantic Council: Iran Task Force, 2010).

Teitelbaum, Joseph. *The Shiites of Saudi Arabia* (Centre on Islam, Democracy and the Future of the Muslim World, 2010). Available from: http://www.currenttrends.org/research/detail/the-shiites-of-saudi-arabia [Accessed: 25 August 2010].

United Nations. *Report of the International Independent Investigation Commission Established Pursuant to Security Council Resolution 1595 (2005).* Available from: http://www.un.org/News/dh/docs/mehlisreport/ [Acccessed: 13 February 2012].

Electronic Resources

08RIYADH649. 'Saudi King Abdullah and senior princes on Saudi policy towards Iraq', (Wikileaks, 20 April 2008). Available from: http://WikiLeaks.as50620.net/cable/2008/04/08RIYADH649.html [Accessed: 7 December 2010].

08RIYADH768. 'Lebanon: SAG FM says UN peace-keeping force needed', (Wikileaks, 14 May 2008). Available from: http://WikiLeaks.ch/cable/2008/05/08RIYADH768.html#par1 [Accessed: 15 December 2010].

2010 Census. Available from: www.cio.gov.bh/CIO_ARA/English/Publications/census/General%20%20%202011%2002%2006%20-%203.pdf [Accessed: 9 February 2012].

Abedin, Mahan. 'Iran at sea over Azerbaijan' (*Asia Times*, 28 September 2004). Available from: http://www.atimes.com/atimes/Middle_East/FI28Ak01.html [Accessed: 12 August 2005]

Ahlul Bayt News Agency. 'Akhtari: Arab spring inspired by Iran 1979 revolution' (10 September 2011). Available from: http://www.abna.ir/data.asp?lang=3&Id=264658 [Accessed: 12 September 2011].

Al Arabiya. 'Saudi Arabia has never given "one single arm" to Syrian opposition: source', (*Al Arabiya*, 10 April 2012). Available from: http://english.alarabiya.net/articles/2012/04/10/206761.html [Accessed: 12 April 2012].

Alfoneh, Ali. *The Basij Resistance Force* (USIP The Iran Primer). Available from: http://iranprimer.usip.org/sites/iranprimer.usip.org/files/The%20Basij%20Resistance%20Force.pdf [Accessed 10 December 2011].

AMEinfo, 'Saudi Arabia- demographic trends to watch for'. (*AMEinfo*, 18 June 2007). Available from: www.ameinfo.com/123859.html [Accessed: 8 September 2010].

Ansari, Massoud. 'We will cut them until Iran asks for mercy'. (*The Telegraph*, 15 January 2006). Available from: http://www.telegraph.co.uk/news/worldnews/middleeast/iran/1507890/We-will-cut-them-until-Iran-asks-for-mercy.html [Accessed: 13 April 2010].

Athanasiadis, Iason. 'Foreign plots and cockroaches in Iran'. (*Asia Times*, 8 June 2006). Available from: http://www.atimes.com/atimes/Middle_East/HF08Ak02.html [Accessed: 15 July 2010].

Aryan, Hossein. *'Blaming Outsiders Won't Solve Iran's Baluchistan Problem'*. Available from: http://www.rferl.org/content/Blaming_Outsiders_Wont_Solve_Irans_Baluchistan_Problem/2104613.html [Accessed: 10 August 2010].

BBC. 'Hamas claims strong Saudi Support'. (*BBC*, 11 March 2006). Available from: http://news.bbc.co.uk/1/hi/world/middle_east/4795574.stm. [Accessed: 12 May 2010].

BBC. 'Holocaust comments spark outrage'. (*BBC*, 14 December 2005). Available from: http://news.bbc.co.uk/1/hi/world/middle_east/4529198.stm. [Accessed: 12 May 2009].

BBC. 'Iran bans Al Jazeera after riots'. (*BBC*, 19 April 2005). Available from; http://news.bbc.co.uk/1/hi/world/middle_east/4459033.stm [Accessed: 22 May 2010].

BBC. 'Iran leader's comments attacked'. (*BBC*, 27 October 2005). Available from: http://news.bbc.co.uk/1/hi/world/middle_east/4378948.stm [Accessed: 26 July 2007].

BBC. 'Iranian forces clash with Kurdish separatist group'. (*BBC*, 27 January 2010). Available from: http://news.bbc.co.uk/1/hi/8482802.stm [Accessed: 11 October 2010].

BBC. 'Iran, Who Holds the Power?' Available from: http://news.bbc.co.uk/1/shared/spl/hi/middle_east/03/iran_power/html/ [Accessed: 12 October 2008].

BBC. 'Islamic Solidarity Games cancelled over Gulf dispute'. (*BBC*, 18 January 2010). Available from: http://news.bbc.co.uk/1/hi/world/middle_east/8465235.stm [Accessed: 18 January 2010].

BBC. 'Lebanon confirms Hariri election win'. (*BBC*, 8 June 2009). Available from: http://news.bbc.co.uk/1/hi/world/middle_east/8089285.stm [Accessed: 13 September 2010].

BBC. 'Q&A: Iran and the nuclear issue'. (*BBC*, 10 January 2011). Available from: http://news.bbc.co.uk/1/hi/world/middle_east/4031603.stm [Accessed: 24 August 2009].

BBC. '"Smoke and screams" on board plane'. (*BBC*, 26 December 2009). Available from: http://news.bbc.co.uk/1/hi/world/americas/8430664.stm [Accessed: 26 December 2009].

BBC. 'Turkmenistan opens new Iran gas pipeline'. (*BBC*, 6 January 2010). Available from: http://news.bbc.co.uk/1/hi/8443787.stm [Accessed: 8 January 2010].

Black, Ian. 'Iran bombing: Profile of Sunni group Jundallah'. (*The Guardian*, 15 December 2010). Available from: http://www.guardian.co.uk/world/2010/dec/15/iran-suicide-bombing-jundallah-profile [Accessed: 15 December 2010].

Black, Ian. 'Saudis blame Hamas amid calls for talks with Fatah'. (*The Guardian*, 1 January 2009). Available from: http://www.guardian.co.uk/world/2009/jan/01/saudi-arabia-hamas-gaza. [Accessed: 12 May 2010].

British Museum, The. *Cyrus Cylinder*. Available from: http://www.britishmuseum.org/explore/highlights/highlight_objects/me/c/cyrus_cylinder.aspx [Accessed: 22 July 2009].

Butler, William. 'Saudi Arabian intervention in Bahrain driven by visceral Sunni fear of Shias'. (*The Observer*, 20 March 2011). Available from: http://www.guardian.co.uk/world/2011/mar/20/bahrain-saudi-arabia-rebellion. [Accessed: 20 March 2011].

Central Intelligence Agency. *The World Factbook-Iran*. Available from: https://www.cia.gov/library/publications/the-world-factbook/geos/ir.html [Accessed: 1 July 2009].

Central Intelligence Agency. *The World Factbook-Saudi Arabia*. Available from: https://www.cia.gov/library/publications/the-world-factbook/geos/sa.html [Accessed: 1 July 2009].

Chulov, Martin. 'Saudi Arabian troops enter Bahrain as regime asks for help to quell uprising'. (*The Guardian*, 14 March 2011). Available from: http://www.guardian.co.uk/world/2011/mar/14/saudi-arabian-troops-enter-bahrain [Accessed 14 March 2011].

Chulov, Martin. 'Saudi women to be given right to vote and stand for election in four years'. (*The Guardian*, 25 September 2011). Available from: http://

www.guardian.co.uk/world/2011/sep/25/saudi-women-right-to-vote [Accessed: 25 September 2011].

CNN, 'Bush State of the Union Address'. (29 January 2002). Available from: http://edition.cnn.com/2002/ALLPOLITICS/01/29/bush.speech.txt/ [Accessed: 13 January 2009].

CNN, 'Iranian leader: Holocaust a "myth"'. (14 December 2005). Available from: http://www.cnn.com/2005/WORLD/meast/12/14/iran.israel/index.html [Accessed: 24 September 2009].

CNN, 'Transcript of interview with Iranian president Mohammad Khatami'. (7 January 1998). Available from: www.cnn.com/WORLD/9801/07/iran/interview.html [Accessed: 1 December 2010].

CNN Wire Staff, 'Yemen-based al Qaeda group claims responsibility for parcel bomb plot'. (6 November 2010). Available from; http://edition.cnn.com/2010/WORLD/meast/11/05/yemen.security.concern/?hpt=T2 [Accessed: 7 November 2010].

Cole, Juan. *Ahmadinejad: We Are Not a Threat to Any Country, Including Israel,* (27 August 2006). Available from: http://www.juancole.com/2006/08/ahmadinejad-we-are-not-threat-to-any.html [Accessed: 26 July 2007].

Constitution of the Islamic Republic of Iran, The. Available from: http://www.iran-chamber.com/government/laws/constitution.php [Accessed: 12 March 2010].

Cornwell, Rupert. 'Iran's new leader accused of role in US embassy siege'. (*The Independent,* 1 July 2005). Available from: http://www.independent.co.uk/news/world/americas/irans-new-leader-accused-of-role-in-us-embassy-siege-497146.html [Accessed: 6 November 2009].

Dehghan, Saeed Kamali. 'Syrian army being aided by Iranian forces'. (*The Guardian*, 28 May 2012). Available from: http://www.guardian.co.uk/world/2012/may/28/syria-army-iran-forces [Accessed: 28 May 12].

Deutsche Welle. 'Iran's supreme leader: Using nuclear weapons is un-Islamic'. (4 June 2006). Available from: http://www.dw-world.de/dw/article/0,,2043328,00.html [Accessed: 7 December 2010].

Drees, Caroline. 'Syria, Iran lack full Hizbullah control: US official'. (*Reuters*, 25 July 2006). Available from: http://www.americanintifada.com/2006/07/07-25-21.htm [Accessed: 27 October 2009].

Economist, The. 'Saudi Arabia: The royal house is rattled too'. (*The Economist*, 3 May 2011). Available from: http://www.economist.com/node/18291511 [Accessed: 4 May 2011].

Energy Information Administration. *Country Analysis Briefs: Iran*. (16 April 2010). Available from: http://www.eia.doe.gov/emeu/cabs/Iran/pdf.pdf [Accessed: 23 January 2009].

Energy Information Administration. *Country Analysis Briefs: Saudi Arabia* (1 April 2011). Available from: http://www.eia.gov/countries/cab.cfm?fips=SA [Accessed: 23 January 2009].

Ertuk, Yakin. 'Turmoil in Syria: failed "Arab Spring" or sectarian nightmare?'. (*Open Democracy*, 8 May 2012). Available from: http://www.opendemocracy.net/5050/yakin-erturk/turmoil-in-syria-failed-%E2%80%9Carab-spring%E2%80%9D-or-sectarian-nightmare [Accessed: 12 May 2012].

Fielding, Nick. 'Saudis paid Bin Laden 200 million pounds'. (*The Sunday Times*, 25 August 2002). Available from: http://www.timesonline.co.uk/article/0,,2089–393584,00.html [Accessed: 21 July 2009].

Finn, Tom. 'I fear for my son, says father of Anwar al-Awlaki, tipped as new Bin Laden' (*The Observer*, 8 May 2011). Available from: http://www.guardian.co.uk/world/2011/may/08/anwar-awlaki-yemen-al-qaida [Accessed: 9 May 2011].

Gause, F. Gregory. 'Is Saudi Arabia really counter-revolutionary?' in Pomeps Briefings, *Arab Uprisings: The Saudi Counter Revolution.* (9 August 2011). Available from: http://www.pomeps.org/wp-content/uploads/2011/08/POMEPS_BriefBooklet5_SaudiArabia_web.pdf [Accessed: 10 August 2011].

Ghanmi, Lamine. 'Morocco cuts ties with Iran over Bahrain'. (*Reuters*, 7 March 2009), Available from: http://af.reuters.com/article/topNews/idAFJOE52601D20090307 [Accessed: 12 January 2011].

Global Security. *Iran-Iraq War (1980–1988).* Available from: http://www.globalsecurity.org/military/world/war/iran-iraq.htm [Accessed: 10 October 2009].

Global Security. *Saudi Hezbollah.* Available from: http://www.globalsecurity.org/military/world/para/saudi-hezbollah.htm [Accessed: 7 November 2010].

Guardian, The. 'US embassy cables: Saudi king urges US strike on Iran'. (*The Guardian*, 28 November 2010). Available from: http://www.guardian.co.uk/world/us-embassy-cables-documents/150519 [Accessed: 28 November 2010].

Guardian, The. 'US embassy cables: Saudi youths "frolic under princely protection". (*The Guardian*, 7 December 2010). Available from: http://www.guardian.co.uk/world/us-embassy-cables-documents/235420 [Accessed: 7 December 2010].

Hakimzadeh, Shirin. *Iran: A Vast Diaspora Abroad and Millions of Refugees at Home* (Migration Information Source, September 2006). Available from: http://www.migrationinformation.org/Profiles/display.cfm?ID=424 [Accessed: 12 July 2009].

Hardy, Roger. *'Hezballah capture marks new escalation'.* (*BBC*, 12 July 2006). Available from: http://news.bbc.co.uk/1/hi/world/middle_east/5172760.stm [Accessed: 12 October 2010].

Henderson, Simon. *A Testing Weekend in Bahrain.* (Washington Institute for Near East Policy, 6 January 2012). Available from: http://www.washingtoninstitute.org/templateC06.php?CID=1790 [Accessed: 27 January 2012].

Henderson, Simon. *Iran's Shadow over Reform in Bahrain.* (Washington Institute for Near East Policy, 11 April 2011). Available from: http://www.washingtoninstitute.org/templateC05.php?CID=3347 [Accessed: 12 April 2011].

Henderson, Simon. *Riot Report Will Force Bahrain to Choose a Direction*. (Washington Institute for Near East Policy, 21 November 2011). Available from: http://www.washingtoninstitute.org/templateC05.php?CID=3424 [Accessed: 22 November 2011].

Henderson, Simon. *Saudi Arabia's Fears for Bahrain*. (Washington Institute for Near East Policy, 17 February 2011). Available from: http://www.washingtoninstitute.org/templateC05.php?CID=3309 [Accessed: 12 October 2011].

Howden, Daniel. 'Saudis jail academics who petitioned for reforms'. (*The Independent*, 18 May 2005). Available from: http://www.independent.co.uk/news/world/middle-east/saudis-jail-academics-who-petitioned-for-reforms-491111.html [Accessed: 15 July 2009].

Al-Husseini, Hassan. 'The expatriate population in Saudi Arabia'. Available from: http://americanbedu.com/2009/06/06/the-expatriate-population-in-saudi-arabia/ [Accessed 8 September 2010].

Inter-Parliamentary Union, *Electoral System*. Available from: http://www.ipu.org/parline-e/reports/2373_B.htm [Accessed: 9 July 2009].

Inter-Parliamentary Union. *General Information*. Available from: http://www.ipu.org/parline-e/reports/2373_A.htm [Accessed: 9 July 2009].

Iran Chamber Society. *History of Iran: Cyrus the Great*. Available from: http://www.iranchamber.com/history/cyrus/cyrus.php [Accessed: 16 August 2009].

Iranian Constitution. *Article 3.16*. Available from: www.alaviandassociates.com/documents/constitution.pdf [Accessed: 24 August 2010].

Al Jazeera. 'Ahmadinejad: Holocaust a myth'. (*Al Jazeera*, 14 December 2005). Available from: http://english.aljazeera.net/archive/2005/12/200849154418141136.html [Accessed: 12 December 2009].

Al Jazeera. 'Leaked cable: Gulf Sates "funded extremism"'. (*Al Jazeera*, 22 May 2011). Available from: http://www.aljazeera.com/news/middleeast/2011/05/2011522154717683995.html [Accessed: 22 May 2011].

Jerusalem Post, The. 'Iran hosts the World Without Zionism'. (*The Jerusalem Post*, 26 October 2005). Available from: http://www.jpost.com/servlet/Satellite?pagename=JPost%2FJPArticle%2FShowFull&cid=1129540603434 [Accessed: 24 July 2007].

Khalaji, Mehdi. *Iran's Continuing Power Struggles*. (Washington Institute for Near East Policy, 20 April 2011). Available from: http://www.washingtoninstitute.org/policy-analysis/view/irans-continuing-power-struggles [Accessed: 14 April 2011].

Khalaji, Mehdi. *Iran's Policy Confusion about Bahrain*. (Washington Institute for Near East Policy, 27 June 2011). Available from: http://www.washingtoninstitute.org/templateC05.php?CID=3376 [Accessed: 1 August 2011].

Khalil, Ashraf. 'Saudi Arabia offers $1 billion to rebuild Gaza as fragile ceasefires hold'. (*Los Angeles Times*, 20 January 2009). Available from: http://articles.latimes.com/2009/jan/20/world/fg-gaza20 [Accessed: 12 May 2010].

Knight, Sam. 'Briefing: the 444-day US embassy siege, Tehran 1979', (*The Times*, 30 June 2005). Available from: http://www.timesonline.co.uk/tol/news/world/article538994.ece. [Accessed: 6 November 2009].

Kohl, Keith. *A Civil War inside OPEC*. (Energy & Capital, 2 February 2007). Available from: http://www.energyandcapital.com/articles/opec-oil-cuts/354 [Accessed: 11 January 2011].

Lyon, Alistair. 'Saudi oil policy not hostage to Iran worries'. (*Reuters*, 29 October 2009). Available from: http://www.reuters.com/article/2009/10/29/us-saudi-iran-oil-analysis-idUSTRE59S30L20091029 [Accessed: 1 May 2010].

MacAskill, Ewan. 'WikiLeaks cables: Saudis proposed Arab force to invade Lebanon'. (*The Guardian*, 7 December 2010). Available from: http://www.guardian.co.uk/world/2010/dec/07/wikileaks-saudi-arab-invasion-Lebanon [Accessed: 8 December 2010].

Mahjoub, Taieb. and Keyrouz, Wissam. 'GCC leaders host Ahmadinejad at summit'. (*Middle East Online*, 3 December 2007). Available from: http://www.middle-east-online.com/english/?id=23340 [Accessed: 20 January 2009].

Mattis, Aaron. 'Oil sheik down: Saudi Arabia's struggle to contain Iran'. (*Harvard International Review*, 1 May 2010). Available from: http://hir.harvard.edu/women-in-power/oil-sheik-down [Accessed: 1 May 2010].

Middle East Media Research Institute, The. *The Holocaust and its Denial* (30 January 2009). Available from: http://www.memri.org/report/en/0/0/0/0/0/0/3060.htm [Accessed: 24 February 2010].

Murphy, Caryle. 'Saudi Arabia's King Abdullah promises $36 billion in benefits'. (*Christian Science Monitor*, 23 February 2011), Available from: http://www.csmonitor.com/World/Middle-East/2011/0223/Saudi-Arabia-s-King-Abdullah-promises-36-billion-in-benefits [Accessed: 28 February 2011].

New York Times, The. 'Excerpts from Khomeini's speeches'. (*The New York Times*, 4 August 1987). Available from: http://www.nytimes.com/1987/08/04/world/excerpts-from-khomeini-speeches.html?pagewanted=all&src=pm [Accessed: 10 June 2009].

New York Times, The. 'Text of Mahmoud Ahmadeinejad's speech'. (*The New York Times*, 30 October 2005). Available from: http://www.nytimes.com/2005/10/30/weekinreview/30iran.html?pagewanted=1&_r=1&ei=5070&en=26f07fc5b7543417&ex=1161230400 [Accessed: 24 February 2010].

Ninth Five-Year Plan Includes $385 Billion in New Spending. Available from: http://www.us-sabc.org/custom/news/details.cfm?id=775 [Accessed: 18 May 2011].

Obaid, Nawaf, 'Stepping into Iraq: Saudi Arabia will protect Sunnis if the U.S. leaves'. (*The Washington Post*, 26 November 2006). Available from: http://www.washingtonpost.com/wp-dyn/content/article/2006/11/28/AR2006112801277.html [Accessed 30 November 2008].

Organisation of the Islamic Conference. Available from: http://www.oic-oci.org/page_detail.asp?p_id=52 [Accessed: 5 May 2011].

Organisation of the Petroleum Exporting Countries. *Annual Statistical Bulletin 2008*. Available from: http://www.opec.org/opec_web/static_files_project/media/downloads/publications/ASB2009.pdf [Accessed: 27 June 2009].

PBS. *Frontline: Saudi Time Bomb* (PBS). Available from: http://www.pbs.org/wgbh/pages/frontline/shows/saudi/interviews/nasr.html [Accessed 18 May 2011].

Pilkington, Ed. 'Ahmadinejad accuses US of "orchestrating" 9/11 attacks to aid Israel'. (*The Guardian*, 23 September 2010). Available from: http://www.guardian.co.uk/world/2010/sep/23/iran-unitednations [Accessed: 24 September 2010].

Pollock, David. 'Saudi Arabia by the numbers'. (*ForeignPolicy.com*, 12 February 2010). Available from: http://www.washingtoninstitute.org/templateC06.php?CID=1414 [Accessed: 19 May 2011].

Press TV, 'Iran-Turkmenistan ties unbreakable'. (*Press TV*, 17 April 2010). Available from: http://www.presstv.ir/detail.aspx?id=123531§ionid=351020101 [Accessed: 18 May 2010].

Press TV, 'Iran, Turkmenistan launch new gas pipeline'. (*Press TV*, 29 December 2009). Available from: http://www.presstv.ir/detail.aspx?id=114878§ionid=351020103 [Accessed: 8 January 2010].

Al Qa'ida in the Arabian Peninsula. *Inspire*. Available from: http://publicintelligence.net/complete-inspire-al-qaeda-in-the-arabian-peninsula-aqap-magazine/ [Accessed 1 August 2010].

Al-Rasheed, Madawi. 'The Saudi response to the "Arab Spring": containment and co-option'. (*Open Democracy*, 10 January 2012). Available from: http://www.opendemocracy.net/5050/madawi-al-rasheed/saudi-response-to-%E2%80%98arab-spring%E2%80%99-containment-and-co-option [Accessed: 15 January 2012].

Al-Rasheed, Madawi. 'Yes, it could happen here: Why Saudi Arabia is ripe for revolution'. (*Foreign Policy*, 28 February 2011). Available from: http://www.foreignpolicy.com/articles/2011/02/28/yes_it_could_happen_here?page=0,0 [Accessed: 28 Febraury 2011].

Ravid, Barak. 'WikiLeaks blows cover off Israel's covert Gulf states ties'. (*Ha'aretz*, 29 November 2010). Available from: http://www.haaretz.com/news/diplomacy-defense/WikiLeaks-blows-cover-off-israel-s-covert-gulf-states-ties-1.327758 [Accessed: 6 June 2011].

Reuters, 'Israel warns Hizbullah war would invite destruction'. (*Reuters*, 10 March 2008). Available from: http://www.ynetnews.com/articles/0,7340,L-3604893,00.html [Accessed: 3 June 2009].

Royal Embassy of Saudi Arabia. *Council of Ministers System*. Available from: http://www.saudiembassy.net/about/country-information/government/council_of_ministers_system.aspx [Accessed: 8 July 2009].

Royal Embassy of Saudi Arabia. *Government*. Available from: http://www.saudiembassy.net/about/country-information/government/ [Accessed: 8 July 2009].

Royal Embassy of Saudi Arabia. *The Basic Law of Governance*. Available from: http://www.saudiembassy.net/about/country-information/laws/The_Basic_Law_Of_Governance.aspx [Accessed: 8 July 2009].

Savage, Charlie, and Shane, Scott. 'Iranians accused of a plot to kill Saudis' US envoy'. (*The New York Times*, 11 October 2011). Available from: http://www.nytimes.com/2011/10/12/us/us-accuses-iranians-of-plotting-to-kill-saudi-envoy.html?_r=1&ref=middleeast [Accessed: 11 October 2011].

Schaeffer, Brenda. 'Iran's volatile ethnic mix'. (*International Herald Tribune,* 6 June 2006). Available from: http://www.nytimes.com/2006/06/02/opinion/02iht-edshaffer.1874687.html?_r=1 [Accessed: 7 July 2009].

Seznec, Jean Francois. 'Saudi Arabia strikes back'. (*Foreign Policy*, 14 March 2011). Available from: http://www.foreignpolicy.com/articles/2011/03/14/saudi_arabia_strikes_back [Accessed: 15 March 2011].

Shalev, Chemi. 'Dennis Ross: Saudi king vowed to obtain bomb after Iran'. (*Ha'aretz*, 30 May 2012). Available from: http://www.haaretz.com/news/diplomacy-defense/dennis-ross-saudi-king-vowed-to-obtain-nuclear-bomb-after-iran-1.433294 [Accessed: 30 May 2012].

Shenker, Jack. 'Saudi Arabia king accused of misjudgement bribery in attempt to avoid unrest'. (*The Guardian*, 24 February 2011). Available from: http://www.guardian.co.uk/world/2011/feb/24/saudi-arabia-king-accused-bribery [Accessed: 24 Febraury 2011].

Siddique, Haroon, and agencies. 'BBC's Panorama claims Islamic schools teach anti-Semitism and homophobia'. (*The Guardian*, 22 November 2010). Available from: http://www.guardian.co.uk/media/2010/nov/22/bbc-panorama-islamic-schools-antisemitism [Accessed: 22 November 2010].

Slackman, Michael. 'The proxy battle in Bahrain'. (*The New York Times*, 19 March 2011). Available from: http://www.nytimes.com/2011/03/20/weekinreview/20proxy.html?pagewanted=all [Accessed: 27 January 2012].

Staff. 'Saudi five-year plan sees stronger private sector'. (*Emirates 24/7 News*, 18 October 2010). Available from: http://www.emirates247.com/news/region/saudi-five-year-plan-sees-stronger-private-sector-2010–10–18–1.305509 [Accessed: 18 May 2011].

Taheri, Amir. 'Why some parts of Iran are beyond Ahmadinejad's reach'. (*Gulf News*, 31 May 2006). Available from: http://gulfnews.com/opinions/columnists/why-some-parts-of-iran-are-beyond-ahmadinejad-s-reach-1.238982 [Accessed: 7 March 2010].

Tahir, Muhammad. *Turkmen Identity on the Wane in Iran.* (Institute for War and Peace Reporting, 27 March 2006). Available from: http://www.iwpr.net/report-news/turkmen-identity-wane-iran [Accessed: 13 April 2010].

Tohidi, Nayereh. 'Iran: regionalism, ethnicity and democracy' *(Open Democracy,* 29 June 2006. Available from: http://www.opendemocracy.net/content/articles/PDF/3695.pdf [Accessed 14.04.10].

Tran, Mark, and Dehghan, Saeed K. 'Iran mosque bombing kills dozens'. (*The Guardian*, 15 December 2010). Available from: http://www.guardian.co.uk/world/2010/dec/15/iran-chahbahar-suicide-bombing-mosque [Accessed: 15 December 2010].

United Nations Economic and Social Council. *E/CN.4/2006/NGO/.* Available from: http://domino.un.org/unispal.nsf/3822b5e39951876a85256b6e0058a

478/258eda552cbb854a852571310058a594?OpenDocument [Accessed: 22 August 2007].

UN Security Council, *SC/9792 Security Council Demands Iran Suspend Uranium Enrichment or Face Possible Economic, Diplomatic Sanctions.* Available from: http://www.un.org/News/Press/docs//2006/sc8792.doc.htm [Accessed: 24 August 2009].

UNPO, *Iran Parliamentary Think Tank Warns of Ethnic Unrest.* Available from: http://www.unpo.org/article/3460 [Accessed: 17 June 2009].

Vidal, John. 'WikiLeaks cables: Saudi Arabia cannot pump enough oil to keep a lid on prices'. (*The Guardian*, 8 February 2011). Available from: http://www.guardian.co.uk/business/2011/feb/08/saudi-oil-reserves-overstated-wikileaks [Accessed: 8 February 2011].

Walsh, Declan. 'WikiLeaks cables portray Saudi Arabia as a cash machine for terrorists'. (*The Guardian*, 5 December 2010). Available from: http://www.guardian.co.uk/world/2010/dec/05/wikileaks-cables-saudi-terrorist-funding [Accessed: 6 December 2010].

White House, The. *The National Security Strategy.* Available from: http://georgewbush-whitehouse.archives.gov/nsc/nss/2006/print/index.html [Accessed: 1 November 2009].

Wood, Paul. 'Life and legacy of King Fahd'. (*BBC,* 1 August 2005). Available from: http://news.bbc.co.uk/1/hi/world/middle_east/4734505.stm [Accessed: 12 November 2009].

Worth, Robert F. 'Iran says capture of rebel is blow to U.S.'. (*The New York Times*, 23 February 2010). Available from: http://www.nytimes.com/2010/02/24/world/middleeast/24insurgent.html [Accessed: 13 April 2010].

Wright, Robin, and Baker, Peter. 'Iraq, Jordan see threat to election from Iran: Leaders warn against forming religious state'. (*The Washington Post*, 8 December 2004). Available from: http://www.washingtonpost.com/wp-dyn/articles/A43980–2004Dec7.html [Accessed: 1 May 2010].

Unpublished Works

Saleh, Alam B., *Identity and Societal Security in Iran* (Unpublished PhD diss., University of Leeds, 2010).

INDEX